LITERACY INSTRUCTION FOR TODAY

LITERACY INSTRUCTION FOR TODAY

Kathryn H. Au
Kamehameha Schools, Honolulu, Hawaii

Jana M. Mason
University of Illinois, Urbana-Campaign, Illinois

Judith A. Scheu
Kamehameha Schools, Honolulu, Hawaii

HarperCollins*CollegePublishers*

Acquisitions Editor: Christopher Jennison
Project Editor: Janet Frick
Design Manager: Wendy Ann Fredericks
Text Designer: Dorothy Bungert
Cover Designer: Kay Petronio
Art Studio: Academy ArtWorks, Inc.
Electronic Production Manager: Valerie A. Sawyer
Desktop Administrator: Sarah Johnson
Manufacturing Manager: Helene G. Landers
Electronic Page Makeup: RR Donnelley Barbados
Printer and Binder: RR Donnelley & Sons Company
Cover Printer: The Lehigh Press, Inc.

For permission to use copyrighted material, grateful acknowledgment is made to the copyright holders on p. 317, which are hereby made part of this copyright page.

Literacy Instruction for Today

Library of Congress Cataloging-in-Publication Data
Au, Kathryn Hu-Pei.
    Literacy instruction for today / Kathryn H. Au, Jana M. Mason, Judith A. Scheu.
        p.   cm.
    Rev. ed. of: Reading instruction for today / Jana M. Mason, Kathryn H. Au. 2nd ed. c1990
    Includes bibliographical references and index.
    ISBN 0-673-46960-3
    1. Reading (Elementary) 2. Language arts (Elementary) 3. Reading comprehension. 4. Children—Books and reading.   I. Mason, Jana M.   II. Scheu, Judith A.   III. Mason, Jana M. Reading instruction for today.   IV. Title
LB1573.M376   1995
372.4—dc20   94-12520
                                                  CIP

94 95 96 97 9 8 7 6 5 4 3 2 1

CONTENTS

PREFACE

Constructivism, whole language, literature-based instruction, process writing, emergent literacy, flexible grouping—these are the concepts and approaches central to *Literacy Instruction for Today.* The textbook replaces our earlier book, *Reading Instruction for Today.*

This book is intended as the main text for a semester-long introductory course on elementary-school reading instruction, typically taken by undergraduates in their second or third year. Our goal is to present the theory and practice of reading and language arts instruction from a constructivist orientation.

Along with an introductory reading-methods textbook, many instructors want to use supplementary books and articles. With nine succinct chapters, this textbook supports this type of arrangement. It addresses central topics and teaching approaches in depth but does not attempt to serve as a compendium.

Many instructors are concerned about giving preservice teachers a sense of the complex, dynamic forms of teaching consistent with a constructivist orientation. To address this concern, the chapters begin with classroom examples showing how theory and practice actually come together. In the body of the chapters, the theory, research, and instructional strategies underlying the classroom examples are explained.

Each chapter contains an overview and a summary and is structured around key concepts. Each chapter also presents students with two or more activities; one involves them in exploring their own literacy, while the other involves them in planning, observing, teaching, and analyzing. Other features include lists of recommended readings and a complete index. An Instructor's Resource Book is available.

Chapter 1 discusses a philosophy for literacy education and the nature of literacy and literacy instruction. Chapter 2 considers emergent literacy, word identification, and the instruction of children in kindergarten and first grade. Chapter 3 deals with literature-based instruction, reader response theory, and children's literature. Chapter 4 focuses on reading informational text and research report writing.

Chapter 5 explains students' vocabulary development and approaches for developing vocabulary in the context of literature-based instruction. Chapter 6 examines classroom organization and management. Chapter 7 explores assessment, with an emphasis on classroom-based forms, especially portfolios. Chapter 8 addresses independence and fostering a love of reading. Finally, Chapter 9 explores the teaching of literacy to all students, including those who find learning to read difficult or who come from diverse cultural and linguistic backgrounds.

We are grateful to Chris Jennison, our editor at HarperCollins, and to Maggie Stuckey, who copyedited the text. We would also like to thank the reviewers of this book, whose feedback was very helpful to us: Victoria Chou, University of Illinois at Chicago; Anne McGill-Franzen, State University of New York, Albany; James H. Mosenthal, University of Vermont; Sam L. Sebesta, University of Washington.

Elementary school teachers have the challenge of putting students on the road toward becoming confident readers and writers, with the ability to use literacy in the ways demanded in a modern technological society. They also have the challenge of helping students see that literacy can be a source of enjoyment and enrichment in their personal lives. We hope that this book gives preservice teachers a good sense of how they can begin to meet these challenges.

Kathryn H. Au
Jana M. Mason
Judith A. Scheu

1 LITERACY, READING, WRITING, AND INSTRUCTION

If we think of education as an act of knowing, then reading has to do with knowing. The act of reading cannot be explained as merely reading words since every act of reading words implies a previous reading of the world and a subsequent rereading of the world. There is a permanent movement back and forth between "reading" reality and reading words—the spoken word too is our reading of the world. We can go further, however, and say that reading the word is not only preceded by reading the world, but also by a certain form of writing it or rewriting it. In other words, of transforming it by means of conscious practical action. For me, this dynamic movement is central to literacy.

Thus, we see how reading is a matter of studying reality that is alive, reality that we are living inside of, reality as history being made and also making us. We can also see how it is impossible to read texts without reading the context of the text, without establishing the relationships between the discourse and the reality which shapes the discourse. This emphasizes, I believe, the responsibility which reading a text implies. We must try to read the context of a text and also relate it to the context in which we are reading the text. And so reading is not so simple. Reading mediates knowing and is also knowing, because language is knowledge and not just mediation of knowledge.

Perhaps I can illustrate by referring to the title of a book written by my daughter, Madalena. She teaches young children in Brazil and helps them learn to read and write, but above all she helps them know the world. Her book describes her work with the children and the nature of their learning. It is entitled *The Passion to Know the World*, not *How to Teach Kids to Read and Write*. No matter the level or age of the students we teach, from preschool to graduate school, reading critically is absolutely important and fundamental. Reading always involves critical perception, interpretation, and "rewriting" what is read. Its task is to unveil what is hidden in the text. I always say to the students with whom I work, "Reading is not walking on the words; it's grasping the soul of them." (Freire, 1985, pp. 18–19)

◀ OVERVIEW

To begin this chapter we describe literacy-learning activities in a third-grade classroom, focusing on the writers' workshop and the readers' workshop. We then discuss the teacher's philosophy of education, proposing five principles to guide the teaching of literacy. Next we examine the nature of literacy and especially of reading. We highlight features of literacy as a social process and emphasize the importance of the reader's background knowledge and purposes for reading. With this background, we address the question of *what* the teacher should teach to provide students with a well-balanced literacy curriculum. The curriculum framework we advocate incorporates six aspects of literacy. Finally, we discuss a model of literacy instruction, suggesting *how* the teacher should teach.

Chapter 1 is organized around the following key concepts:

KEY CONCEPT 1: Teachers should have a sound philosophy for literacy education, drawing upon constructivist principles.

KEY CONCEPT 2: Teachers should understand the nature of literacy as a social process involving active meaning-making.

KEY CONCEPT 3: Teachers should be guided by a curriculum framework that recognizes the importance of both the affective and cognitive dimensions of literacy.

KEY CONCEPT 4: Teachers should help students with difficult literacy tasks, then gradually release responsibility for these tasks to the students.

◀ **PERSPECTIVE**

Literacy Instruction in a Third-Grade Classroom

Susan Meyer teaches third grade in a school in a low-income urban neighborhood. Her students are from many different ethnic groups, including African-American, Hispanic-American, and Asian-American. This morning in October, just before the bell rings to start the school day, Susan looks around the room to see how her students are doing. Most of them are already settled at their desks, reading a book or chatting quietly with friends. A few are returning books they borrowed the night before and signing out new ones.

"Ms. Meyer," Jennifer calls out, "me and Brenda are going to read another Baby-sitters' Club book." Susan nods and smiles. Jennifer and Brenda have been doing buddy reading, reading a chapter a night in a novel and getting together in school the next day to discuss it. Susan is pleased about the amount of reading they are doing, but she thinks that in a few weeks she might suggest that they branch out to other kinds of books.

Sam approaches Susan with the draft of his story. "I think I need a conference with you. I can't figure out a good ending for my story."

"Have you already had a conference with someone else in the class, Sam?"

"No, not yet."

"Well, maybe you'd like to meet with Reggie. He's writing an adventure story too. But I'll be glad to meet with you after that." Sam agrees, and Susan makes a mental note to remind the students that they can get help with their writing from classmates as well as from the teacher.

After student helpers lead the class in the Pledge of Allegiance and take attendance and the lunch count, it's time for the writers' workshop, a period devoted to having students write on a topic of their own choosing. The term *workshop* is used to convey the idea that individuals will be at different points in completing their projects and so will not all be doing the same thing at the same time. Susan calls the students to gather on the carpet. She sits in the author's chair (Graves & Hansen, 1983), a special chair at the front of the room, and begins by reading to the students from her own notebook. She has written about how her daughter learned to swim. The short piece concludes:

> Amy jumped up and down in the water several times, as if she were gathering all her courage. Then she started to dog paddle toward me, legs and arms working hard. She swam about six feet. Her father and I cheered for her, and she was as proud and excited as if she had won an Olympic medal.

Kenyatta raises her hand. "Why did you want to write about how Amy learned to swim?" Susan smiles because she hears her own words coming back to her. Since the beginning of the school year, she has asked her students to think about why what they have written is important to them. "Well," Susan replies, "I guess because Amy wanted to swim very badly but she was a little afraid of the water. So when she finally swam I really thought she had accomplished something, and I was so happy that I was there to see it."

The students continue to ask questions, and several talk about how they learned to swim. Then Susan says, "You might want to write about how you learned to do something that was important to you. It might be swimming or it might be something else." Shontelle thinks that she will write about learning to skate with rollerblades, and Michael thinks that he will write about his uncle teaching him to play the harmonica.

Susan excuses the students to return to their desks, and they begin to work on their own pieces. Susan notices that some of their drafts are quite long and that many students do not know how to use paragraphs to signal the start of a new set of ideas. She decides to give a lesson tomorrow on the use of paragraphs and asks Ming if she can use his draft as an example. Ming agrees.

Several other students, including Sam, meet in peer conferences to find out if their pieces make sense and to get suggestions. Esteban, whom the other students know to be a good speller, helps Reggie edit his piece.

Laura is working on the illustrations for a book on her great-uncle. He kept pigeons and after he died, Laura and her family had to let all the pigeons go. Laura's piece ends:

> I watched the pigeons fly into the sky until they were out of sight. Even though Uncle Frank isn't there any more, I think the pigeons will all come back again.

Laura tells Susan that she will finish her illustrations today and would like to sit in the author's chair and share the book with the class tomorrow. Susan says she thinks this is a good plan.

The writers' workshop comes to an end, and it is time for the readers' workshop. Susan sets aside about one hour each day to emphasize writing and one hour to emphasize reading. However, she sees the two processes as highly interrelated, and she has her students both reading and writing almost all day long.

For the readers' workshop, Susan has organized the class into three small groups. Right now the class is working on a unit featuring Tomie dePaola, a well-known author and illustrator. Each small group is reading a different picture storybook by dePaola: *The Art Lesson* (1989), *Now One Foot, Now the Other* (1981), and *Strega Nona's Magic Lessons* (1982).

Susan calls the group reading *The Art Lesson* to meet with her. In the meantime, students in the group reading *Now One Foot, Now the Other* are working individually at their desks. Some are writing summaries of the story and illustrating them with drawings. Others have completed their summaries and are writing about the connection between the story and their own lives. For example, Crystal began by writing:

> I think Bobby [the main character in the story] is so lucky because his grandfather helped him when he was a baby and then he got to help his grandfather. My grandfather died before I was born so I never even knew him.

The group reading *Strega Nona's Magic Lessons* has already finished reading and writing about the book. They enjoyed the story and decided they wanted to share it with the class through a play. The eight children in the group are working in pairs to write the script for four different scenes in the story. Michael and Bobby are writing the script for the scene when Big Anthony appears at Strega Nona's door dressed as a girl.

Michael: We can use what it says right here, where he's saying "All my life I wanted to learn your magic." We can just copy that.

Bobby: Yeah, yeah, and then we can write to be sure to talk in a really high voice. (He reads the lines in a high voice to illustrate, and both boys laugh.)

The students reading *The Art Lesson* seat themselves in a semicircle at two tables in front of Susan. She asks for volunteers to read their predictions about how the story will end. Boun volunteers.

Boun: (reading from his paper) "I predict that Mrs. Bowers will let Tommy draw whatever he wants and use his own crayons."

Teacher: Okay, and what reason did you give?

Boun: I wrote, "The reason for my prediction is because Mrs. Bowers might be an artist and she might understand what Tommy wants to do."

Teacher: Oh, that's a good reason. What makes you think Mrs. Bowers, the art teacher, might be an artist herself?

Boun: (shrugs)

Tamekia: Well, our art teacher, Mr. Wilson, is a good artist so maybe that other art teacher could be a good artist too.

Notice that, in addition to having students make predictions, Susan also makes them write justifications for their predictions. She uses group discussion time to have students extend their thinking further.

Next Susan asks if other students have predictions similar to Boun's. Two students do, and they read their predictions and reasons. Then Susan asks the students with different predictions to read what they have written. Brenda has written that Mrs. Bowers won't let Tommy use his own crayons "because it won't be fair for the other kids." Susan then leads the students in a discussion of which predictions make sense and have good reasons to support them. She asks the students to return to their seats to finish reading the story, then to write about whether their prediction was accurate and how they liked the ending of the story. As students return to their seats, Susan asks Tamekia to sit next to Lindsey while they read. Tamekia has been able to read the story with ease, while Lindsey has been struggling, and this way she will be able to ask Tamekia for help.

Susan conducts a discussion lesson with the group reading *Now One Foot, Now the Other*, again basing the discussion on the writing the students have done about the story. Then she goes around to check on the students who are writing the play, and she is satisfied that all of the pairs have at least made a start.

Next Susan calls up Lindsey and four other students for a brief lesson on compound words. She has selected words from the stories the students are reading: *birthday, hallway, grandfather, fireworks, headache.* The students read the sentences containing the words, and those who can figure out the compound word explain the strategies they used.

> *Lindsey:* I knew it was *birthday* because of the balloons, and I saw paper and ribbon on the floor.
>
> *Teacher:* Good job, Lindsey, you looked at the picture to help you. But is there anything about the letters in the word that could help?
>
> *Daniel:* It starts with *b.*
>
> *Lindsey:* And it has *d-a-y.*
>
> *Daniel:* Wait, I see, I can draw a line between the *birth* and the *day.*

As this example shows, Susan uses questioning to encourage students to develop new strategies for identifying words, beyond those they are presently using.

Just before the readers' workshop ends, Susan asks the children to return to their seats and get out the book they are reading on their own. She asks for volunteers to tell the class something about their books. Jennifer and Brenda discuss their latest Baby-sitters' Club book. Esteban talks about *The Trading Game* by Alfred Slote (1990). As these students share, other students ask questions.

After praising the students for their contributions, Susan says, "You know that I really like Tomie dePaola's books, and I think most of you are enjoying them too, so today I brought another one to share with you." She holds up a copy of *The Legend of the Bluebonnet* (dePaola, 1983) and gives a brief description of the problem faced by the people in the story. She says that she will put the book in the classroom library for the students to borrow.

Through these brief book talks, given by her or by students, Susan seeks to encourage her students to engage in voluntary reading (discussed in depth in Chapter 8).

After school is over, Susan takes a few minutes to write in her journal.

> I definitely need to keep making the time to meet with Lindsey, Daniel, Bobby, and Michael as a group to work on skills. Bobby is the one who worries me most. I've found children who don't mind pairing up to help the others read, but that hasn't worked with Bobby. Reading is so difficult for him that he doesn't stick with it long and ends up causing trouble for the person reading with him. I need to think more about how to help him.
>
> This is the first year I've had an author unit on Tomie dePaola and the kids really like the literature. I've enjoyed teaching it, too, maybe because dePaola is one of the few authors who writes some books that are humorous and some that are serious. However, next year I think I'll replace *Strega Nona's Magic Lesson* with another book. It's a fun story but there isn't as much for the children to think about, and it's a book they can just enjoy reading on their own.

Later in the week, Susan will meet with the other two third-grade teachers in her building. All three are experimenting with new ideas in the readers' workshop. At their weekly meetings they share the writing in their journals and help one another solve problems. This week, Susan thinks that she will ask the other teachers for advice about how she can help Bobby.

KEY CONCEPT 1   TEACHERS SHOULD HAVE A SOUND PHILOSOPHY FOR LITERACY EDUCATION, DRAWING UPON CONSTRUCTIVIST PRINCIPLES.

GUIDING PRINCIPLES

Susan Meyer feels that she has grown since she began teaching ten years ago. In her first years in the classroom, she geared her reading and writing instruction toward skills. In reading she was concerned that her third-grade students know such skills as base words, prefixes, and suffixes; in writing she wanted to make sure they could use cursive writing and knew the difference between a noun and a verb. About four years ago, Susan became interested in a philosophy of education known as *whole language.* She learned that whole language and the process approach to writing are both forms of a broad intellectual movement known as *constructivism* (Applebee, 1991).

As Susan learned more about constructivism and whole language, she changed her views. She began to see that in reading, it was important for her students to enjoy and appreciate good literature and to be able to understand and interpret the books they read. In writing, Susan realized that it was important for her students to know that they had something to say and could get their messages across through writing.

According to constructivism, learning is a process in which individuals construct their own understandings. Learning is not a matter of passively absorbing knowledge from someone else. Rather, learners must be actively involved in putting ideas together in a way that makes sense from their own point of view. The knowledge that one learner constructs might well be different from the knowledge another learner constructs, due to differences in what they bring to the learning situation and the way they experience the learning situation. In this view, knowledge is not absolute. Rather, we can say only that knowledge is "right" or "wrong" from a certain perspective (Bruner, 1990).

Motivation is an important factor in constructivism. If learners are not willing to be actively involved in constructing meaning, and instead sit back passively, little learning can take place. Learners are most likely to be motivated to learn if they can understand the purpose for a particular learning activity and if they themselves have chosen to pursue it.

Constructivism includes the idea that people's learning is always influenced by the society around them (Vygotsky, 1978). What we learn or understand comes through our interactions with other people. In a sense, there is no such thing as individual learning (Bakhtin, 1986; Wertsch, 1990). Even when reading a book alone, the reader is being influenced by other people—the author, obviously, but also the people who influenced the author. Also, the language shared by the author and the reader has been developed as the result of many social influences on them both.

Moving toward a constructivist and whole-language orientation led Susan to change her teaching. She now spends less time lecturing her students and giving them skill lessons, and more time involving them in real reading and writing activities. She tries to engage her students in authentic literacy activities that they find purposeful and meaningful, so that they will be motivated to construct their own understandings of literacy.

Susan sees important practical implications in the idea that learning is a social process. She understands that learning will take place only if the social situation in the classroom provides learners with an adequate degree of support.

Susan is aware that literacy learning is easy for some of her students but very difficult for others, such as Lindsey and Bobby. She has found that a constructivist perspective is especially important with students who struggle with reading and writing (for further information about students with special needs, refer to Chapter 9). In keeping with a constructivist perspective, Susan understands that she must keep adjusting the learning situations in her classroom to provide all of her students with the help they need. She now assumes that, if students are not learning, it is because the situation is not yet supporting their learning. Susan feels that she has come up with arrangements that support Lindsey and all of the other students except Bobby. But with ideas from her colleagues and some further reading, she is certain that she will come up with ways to help Bobby.

Susan knows that constructivism and whole language are rich and complex philosophies, and that she will always be discovering more about what they mean for classroom teaching. Over the past few years, Susan and many other teachers have found certain constructivist principles useful in guiding their teaching of literacy. Some of these principles follow.

1. When I am teaching literacy, I use authentic activities with purposes that students can recognize as important.

Literacy, the ability to use reading and writing, is important in Susan's own life, and she wants to make sure it is important in her students' lives as well. For this reason, she provides her students with what are termed *authentic* literacy activities, meaning those that might be found in social situations in the home and community, as well as in the classroom. She believes that these activities will be highly motivating for her students. Students read and share their ideas about books, and they write about their own experiences and create their own stories. Susan also has her students read magazines, write letters, make lists, and take notes. All of these are authentic activities that are part of the lives of many adults in the community. Susan makes it a point to discuss with her students how different literacy activities, such as reading a book or writing a letter, can be useful or enjoyable in their own lives.

Keeping the concept of authentic literacy activities in mind helped Susan to cut down on the use of worksheets to practice skills. She found that students picked up skills just as well, if not better, when they were involved in real reading and real writing, with skill lessons provided as needed. It seemed, just as the experts on whole language claimed, that her students *did* learn to read by reading and to write by writing (Smith, 1988).

2. When I am teaching literacy, I have my lessons proceed from whole to part, rather than from part to whole.

Susan knows from experiences with her own two children that literacy learning begins with an understanding of the whole, or the purposes that people have for using literacy. In a sense, children learn literacy in the same way that they learn to speak, by trying to communicate and by receiving the help of someone who is already adept (Holdaway, 1979).

Susan begins by involving her students in the full process of reading a book or writing a story, following a natural learning approach. Then, once students are engaged in a full literacy activity with a purpose they understand, Susan can develop their higher-level thinking skills—identifying words, spelling, grammar, and so on.

Susan finds the approach of moving from whole to part much more effective than moving from part to whole. Her experience has been that when lessons move from part to whole, or start with skills or small bits of literacy, students often show poor motivation. They lack interest because they do not see the purpose for learning the skills. Beginning with the whole, with an authentic literacy activity, helps students to become motivated and to recognize that skills can help them to carry out the activity successfully. For example, students can see that learning a skill such as compound words will help them to read books.

3. When I am teaching literacy, I encourage students to construct their own understandings of text.

Susan knows from research on schema theory (to be discussed later in this chapter) that texts do not have a fixed meaning or the same meaning for all readers. Susan teaches her students about the points that readers might agree on (such as the characters or the order of events in a story) but encourages them to construct their own meaning, to express their own views about the theme or author's message, and to draw connections between the text and their own lives. Susan does not accept just any answer, but she does accept all answers for which students can provide good justifications. In other words, she emphasizes the process of constructing meaning from text, rather than correct answers.

Susan believes it is very important for her students to make personal connections to the stories they read, because she feels that they need to know that books can be personally meaningful in their own lives. Only then will they be motivated to read on their own. Some of Susan's students read books for their own enjoyment, but many do not yet do so. Susan wants *all* of her students to reach the point where they will make books a part of their lives.

4. When I am teaching literacy, I act as a "knowledgeable other" by providing demonstrations and scaffolding for students.

The concepts of the "knowledgeable other" and of scaffolding will be discussed in detail later in this chapter under Key Concept 4. At this point, it should simply be noted that while Susan gives her students ample opportunity to read and write on their own, she also takes specific steps to move them forward in reading and writing. In part, she does this by demonstrating how literacy works in her own life; for example, by sharing from her own notebook or by telling them about the connection she sees between a story and her own life. She also moves students forward by guiding them through the process they could use in the future to tackle a reading or writing problem on their own. You will see an example of how Susan provides guidance or scaffolding in a situation involving Ming, a student who comes upon an unknown word.

5. When I am teaching literacy, I encourage students to interact with one another as well as with me.

Sometimes Susan provides students with guidance or scaffolding not by helping them herself but by linking them up with other students. For example, she asked Sam to participate in a peer conference with Reggie, and she had Lindsey read with Tamekia. Susan wants students to realize that their classmates, as well as the teacher, may be knowledgeable others or sources of help.

When students are sharing their literacy with one another, Susan believes, the classroom becomes a literate community (Hansen, 1987). In a literate community, readers and writers respond to one another's ideas and offer assistance and encouragement. Susan relates to each of the students and supports each one's growth in literacy, but she believes her students will move forward more quickly if they also help and motivate one another. Having a literate classroom community makes it likely that all students will receive the social support they need to progress well as readers and writers.

KEY CONCEPT **2**   TEACHERS SHOULD UNDERSTAND THE NATURE OF LITERACY AS A SOCIAL PROCESS INVOLVING ACTIVE MEANING-MAKING.

THE NATURE OF LITERACY

Susan Meyer and other teachers recognize that literacy plays an increasingly important role in today's world. For example, while at work, people in the United States spend an average of more than two hours a day reading, and the materials they read are usually at the tenth- to twelfth-grade level in difficulty (Mikulecky, 1982). Nearly all adults in the United States read magazines (Montieth, 1981), and about two-thirds read a newspaper daily (Guthrie, 1981). Older adults read an average of almost a book a month (Ribovich & Erickson, 1980). Literacy is pervasive not only in school but in the workplace, home, and community.

Susan Meyer wants her students to enjoy reading and writing and to read and write for their own purposes. She is also concerned that they become functionally literate, or able to use literacy to meet the basic demands of daily life.

What it means to be functionally literate varies from society to society. In some societies people may not need literacy to live fulfilling lives. However, high levels of literacy are required of people who wish to take full advantage of opportunities offered by complex societies like the United States. Susan Meyer's third-grade students will need to be literate to qualify for good jobs, to carry out household tasks, to be informed citizens, and to participate in community activities.

Different levels of literacy are recognized. For example, the National Assessment of Educational Progress (NAEP, 1987), describes these five levels:

1. *Rudimentary.* Able to carry out simple reading tasks, such as following brief written directions or selecting the phrase to describe a picture.
2. *Basic.* Able to understand specific or sequentially presented information, such as locating facts in uncomplicated stories and news articles.
3. *Intermediate.* Able to see the relationship among ideas and to generalize, such as making generalizations about main ideas and the author's purpose.

4. *Adept.* Able to understand, summarize, and explain complicated information, such as analyzing unfamiliar material and providing reactions to whole texts.
5. *Advanced.* Able to synthesize and learn from specialized reading materials, such as extending and restructuring ideas in scientific articles or literary essays.

From studies conducted by NAEP, we know that almost all 17-year-olds have achieved a basic level of literacy; about 84 percent of them have achieved an intermediate level (about the eighth-grade level), and about 40 percent an adept level. However, only 5 percent can function at an advanced level of literacy (Applebee, Langer, & Mullis, 1985).

Susan Meyer and other teachers have the important task of helping their students become literate. In preparing students to meet the challenges of the future, they know that they will need to take their students well beyond basic literacy. Their goal is to lead students toward becoming literate at the adept and advanced levels.

That is why Susan emphasizes literacy activities that require her students to do lots of higher-level thinking. In the writers' workshop students must decide on their own topics, plan their writing, put their ideas down on paper, and make sure their ideas make sense to others. In the readers' workshop students must comprehend the text, write down their feelings and interpretations, summarize, and identify points that need clarification.

Susan also teaches her students many skills, such as the use of paragraphs and punctuation, spelling, prefixes and suffixes, plurals, and verb endings. However, she knows from the NAEP results that knowledge of specific skills is not the weak area for most American students today. Students do need to know specific skills, but most of all they need to be able to do the kind of higher-level thinking that will help them become literate at the adept and advanced levels.

The Importance of Literacy in Everyday Life

When we say that literacy is a social process, we mean that it is one of the means people use to communicate with one another and to go about their daily lives in our society. In her classroom Susan has created a literate community in which students must read and write to participate fully and to feel a sense of belonging. The world outside Susan Meyer's classroom consists of many other literate communities.

We all participate in these literate communities, usually without giving our uses of literacy a second thought. In fact, most of us can hardly imagine going through a day without reading and writing. This is because literacy has many different functions; that is, we use

For all children, literacy begins at home. That is why it's important for teachers to be aware of children's home experiences with literacy, such as family storybook reading.

it to accomplish so many different purposes (Heath, 1980). When we check price tags or street signs, we are reading to deal with the practical problems of everyday life. When we exchange letters and greeting cards, we are reading and writing to maintain social relationships. When we peruse the front page of the newspaper, we are reading to learn about distant events. And when we curl up with a good book, we are reading for recreation and enjoyment.

Susan Meyer remembers her parents reading books to her when she was a child, and she and her husband Ron have continued this practice with their daughters, Amy and Kristy. Research by Denny Taylor (1983) shows that reading is a social process with roots in the family, as Susan Meyer's experience suggests. Taylor set out to learn about young children's earliest experiences with literacy. She looked at six families, each with a child who was successfully learning to read and write. She found that the styles and values of literacy were transmitted to the children by their parents, and in turn were shaped by the personalities and preferences of the children themselves.

Taylor discovered that the children attended more to the *uses* of print in everyday life than to the print itself. They often tried to communicate through print even though they did not yet know how to write letters and spell words. In their own home, Susan and Ron Meyer have seen many examples of their two daughters' efforts to communicate through print. For example, one day when she was three, Kristy came to Susan with a sheet of paper with several scribbles, one below the other. She told Susan this was her shopping list and asked to have it put on the refrigerator next to the shopping lists that Susan and Ron keep there. Kristy could not yet write any letters, but she showed her understanding of one of the uses of print.

Reading and writing are ways of engaging in and making sense of everyday life. Children learn about the way print can be used to accomplish different purposes before they learn about the alphabet and the conventions of writing. As Taylor's work demonstrates, reading and writing are part of the larger process of being literate and participating in a literate society.

We can think of literacy as a social process involving different kinds of contexts. Smith, Carey, and Harste (1982, p. 22) suggest the following three contexts, which can all apply to writing as well as reading:

> Linguistic context is the written text per se, that which appears visually on the page.
>
> Situational context . . . is the setting in which a reading-event occurs; it includes the linguistic text, the individuals involved (e.g., a student and a teacher), the location (e.g., in a classroom or at home), the expectations (e.g., that a recall test will be given over the material), and all such other factors impinging immediately on the event.
>
> Cultural context is the social/political matrix in which the situation of reading has come about.

These abstract ideas can be made more concrete by considering the example of the readers' workshop in Susan Meyer's classroom. The linguistic context is stories by Tomie dePaola. The situational context includes the 25 students in the class but just one teacher. The lesson takes place in a classroom, which in turn is in a school building. Some of the time the children are discussing the text, either with Susan or their classmates. They also read silently or with a partner, write down their ideas, and work on projects.

But how did these students come to be involved in reading discussions and other activities every day? To answer this question we must consider the cultural context. It includes such diverse factors as the value the children and their families attach to education, the need for children to be occupied while their parents are off at work, laws requiring children to be in school, and the way schools are organized into grade levels and classes.

Notice, as in Taylor's view, that the linguistic context or the printed page is only one of the contexts or factors to be considered in the act of reading. Since literacy reading is a social process and a form of communication, it is equally important to consider its larger situational and cultural contexts as well.

Susan Meyer's students come from a number of different ethnic groups, and she knows that their family backgrounds and home experiences with literacy differ a great deal. Susan has discussed literacy practices outside of school with her students, their parents, other community members, and other educators in her building. From these conversations, as well as her reading of professional articles, Susan knows that many of her students come to school with literacy experiences quite different from those of her two daughters, who are growing up in a mainstream environment. For example, Esteban's family speaks Spanish at home, and his older sister often translates notes from school into Spanish for her parents, then writes their reply in English. Ming's parents did not read to him as a child, but he often saw them reading Chinese-language newspapers and writing letters in Chinese.

Susan is aware that different beliefs about literacy may be held in different communities and cultural groups within the United States. For example, in some communities people believe that the written word itself carries meaning and authority and that reading is a process of understanding the text at a literal level (Heath, 1983). In other communities people have the idea that texts should be interpreted on the basis of one's own beliefs and knowledge and that it is important to find a personal connection to the text.

The key concept of literacy as a social process has an important practical implication for Susan and other classroom teachers. As a social process, literacy may have a different meaning for different people. Teachers need to be alert to the overall meaning of literacy to their students. Children have larger lives outside the school that may lead them to see the situational and cultural contexts of literacy in the classroom in a different way from the teacher.

Young students of diverse backgrounds, in particular, are best taught in situations responsive to their cultural backgrounds. Kathryn Au and Jana Mason (1983) studied the issue of culturally responsive instruction with students of Polynesian Hawaiian ancestry. Teachers who insisted that Hawaiian children speak one at a time in answering their questions had great difficulty conducting effective reading lessons. On the other hand, teachers who allowed the children to cooperate or speak together in answering questions could conduct highly effective lessons.

Teachers who used this second style of interaction were teaching in a manner consistent with the rules for talk story, an important community speech event for Hawaiian children. In talk story, speakers cooperate with one another in telling stories. Rather than one person telling the whole story, two or more speakers take turns, each narrating just a small part. Talk story was important to the students, perhaps because it reflects the value many Hawaiians attach to the performance and well-being of the group or family as opposed to the individual.

In short, teachers need to take a broad view of the contexts of literacy and learning to read and write, in order to teach effectively. In the study by Au and Mason, the text itself was not the problem at all. Rather, the barrier to effective instruction was found in the situational and cultural contexts. Teachers like Susan Meyer, whose students are from diverse cultural and linguistic backgrounds, need to be aware of teaching in ways that permit comfortable communication with students, so that literacy learning can take place.

You have just learned about the importance of the social context for reading. Figure 1.1 displays the interaction among a person, a text, and a particular social context. When thinking about literacy instruction, then, Susan Meyer and other teachers need to consider three factors: (1) the people (students) and their backgrounds: (2) the texts being used for instruction whether written by others or by the students themselves; and (3) the context provided by the classroom and society.

Constructing Meaning from Text

We have suggested that reading and writing are both processes of constructing meaning from text. This idea is easier to understand in the case of writing, because it is obvious that the writer must create the text. But let us consider what this idea means in terms of reading. Many people have the impression that reading is a simple matter of being able to identify words, to put words into sentences, sentences into paragraphs, and so on. According to this commonsense notion, texts have some inherent, fixed meaning that will become evident to a reader who knows all the words.

Susan Meyer remembers being taught to read in elementary school by teachers who held this commonsense view. They focused their reading lessons on letters and words rather than on meaning. However, with the knowledge now available to her about the reading process and learning to read, Susan does things differently in her

FIGURE 1.1
Reading as an Interaction Among Person, Text, and Social Context

own classroom. She approaches reading as an active process of making meaning.

Susan's views about reading instruction have been influenced by current research that supports the view that reading is an active process of thinking, in which the reader must work to make a meaning for the text. Making meaning is not just a matter of knowing all the words. It is possible to know all the words in a passage yet still be uncertain about its meaning. To understand how this can be so, consider the following passage:

The procedure is quite simple. First you arrange things into different groups. Of course, one pile may be sufficient depending on how much there is to do. If you have to go somewhere else due to lack of facilities that is the next step, otherwise you are pretty well set. It is important not to overdo things. That is, it is better to do few things at once than too many. In the short run this may not seem important but complications can easily arise. A mistake can be expensive as well. At first the whole procedure will seem complicated. Soon, however, it will become just another fact of life. It is difficult to foresee any end to the necessity for this task in the immediate future, but then one can never tell. After the procedure is completed one arranges the materials into different groups again. They can be put into their appropriate places. Eventually they will be used once more, and the whole cycle will then have to be repeated. However, this is part of life. (Bransford & Johnson, 1977, p. 400)

This passage was written to show that the reading process depends on the reader's background knowledge and interpretations and not just on being able to read the words. Most people who read the passage have no difficulty with any of the words, yet feel they do not understand the passage or know what it is really about. However, once they are told that it is about doing laundry, they can reread the text and experience the "click" of comprehension.

With this view of reading as an active search for meaning, we see the importance of the reader as a person. We realize that letters and words do not carry meaning and value in themselves, but take these on as they become the objects of the reader's attention. Teachers like Susan Meyer understand that the job of teaching children to read is one of helping them learn to construct meaning from text. Teaching children to identify words is important, but it is not enough to help them become good readers.

Much has been learned about the reading process by researchers investigating *schema theory* (Spiro, Bruce, & Brewer, 1980). A schema is a "packet" or structure of knowledge in the human mind (Rumelhart, 1981). Schema theory is a way of trying to explain how people store knowledge in their minds, how they use the knowledge they have, and how they acquire new knowledge. According to schema theory, most texts do not tell us very much at all. Rather, a text is nothing more than a linguistic blueprint (Langer, 1982) that we are able to comprehend only because we fill in the gaps with knowledge we already have (background knowledge or prior knowledge). To understand the importance of prior knowledge, think about the following passage (adapted from Collins, Brown, & Larkin, 1980, p. 387):

> He plunked down $12.00 at the window.
> She tried to give him $6.00 but he refused to take it.
> So when they got inside, she bought him a large bag of popcorn.

When reading just the first sentence, some people think the man is at a racetrack window placing a bet, and many others see him at the window of a bank or theater. At any rate, the first sentence is rather ambiguous. Upon reading the second sentence, some people think that the "she" refers to a cashier who is trying to give the man change. With this interpretation, it is somewhat puzzling when the man refuses the money. Upon reading the third sentence, most people arrive at the conclusion that the woman is probably the man's date and that they are going to a movie. She wanted to pay for her own ticket but he didn't agree, and she then decided to use the money to buy him some popcorn.

As this passage suggests, when readers progress through a text they construct a vision, envisionment, or mental model of it (Langer, 1984; Collins, Brown, & Larkin, 1980). They begin with certain hypotheses, and as these hypotheses are confirmed or disconfirmed, their vision of the text becomes increasingly refined.

Readers find it easier to envision a text if they have prior knowledge, not only about the topic (such as going to the movies) but also about that particular kind of text. For example, there are different genres or forms of literature, as will be discussed in detail in Chapter 3. Susan Meyer enjoys reading murder mysteries. When she starts a new mystery book, she reads to discover what case the detective faces, and she is alert to clues about the criminal. When Susan reads a novel, she expects to identify the main characters, to see an interesting plot unfold, to watch the characters develop over the course of the story, and to discover a resolution to the problems posed. She has different expectations depending on whether she is reading a mystery, a novel, a biography, a professional article, and so on.

You can see, then, that background or prior knowledge is one of the major factors influencing the reader's comprehension or understanding of the text. The effect of prior knowledge is so strong that readers with different perspectives may have entirely different understandings of the same text. To see how this can be so, read the following passage and decide what it is about.

> Rocky slowly got up from the mat, planning his escape. He hesitated a moment and thought. Things were not going well. What bothered him most was being held, especially since the charge against him had been weak. He considered his present situation. The lock that held him was strong but he thought he could break it. He knew, however, that his timing would have to be perfect. Rocky was aware that it was because of his early roughness that he had been penalized so severely—much too severely from his point of view. The situation was becoming frustrating, the pressure had been grinding on him for too long. He was being ridden unmercifully. Rocky was getting angry now. He felt he was ready to make his move. He knew that his success or failure would depend on what he did in the next few seconds. (Anderson, Reynolds, Schallert, & Goetz, 1977)

What do you think this passage is about? Anderson and colleagues asked two groups of subjects to read this passage: college students majoring in music, and students majoring in physical education. The two groups interpreted the passage very differently. The music majors thought they were reading about a jailbreak; the physical education majors thought they were reading about a wrestling match. If you look back, you will see that the passage lends itself equally well to both interpretations. The deciding factor was the subjects' background knowledge. As this experiment demonstrated, two individuals may read the same text but arrive at very different interpretations of it.

In summary, you can see that reading is a complex social process, and different communities may have different views of reading. In all cases, however, reading depends on much more than simply knowing the words in a text. Rather, the reader must actively construct meaning from text, knowing how the words go together to convey messages, sometimes subtle and sometimes more obvious. Background experiences and knowledge affect a person's understanding of literacy, participation in literacy events such as discussions of books, and interpretations of text.

KEY CONCEPT 3   TEACHERS SHOULD BE GUIDED BY A CURRICULUM FRAMEWORK THAT RECOGNIZES THE IMPORTANCE OF BOTH THE AFFECTIVE AND COGNITIVE DIMENSIONS OF LITERACY.

SIX ASPECTS OF LITERACY

You have just learned about the complexities of reading and writing and the importance of literacy in people's everyday lives. You might well be wondering: if I want my students to become literate in the ways required by life in our complex society, what should I teach? Specifically, what should I be helping my students to learn?

Susan Meyer has spent a great deal of time wrestling with these questions. Although she recognizes that literacy and literacy learning are holistic processes, she finds it focuses her teaching to think of literacy as having six major aspects. These six aspects (shown in Figure 1.2) form the curriculum framework that Susan uses to guide her teaching.

Ownership

The overarching goal of this curriculum framework—students' ownership of literacy—is shown at the top of the figure. Ownership involves students valuing their own ability to read and write (Au, Scheu, & Kawakami, 1990). Students who "own" literacy are those who choose to use literacy for purposes they have set for themselves, at home as well as at school. The need to be concerned about ownership is highlighted in research suggesting that many students have the ability to read and write but do not choose to do so on their

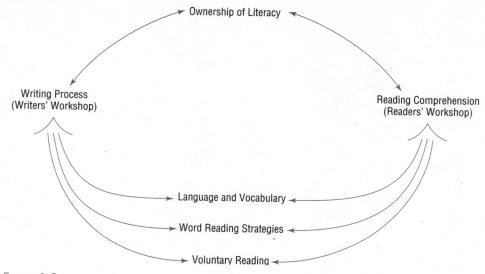

Ownership of Literacy

Writing Process
(Writers' Workshop)

Reading Comprehension
(Readers' Workshop)

Language and Vocabulary

Word Reading Strategies

Voluntary Reading

FIGURE 1.2
Six Aspects of Literacy
Source: From Au, Scheu, Kawakami, & Herman, 1990.

own. For example, a surprising number of fifth-grade students never choose to read a book in their free time (Fielding, Wilson, & Anderson, 1986).

Susan feels that seeing ownership as the overarching goal has changed her thinking about the teaching of reading and writing. She now understands the importance of students wanting to put their reading and writing skills to work. On the one hand, Susan has found that ownership of literacy does not come automatically, just because a student is a capable reader and writer. Marlon, for example, is an able reader but does not read for his own enjoyment. On the other hand, Susan has found ownership of literacy to be high among some students who struggle with reading and writing. Lindsey struggles with reading but she is highly motivated to read books on her own. In school she looks for books that she can read aloud at home to her four-year-old brother. Because Lindsey is so motivated to read, she is very receptive to instruction and suggestions, and Susan feels confident that Lindsey will make good progress in learning to read this year.

Listed below ownership in the figure are the next two aspects of literacy: the writing process and reading comprehension. As you saw in the description of Susan's classroom, the writing process serves as the focal point for the writers' workshop. Reading comprehension serves as the focal point for the readers' workshop, which will be discussed in more detail in Chapters 3 and 4. The remaining three aspects of literacy—language and vocabulary, word-reading strategies, and voluntary reading—are all developed within both the writers' workshop and the readers' workshop.

Writing Process

Writing involves a process of using print (or for younger children, drawing) to compose meaning and communicate a message. Students experience ownership of writing when they write on self-selected topics and come to see themselves as authors. In this curriculum framework writing is seen as a dynamic, nonlinear process that includes activities such as planning, writing or drafting, revising, editing, and publishing (see Graves, 1983). Typically, writers go back and forth among these different activities. While revising, for example, they may decide to abandon the draft and begin another piece based on a new idea. Susan studied the writing process for a summer during which she participated in a writers' workshop with teachers from other schools. She learned that students progress well as writers when they see writing as a means of communicating a message to a certain audience, when they have the opportunity to write about self-selected topics, and when they can discuss and share their writing with real audiences, including other students, the teacher, and adults outside school.

Hampton loves to write and has even written several short pieces at home. Right now in the writers' workshop, he is writing about a visit to his grandmother's house this past summer. Hampton can get his ideas down on paper with relatively little difficulty, but he tends to jump from one thing to the next without developing any idea in

His classmates respond with interest to the story being read by its creator, seated in the author's chair.

depth. Susan is concentrating on helping Hampton learn to revise his writing by fleshing out ideas with further information, especially interesting details. Hampton has decided that he wants to turn his piece into a book and has made sketches for several of the illustrations. He is going to dedicate his book to his grandmother and has already asked if Susan will make a copy that he can mail to her.

Reading Comprehension

As you have already learned, reading comprehension involves the reader's ability to respond to the text and to construct or compose meaning from text, using background knowledge as well as text information. Reading is viewed as the dynamic interaction among the reader, the text, and the situation or social context in which reading takes place (Wixson, Peters, Weber, & Roeber, 1987). Susan tries to take all these factors into consideration when she is having her students read and discuss books during the readers' workshop. The teaching of reading comprehension is discussed in detail in Chapters 3 and 4.

Tamekia is progressing well in reading comprehension. She participates actively in discussions and is able to provide reasons for her answers. She knows how to refer back to the text to verify her answers. But while she reads carefully and can grasp details, Tamekia needs guidance in constructing a theme for the story and in making connections between the story and her own life. Susan feels that Tamekia will benefit from small-group discussions in which students can be guided to think about possible themes for a story and the connections between the story and their own lives.

Language and Vocabulary

This aspect of literacy refers to students' ability to understand and use appropriate terms and structures in both spoken and printed English and to learn the meanings of new words. Students' knowledge of language and vocabulary grows when they are engaged in meaningful communication about a variety of topics (Weaver, 1990). As children read and listen, they encounter new language structures and vocabulary that they are gradually able to use when writing and speaking. Language and vocabulary grow when children are involved in communicating for real purposes in social situations (Pinnell & Jaggar, 1991).

According to the knowledge hypothesis (Mezynski, 1983), vocabulary represents the knowledge a person has of particular topics, not just dictionary definitions. People learn the meaning of new words in increments over time, through repeated encounters. That is, each time we encounter a new word, we learn a little more about its meaning. The major source of vocabulary learning is wide independent reading, when students encounter many new words (Nagy, Herman, & Anderson, 1985). Teachers can help build students' vocabulary knowledge by heightening their interest in words, by teaching them strategies for inferring word meanings from text, and by encouraging them to do wide independent reading. Vocabulary instruction is discussed in detail in Chapter 5.

Esteban speaks Spanish at home, although he can use English well to communicate in class and on the playground. However, Susan understands that there is a difference between the language skills needed for everyday communication and those needed for academic learning (Cummins, 1979). She wants to make sure that Esteban develops the ability to use the formal, standard English necessary for success in school and in the workplace. Esteban is an avid reader, and Susan wants to promote his vocabulary growth by teaching him strategies for learning the meanings of the words he encounters when reading on his own.

Word-Reading Strategies

As explained earlier in this chapter, the roots of children's ability to deal with print are found in their home experiences with literacy (Taylor, 1983). Storybook reading is an especially important home literacy experience. Through storybook reading, children learn concepts about print; for example, that the left page is read before the right and that words run from left to right. Learning concepts about print sets the foundation for word-reading strategies, including spelling (for further information, see Chapter 2).

Students need to have word-reading strategies if they are to read words accurately and quickly. Fluent readers, those who experience a smooth and easy flow through the text, integrate knowledge of the different cue systems (Clay, 1985). That is, they figure words out by considering the cues provided by the *meaning* of the text as a whole, as well as the particular sentence containing the unknown word. They consider the grammatical *structure,* which indicates, for example, that the unknown word is a plural noun or an adjective. They also consider the *visual* cues provided by the letters that make up the unknown word.

Instruction in word-reading strategies involves helping students to use the three cue systems mentioned above in a balanced manner. Students must learn to check their guesses about words by using not just one but all three cue systems, and then they must correct their guesses. Once students learn to use the three cue systems in a balanced manner, they usually stumble only over multisyllable words. At this point, they can benefit from learning about root words and affixes, including plural endings, prefixes, and suffixes. Cue systems and word-reading strategies are discussed in Chapter 2; strategies for dealing with multisyllable words appear in Chapter 5.

Jennifer, like many of the students in Susan Meyer's class, has reached the point where she can easily read shorter words (those of one or two syllables), but she is often stumped when she comes to longer ones. This is a critical problem for students at the third grade and above, because the books they read are beginning to contain many longer and unfamiliar words, such as *fascinating, prehistoric,* and *humiliation.* Susan wants to help Jennifer learn to deal with these longer words by looking for root words, affixes, or common syllables such as *-tion.* Once Jennifer has developed some strategies for dealing with longer words, Susan will encourage her to use these strategies independently.

Voluntary Reading

The final aspect of literacy in the curriculum framework is voluntary reading. Like ownership, voluntary reading has to do with the affective side of literacy. In voluntary reading, the students themselves select the materials they wish to read, either for information or for pleasure (Spiegel, 1981). Students read to fulfill personal goals, not simply to meet the expectations of others. Ideally, students also choose the times when they will read.

Voluntary reading is valuable for a number of reasons. First, students who develop the habit of voluntary reading have gained a source of pleasure to be carried with them throughout their lives. Voluntary reading is one of the ways students demonstrate their ownership of literacy. Second, voluntary reading contributes to students becoming better writers and readers. As mentioned above, literature may provide students with models to follow in their own writing. Voluntary reading can also improve students' comprehension, vocabulary, and word-reading strategies, because they apply and practice skills in all these aspects of literacy when they read on their own.

In September, it seemed to Susan that Reggie was not very interested in books. He read during the time scheduled for sustained silent reading (see Chapter 8), when all the students in the class, and Susan as well, were supposed to read silently from a book of their choice. However, Reggie seldom borrowed books from the class library to read at home, and he told Susan he much preferred to spend his time playing video games. Susan tried recommending different books to Reggie, to see if she could find something that would spark his interest. One day Reggie became fascinated by a book about the *Titanic* that Susan had suggested. Ever since then he has been eagerly reading about lost ships, treasure hunts, and related topics. Susan hopes that she will have similar success with other reluctant readers.

In short, many teachers will find it useful, as Susan does, to follow a curriculum framework highlighting these six aspects of literacy. Putting ownership as the overarching goal reminds teachers of the importance of pursuing affective as well as cognitive goals when promoting students' literacy development. Traditional skill areas, such as word-reading strategies and vocabulary, are still taught. However, skills are embedded in a larger framework emphasizing reading and writing for authentic purposes of learning, communication, and enjoyment.

KEY CONCEPT 4

TEACHERS SHOULD HELP STUDENTS WITH DIFFICULT LITERACY TASKS, THEN GRADUALLY RELEASE RESPONSIBILITY FOR THESE TASKS TO THE STUDENTS.

A MODEL OF INSTRUCTION

The ideas behind this key concept come from the theory developed by Lev Vygotsky (1978). Vygotsky points out that children learn higher-level mental processes, such as those involved in reading, through the help of knowledgeable others. Before they come to school, children have parents and other relatives to assist them, and after they come to school, they also have teachers to help them learn. Learning is an external, social process, which takes place during interactions between children and adults. You can see that these ideas relate to those in Key Concept 2, where we discussed literacy and literacy learning as social processes.

Susan Meyer can understand the importance of knowledgeable others in the way her own children and her students are learning to read. At home, Susan has not tried to teach Amy and Kristy to read through formal lessons, but she is aware of teaching them in many informal ways throughout the day. She and Ron read to Amy and Kristy every night before bedtime and answer questions the girls have about the stories. Amy and Kristy have paper and crayons so that they can draw and experiment with letters if they wish. Amy was interested in knowing how to write *Amy, Mom, Dad,* and *Kristy* and so Susan wrote those words for her to copy. She and Ron point out signs and labels when they are in the car or shopping at the supermarket, and Amy and Kristy can recognize the signs for McDonald's and other fast-food chains.

At school, Susan Meyer acts as the knowledgeable other to help her students learn to read and write. She talks with her students about the processes of reading and writing and the kinds of reasoning that she and other adults do with text. For example, when Susan decided that one of the groups would read *The Art Lesson,* she thought about the theme she would guide the students to understand. The theme she chose was the importance of having goals in your life and how the people around you can help you achieve them. When the students had finished reading the story, Susan wanted them to make connections between the story and their own lives. To show them the kind of reasoning involved, she gave an example from her own life. Here's what Susan told her students:

> Today we're going to think about connections between the story and our own lives. Here's the connection that I see to my own life. When I think about what happened to Tommy in *The Art Lesson,* it reminds me about when I was in school. But I didn't want to be an artist. In fact, I didn't know what I wanted to be when I grew up. Then when I was in high school, I had a history teacher named Mrs. Hunter, who took a lot of interest in me and really seemed to enjoy teaching. That convinced me. I decided that I wanted to be a teacher just like Mrs. Hunter.
>
> I wonder if any of you can think about a connection between the story and your own life? It could be a time when you had a goal, or maybe you can think of another connection.

The teacher's "thinking out loud" is very important in helping students learn, because the thinking readers do while reading is otherwise invisible. When children watch an adult read silently, about all they see is eyes moving back and forth and a hand occasionally turning a page. Nothing can be known about the adult's thinking, unless the adult talks about it. That is why Susan talks to her students about the thinking processes she uses when she reads.

Similarly, when children read, their thinking generally is invisible to their teachers. However, teachers can find out about children's mental processes by engaging them in discussions. For example, you saw how Susan asked her students questions about their thinking when making predictions about the story. Through social interactions, which may be formal lessons or informal conversations, teachers provide students with the help they need to think about and construct meaning from text.

Susan Meyer realizes that she must be careful about the assistance she gives her students, because some kinds of assistance might not be at all beneficial to their literacy development. Susan knows that she should not be helping students with tasks they could just as well do alone. She also knows that she should not present students with impossibly difficult tasks but those that are slightly beyond their reach, and then provide just enough help so they can be successful.

In Vygotsky's terms, a task that is just beyond the child's reach is said to be in the *zone of proximal development*—the next step forward in mental development. A task in the zone of proximal development is too difficult for the child to accomplish independently but not too difficult if the guidance of a knowledgeable other is available.

The term *scaffolding* is used to describe the kinds of support a teacher might give a child dealing with a literacy task in the zone of proximal development. The word *scaffolding* reminds us that the support is necessary at the time but temporary (Wood, Bruner, & Ross, 1976). The scaffolding or extra support is to be adjusted, reduced, and finally taken away.

Here is an example of how Susan Meyer provided scaffolding when her students were confused about the sequence of events in a story. Susan traced the difficulty to the fact that the story had a flashback.

> *Teacher:* Maybe it would help if we made a timeline showing the events in the story in order. Now, when we read the story, what part did the author write about first?
>
> *Esteban:* How Maria is at home and she doesn't want to go to art class.
>
> *Teacher:* Right, let me write that part on the chart. Now, the next part of the story is what's called a flashback. In a flashback, the author goes back in time and tells you about something that happened before. What happened to Maria before?
>
> *Jennifer:* She was going to art classes every Saturday and she really liked it.
>
> *Teacher:* Okay, good, let me put that part near the beginning of our timeline. Then what happened that all of a sudden made her feel she didn't want to go to art classes any more? Brenda?
>
> *Brenda:* They were supposed to do a drawing of their home and she's ashamed of where she lives.

Under Susan's guidance, the students recounted the events in the story. Later, when they reviewed the timeline that Susan had written on chart paper, they were able to get a clear picture of the sequence of events.

Here is an example of how Susan Meyer provided scaffolding when a student came across an unknown word.

> *Ming:* Ms. Meyer, I don't know this word. I think it's something like *hum-mil-ation.*

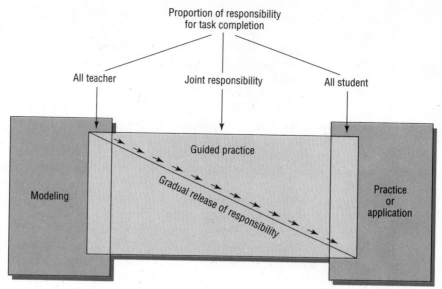

Proportion of responsibility
for task completion

All teacher   Joint responsibility   All student

Modeling   Guided practice   Practice
or
application

Gradual release of responsibility

FIGURE 1.3
The Gradual Release of Responsibility Model of Instruction
Source: Pearson, 1985, p. 732.

Teacher: That's a good try. It's *humiliation.* So what do you think it means?

Ming: (shrugs)

Teacher: Well, let's see if we can figure it out. First of all, what's happening in this part of the story?

Ming: The lion's just been caught in the net and he's really upset.

Teacher: Uh-huh, so this is something the lion's saying when he's upset. Read this part for me (points).

Ming: "Me—the King of Beasts—caught like a mouse in a trap! Oh the shame of it all! The humiliation!"

Teacher: So what would you guess *humiliation* means?

Ming: Could be like when you feel ashamed.

Teacher: Um-hm, that's what I think too.

Notice in both of these examples of scaffolding that Susan did very little telling. Instead, through careful questioning, she guided students through the process of working the answers out for themselves.

Pearson (1985) refers to the careful adjusting and removal of scaffolding as the *gradual release of responsibility.* This process is shown in Figure 1.3. On the left, we see that instruction begins with the teacher modeling or showing the students how the task can be accomplished. At this point, responsibility for the task rests with the teacher.

In the center of the diagram, the teacher involves the students in guided practice, and the teacher and students have joint responsibility for the task. The two examples just presented showed this kind of joint responsibility. In one case responsibility was shared by Susan and a group of students, and in the other case by Susan and just one student. The diagonal line going from upper left to lower right shows how the teacher reduces the scaffolding and gradually releases responsibility for the task to the students. The teacher assumes less and less responsibility, while the students take on more and more.

On the right, we see that the teacher has arranged for the students to practice the task on their own and to apply what they have learned. Now all the responsibility for the task has been transferred from the teacher to the students. Through a process in which the teacher gradually released responsibility, the students have become capable of performing the task on their own.

In brief, we can think of the teacher's role as that of helping students through the zone of proximal development, or helping them to take the next step forward in learning to read. Effective instruction involves proceeding along a continuum in which the teacher releases responsibility to the students, not all at once but little by little. In the end, students will set their own goals and determine for themselves whether teacher assistance is necessary (Gavelek, 1986).

SUMMARY

One way to organize literacy instruction is through a writers' workshop and a readers' workshop, as you saw in the example of Susan Meyer's classroom. In Key Concept 1 you learned that effective teachers like Susan Meyer have a well-defined philosophy that guides literacy instruction in their classrooms. Their philosophy includes principles such as using authentic literacy activities, teaching from whole to part, providing demonstrations and scaffolding, and encouraging students to learn from one another. In Key Concept 2 you learned about the complex nature of reading as a social process. Reading is not just one kind of behavior. There are different ways of reading, depending on such factors as the way the community views reading and the purposes the reader has for reading. Reading for meaning is not just a matter of words but depends on the social situation and the reader's background knowledge.

You learned in Key Concept 3 that teachers should be aware of fostering students' development in six aspects of literacy: ownership, the writing process, reading comprehension, language and vocabulary knowledge, word-reading strategies, and voluntary reading. These aspects address the affective as well as the cognitive dimensions of literacy. Finally, in Key Concept 4 you learned of a model for literacy instruction based on the concepts of the zone of proximal development and the gradual release of responsibility. These concepts highlight the teacher's role in guiding students toward independence in literacy.

◀ **ACTIVITIES**

Reflecting on Your Own Literacy

For a period of two or three days, keep a log of all your reading and writing activities. What kind of reading and writing did you do? What are the functions or purposes of these different literacy activities? Compare your log to that of someone else. What similarities and differences can you find?

Applying What You Have Learned to the Classroom

Observe reading instruction taking place in an elementary school classroom. Make notes of what you see the teacher and students doing. Then consider the six aspects of literacy discussed in Key Concept 3. Which aspects of literacy did you see being addressed in the classroom? How were they being addressed? Which aspects, if any, were not being addressed?

BIBLIOGRAPHY

References

Anderson, R. C., Reynolds, R. E., Schallert, D. E., & Goetz, E. T. (1977). Frameworks for comprehending discourse. *American Educational Research Journal, 14*(4), 367–381.

Applebee, A. (1991). Literature: Whose heritage? In E. H. Hiebert (Ed.), *Literacy for a diverse society: Perspectives, practices, and policies.* New York: Teachers College Press, pp. 228–236.

Applebee, A., Langer, J., & Mullis, I. (1985). *The reading report card: Progress toward excellence in our schools.* Princeton, NJ: National Assessment of Educational Progress, Educational Testing Service.

Au, K. H., & Mason, J. M. (1983). Cultural congruence in classroom participation structures: Achieving a balance of rights. *Discourse Processes, 6*(2), 145–167.

Au, K. H., Scheu, J. A., & Kawakami, A. J. (1990). Assessment of students' ownership of literacy. *The Reading Teacher, 44*(2) 154–156.

Au, K. H., Scheu, J. A., Kawakami, A. J., & Herman, P. A. (1990). Assessment and accountability in a whole literacy curriculum. *The Reading Teacher, 43*(8), 574–578.

Bakhtin, M. M. (1986). *Speech genres and other late essays.* C. Emerson & M. Holquist (Eds.), trans. V. W. McGee. Austin, TX: University of Texas Press.

Bransford, J. D., & Johnson, M. K. (1977). Considerations of some problems of comprehension. In W. C. Chase (Ed.), *Visual information processing.* New York: Academic Press.

Bruner, J. (1990). *Acts of meaning.* Cambridge, MA: Harvard University Press.

Clay, M. M. (1985). *The early detection of reading difficulties* (3rd ed.). Auckland, New Zealand: Heinemann.

Collins, A., Brown, J. S., & Larkin, J. M. (1980). Inference in text understanding. In R. J. Spiro, B. C. Bruce, & W. F. Brewer (Eds.), *Theoretical issues in reading comprehension.* Hillsdale, NJ: Erlbaum.

Cummins, J. (1979). Linguistic interdependence and the educational development of bilingual children. *Review of Educational Research, 49,* 22–51.

Cunningham, P. (1975–1976). Investigating a synthesized theory of mediated word recognition. *Reading Research Quarterly, 11,* 127–143.

Fielding, L., Wilson, P., & Anderson, R. C. (1986). A focus on free reading: The role of tradebooks in reading instruction. In T. E. Raphael (Ed.), *The contexts of school-based literacy.* New York: Random House, pp. 149–160.

Freire, P. (1985). Reading the world and reading the word: An interview with Paulo Freire. *Language Arts, 62*(1), 15–21.

Gavelek, J. R. (1986). The social contexts of literacy and schooling: A developmental perspective. In T. E. Raphael (Ed.), *The contexts of school-based literacy.* New York: Random House, pp. 3–26.

Graves, D. (1983). *Writing: Teachers and children at work.* Exeter, NH: Heinemann.

Graves, D., & Hansen, J. (1983). The author's chair. *Language Arts, 60*(2), 176–183.

Guthrie, J. T. (1981). Acquisition of newspaper readership. *Reading Teacher, 34,* 616–618.

Hansen, J. (1987). *When writers read.* Portsmouth, NH: Heinemann.

Heath, S. B. (1980). The functions and uses of literacy. *Journal of Communication,* Winter, 123–133.

Heath, S. B. (1983). *Ways with words: Language, life, and work in communities and classrooms.* Cambridge: Cambridge University Press.

Holdaway, D. (1979). *The foundations of literacy.* Sydney, Australia: Ashton Scholastic (distributed in the United States by Heinemann).

Langer, J. A. (1984). Examining background knowledge and text comprehension. *Reading Research Quarterly, 19*(4), 468–491.

Langer, J. A. (1982). The reading process. In A. Berger & H. A. Robinson (Eds.), *Secondary school reading: What research reveals for classroom practice.* Urbana, IL: National Conference on Research in English and ERIC Clearinghouse on Reading and Communication Skills.

Mezynski, K. (1983). Issues concerning the acquisition of knowledge: Effects of vocabulary training on reading comprehension. *Review of Educational Research, 53,* 253–279.

Mikulecky, L. (1982). Job literacy: The relationship between school preparation and workplace actuality. *Reading Research Quarterly, 17,* 400–417.

Monteith, M. K. (1981). The magazine habit. *Language Arts, 58,* 965–969.

Nagy, W. E., Herman, P., & Anderson, R. C. (1985). Learning words from context. *Reading Research Quarterly, 20,* 233–253.

National Assessment of Educational Progress (1987, June). Reading objectives, 1986 and 1988 assessments. Princeton, NJ: National Assessment of Educational Progress, Educational Testing Service.

Pearson, P. D. (1985). Changing the face of reading comprehension instruction. *The Reading Teacher, 38*(8), 724–738.

Pinnell, G. S., & Jaggar, A. M. (1991). Oral language: Speaking and listening in the classroom. In J. Flood, J. M. Jensen, D. Lapp, & J. R. Squire (Eds.), *Handbook of research on teaching the English language arts.* New York: Macmillan, pp. 691–720.

Ribovich, J. K., & Erickson, L. (1980). A study of lifelong reading with implications for instructional programs. *Journal of Reading, 24,* 20–26.

Rumelhart, D. E. (1981). Schemata: The building blocks of cognition. In J. T. Guthrie (Ed.), *Comprehension and teaching: Research reviews.* Newark, DE: International Reading Association.

Smith, F. J. (1988). *Understanding reading* (2nd ed.). Hillsdale, NJ: Lawrence Erlbaum.

Smith, S. L., Carey, R., & Harste, J. C. (1982). The contexts of reading. In A. Berger & H. A. Robinson (Eds.), *Secondary school reading: What research reveals for classroom practice.* Urbana, IL: National Conference on Research in English and ERIC Clearinghouse on Reading and Communication Skills.

Spiegel, D. L. (1981). *Reading for pleasure: Guidelines.* Newark, DE: International Reading Association.

Spiro, R. J., Bruce, B. C., & Brewer, W. F. (Eds.) (1980). *Theoretical issues in reading comprehension.* Hillsdale, NJ: Erlbaum.

Taylor, D. (1983). *Family literacy: Young children learning to read and write.* Portsmouth, NH: Heinemann.

Vygotsky, L. S. (1978). *Mind in society.* In M. Cole et al. (Eds.). Cambridge, MA: Harvard University Press.

Weaver, C. (1990). *Understanding whole language: Principles and practices.* Portsmouth, NH: Heinemann.

Wertsch, J. V. (1990). The voice of rationality in a sociocultural approach to mind. In L. C. Moll (Ed.), *Vygotsky and education: Instructional implications and applications of sociohistorical psychology.* Cambridge: Cambridge University Press, pp. 111–126.

Wixson, K. K., Peters, C. W., Weber, E. M., & Roeber, E. D. (1987). New directions in statewide reading assessment. *The Reading Teacher, 40*(8), 749–754.

Wood, D., Bruner, J., & Ross, G. (1976). The role of tutoring in problem solving. *Journal of Child Psychology and Psychiatry, 17,* 89–100.

Suggested Classroom Resources

dePaola, T. (1981). *Now One Foot, Now the Other.* New York: G. P. Putnam's Sons.

dePaola, T. (1982). *Strega Nona's Magic Lessons.* Orlando, FL: Harcourt Brace Jovanovich.

dePaola, T. (1983). *The Legend of the Bluebonnet.* New York: G. P. Putnam's Sons.

dePaola, T. (1989). *The Art Lesson.* New York: G. P. Putnam's Sons.

Slote. A.(1990). *The trading game.* Philadelphia: Lippincott.

Further Readings

Applebee, A. N., Langer, J. A., & Mullis, I. V. S. (1988, February). *Who reads best: Factors related to reading achievement in grades 3, 7, and 11.* Princeton, NJ: National Assessment of Educational Progress, Educational Testing Service.

Goodman, K. (1986). *What's whole in whole language?* Portsmouth, NH: Heinemann.

Powell, R. E. (1992). Goals for the language arts program: Toward a democratic view. *Language Arts, 69* (5), 342–349.

Spiegel, D. L. (1992). Blending whole language and systematic direct instruction. *The Reading Teacher, 46* (1), 38–44.

2 EMERGENT LITERACY AND BEGINNING INSTRUCTION

Anne-Marie made me sit down in front of her, on my little chair; she leant over me, lowered her eyelids and went to sleep. From this mask-like face issued a plaster voice. I grew bewildered: who was talking? about what? and to whom? My mother had disappeared; not a smile or trace of complicity. I was an exile. And then I did not recognize the language. Where did she get her confidence? After a moment, I realized: it was the book that was talking. Sentences emerged that frightened me: they were like real centipedes; they swarmed with syllables and letters, spun out their diphthongs and made their double consonants hum; fluting, nasal, broken up with sighs and pauses, rich in unknown words, they were in love with themselves and their meandering and had no time for me: sometimes they disappeared before I could understand them; at others, I had understood in advance and they went on rolling on nobly towards their end without sparing me a comma. These words were obviously not meant for me. The tale itself was in its Sunday best: the wood-cutter, the wood-cutter's wife and their daughters had acquired majesty; their rags were magnificently described, words left their mark on objects, transforming action into rituals and events into ceremonies. (Sartre, 1964, quoted in Britton, 1970, pp. 150–151)

◀ OVERVIEW

In this chapter we describe emergent literacy, or the beginnings of children's development as readers and writers. We focus on kindergarten and first-grade classrooms and the need for a holistic, meaningful approach to instruction that fosters children's efforts and interests in literacy. Teachers promote literacy both informally and through planned instruction, by following children's interests in the new and allowing them to practice the old. As Sartre eloquently states in the introductory quotation, some children may be surprised by the novelty of having adults read aloud instead of talking to them, and they may at first be overwhelmed by the formality and complexity of written language forms. However, many children come to school with considerable experience with the reading aloud of stories and other literacy activities, such as writing shopping lists or sending greeting cards.

We present four key concepts in this chapter. The first deals with the concept of emergent literacy. The second addresses the role of a

35

meaningful context, along with opportunities for play and discovery, in children's emergent literacy. The third discusses shared reading as a key approach for instruction in kindergarten and first grade. The fourth deals with word-reading strategies, including phonics.

KEY CONCEPT 1: Kindergarten and first-grade students should receive instruction and engage in activities consistent with the concept of emergent literacy.

KEY CONCEPT 2: Kindergarten and first-grade students should learn about literacy in a classroom community with meaningful contexts for systematic instruction, informal instruction, and opportunities for discovery.

KEY CONCEPT 3: Kindergarten and first-grade students should participate in shared reading, with instruction moving from whole (the story) to part (the words and letters).

KEY CONCEPT 4: Kindergarten and first-grade students should learn to use a combination of cue systems, including letter-sound relationships, so they will be able to identify words accurately.

◀ **PERSPECTIVE**

Reading and Writing in a Kindergarten Classroom

Some of Hally Simmons' kindergarten students, those who lived in the neighborhood, arrived at school long before the bell rang, because their parents had jobs that began early. Other students came on the bus from other parts of the city. After doffing their outdoor clothes, the children took picture books from the classroom library, or big or little predictable books from a display at the side of the room, to read with their friends. (Big books are oversized books with enlarged text and illustrations, while little books are normal-sized versions of the same material. These books are termed *predictable* when the events and language follow a pattern that children can anticipate.) Of course, most of the children were not reading in the way that mature readers read. With picture books, they often looked at the illustrations and told the story in their own words, inserting familiar phrases such as "once upon a time." With predictable books that they had previously read with Hally, they had memorized the words and so could recite the text from memory: "Brown bear, brown bear, what do you see?"

Hally began the day's instruction by gathering the children on the carpet at the front of the room. Brian, the leader for the day, chose a favorite nursery rhyme, "Little Boy Blue," and led the class in reciting it by using a pointer to indicate the words on the chart.

Then it was time for the morning message. As Hally stood before the group, she pondered out loud for a moment: "Let's see, what should I write? I know, I'll write about something special that will be happening today." Then Hally wrote on the chalkboard:

Good morning, girls and boys.
Today is Tuesday, October 12.
Today is Sara's birthday.
Sara's mother sent a snack for us.

As Hally wrote, children called out some of the words. "That's my name!" Sara said excitedly. When Hally was finished, she had the class read the message together. The first two lines were very familiar to the students, since Hally used a greeting and the date every day. Several of the children noticed that *Today is* was repeated, and so were able to start the third line. They recognized Sara's name and knew that it was her birthday.

The word *snack* posed a problem for the children. Hally asked for guesses about what a mother might send to school for a child's birthday, and the children came up with ideas such as cake, ice cream, and cookies. Hally wrote these guesses on the board, and the children could see that none of them matched. She cued the children by saying that the word started with a *ssss* sound, adding that "when you're hungry and it's not time for dinner yet, your mother might fix you a _____." With these cues the children figured out that the word must be *snack*. Other activities that Hally built around the morning message are described in Key Concept 2.

After work with the message, Hally began the writers' workshop. She started the workshop with a mini-lesson on using invented spelling. "Yesterday," Hally said, "Carlton told me a story about something that happened to him. I'm going to show you Carlton's drawing and ask him to tell you the story." Carlton explained how his mother had gone to the hospital to have a baby, and how his father had held him up so he could look through the window at his new baby sister. His drawing showed a row of babies in cribs, and his father lifting him up to see them. Hally helped Carlton phrase what he might want to write to go with his picture: "I have a new baby sister. Me and my dad went to the hospital. My dad lifted me up so I could see." Hally asked the children if they knew what letter Carlton could use to write *sister*. Some children knew it was an *S*. Hally suggested that Carlton might want to write an *S* to show which baby was his sister. She urged the children to use letters to label the things they were drawing. Then she held up a writing folder and the children called out the name of the classmate who should come up and get it. (A writing folder is a manila folder that contains the

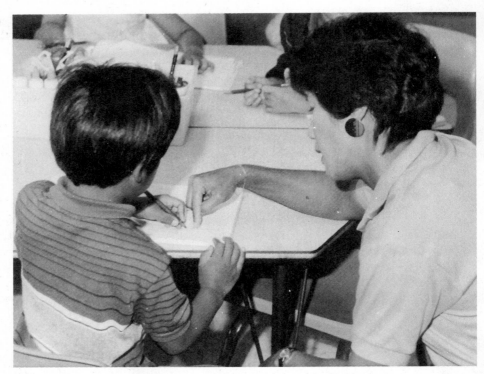

In a brief writing conference with his teacher, this kindergartner receives help with his draft. The teacher first praises his efforts and then gives him one specific suggestion about how to proceed.

drafts of a child's writing. Each folder is labeled with the child's name.) This process continued until all the folders were distributed.

The children returned to their seats and began working. Many started drawing on new sheets of paper. A few took out the drawings they had done the day before and tried to use letters to label, as Hally had suggested. Hally moved from one table to the next, conferring briefly with individual children. "Sara, tell me what you're planning on drawing today. Marco, which one is you and which one is your brother? Good, you can write *Marco* there, then think about what letter you want to put so we'll know the other person is your brother."

After 15 minutes, Hally had the children clean up and come to the carpet again with their folders. She selected four children to share, including Marco. Each of these children had completed a drawing and made an attempt at labeling. Hally wanted to encourage the children to work on a drawing for more than one day and to do a set of drawings on the same sequence of events. In this case, she suggested that Carlton might want to draw something else about his baby sister, and that Marco might want to add to his story about how his brother was teaching him to play soccer.

After the writers' workshop the children had about 15 minutes to go to a center of their choice. Hally's classroom had seven: a library center, a message center, a home center, a computer center, a blocks center, a science center, and an art center. Hally had introduced the centers one at a time, so the children would know what they could do at each center and how many could be there at the same time. For example, the children had learned that at the blocks center they could build block structures alone or with their friends, and that they were responsible for putting the blocks back on the shelf when they were finished.

Some of the centers, such as the library and computer centers, involved children in literacy directly. At the library center they read books, while at the computer center they played games that taught them about letters. At the other centers, Hally made it easy for the children to experiment with literacy if they chose to do so. For example, she put Post-its and crayons in the blocks center, so children could label the structures they made. She put paper and pencil in the home center so children could play at taking phone messages or writing shopping lists.

After morning recess Hally involved the whole class in the shared reading of a big book, as described in Key Concept 3. This lesson usually lasted for about 20 minutes. Then the children were free to return to the centers again. Soon, when the children are thoroughly familiar with the centers, Hally will begin calling small groups for 15-minute reading lessons based on predictable little books (often with the same text as the big books). For now, she circulated to the different centers, talking to children about what they were doing and taking anecdotal notes about both their social and academic behaviors.

Before lunch, Hally called the children back to the carpet again, this time to listen to a story. Hally's selections ranged from *The Very Hungry Caterpillar* by Eric Carle (1969) to *First Pink Light* by Eloise Greenfield (1976) to *Millions of Cats* (1928) by Wanda Gag. These stories were more complex in language and events than those used for shared reading. Hally encouraged the children to discuss their feelings about the story and to make personal connections to it. Today, having heard *First Pink Light,* Marco discussed wanting to stay up late until his older brother got home but having his parents send him to bed.

In Hally Simmons' kindergarten the morning passed quickly, with a mixture of group and individual activities that allowed children to become involved with literacy at their own levels. Some children experimented with letters while others drew. Some were highly familiar with storybook reading and able to pick out a word or two on the page, while others had had little prior experience with storybooks and were not yet attending to print. Using a range of activities that permitted a range of responses, Hally was able to further the literacy of all the children in her class.

KEY CONCEPT 1 STUDENTS IN KINDERGARTEN AND FIRST GRADE SHOULD RECEIVE INSTRUCTION AND ENGAGE IN ACTIVITIES CONSISTENT WITH THE CONCEPT OF EMERGENT LITERACY.

EMERGENT LITERACY

The phrase *emergent literacy* (or *emerging literacy*) is used to describe the reading and writing efforts shown by young children before they are able to read and write in conventional ways that adults would recognize as reading and writing. William Teale (1987) notes that, from the perspective of emergent literacy, children are continuously in the process of becoming literate, probably from the time they are just a few months old. For example, infants can scan the illustrations in a picture book and listen as their parents read to them or to their older siblings. Through these and other experiences, children at the ages of one, two, or three are already learning about literacy.

Research on emergent literacy is consistent with the notion of constructivism, discussed in Chapter 1, in verifying that young children are actively constructing their own understandings of reading and writing. Children are not merely copying what adults do, because, as discussed in detail below, they read and write in ways quite unlike those of adults. Given opportunities to read and write, they try different ways following their own (not adult) logic.

This process of literacy learning has been described as one of *successive approximation* (Holdaway, 1979). That is, the child learns by engaging in the full processes of reading and writing, and through trial and error gradually moves closer and closer to reading and writing in conventional ways. In this view, children's reading and writing will often show what we might think of as errors. For example, the child may tell the story by referring to the pictures, instead of decoding the print, or may use just the letter *S* to write *sister*. However, from the point of view of emergent literacy, these efforts are not errors but steps along the way to conventional literacy.

Having some background about research in emergent literacy will help teachers to recognize and celebrate the signs of progress young children show in the process of successive approximation. For example, research conducted by Elizabeth Sulzby (1985) shows that young children's attempts to read picture storybooks fall into several categories. (Sulzby's research involves 11 different vari-

Category	Example
1. Children refer to the pictures, using their own oral language to label objects or make comments.	Child: There's the pig. And the wolf.
2. Children refer to the pictures, using their own oral language to tell the story.	Child: So the pig got the straw, and he was building his house. Then the wolf wanted to eat the pig, so he blew the house down.
3. Children refer to the pictures, using a mixture of their own oral language and the language of the book to tell the story.	Child: No—no way, said the pig. Then I'll huff and I'll puff and I'll blow your house in, said the wolf.
4. Children refer to the pictures, using the language of the book to tell the story. Children have memorized the story.	Child: Little pig, little pig, let me come in. No, no! Not by the hair of my chinny chin chin.
5. Children refer to the print. Children may refuse to read if they cannot identify the words.	Child: B—uh, what's this word? (Refuses to continue until told the word.)

(Adapted from Sulzby, 1985)

FIGURE 2.1
Categories of Storybook Reading

ables, and the 5 categories presented here are an adaptation of her work.) In this study kindergarten students were asked to choose a favorite storybook, one that had been read to the class several times, to read to an adult. An overview of the categories of storybook reading identified by Sulzby is shown in Figure 2.1.

Children in the first category turned through the pages of the book, labeling objects or making comments: "There's the pig. And the wolf." In the second category, children did not just comment but told the story by referring to the pictures. They recounted the story in their own oral language, not the language of the book: "So the pig got the straw, and he was building his house. Then the wolf wanted to eat the pig, so he blew the house down."

In the third category, children told the story by referring to the pictures, but now they used a mixture of their own oral language and the language of the book: "No, no way, said the pig. Then I'll huff and I'll puff and I'll blow your house in, said the wolf." Notice in this example that the child had memorized some phrases from the text ("Then I'll huff and I'll puff") and was also using other phrases ("said the pig") that would appear in books but would not usually be heard in oral conversations. In the fourth category, children told the story in the language of the book, often word for word: "Little pig, little pig, let me come in. No, no! Not by the hair of my chinny chin chin." In this example the child had memorized nearly the entire text and so could tell the story almost word for word as it appeared in the book, without using his own oral language. In short, children in these four categories, when asked to read a favorite picture storybook to an adult, did so by referring to the pictures, not to the words on the page.

Children in the fifth category attempted to read familiar story-books by attending to print. These children often pointed to the words, showing that they were tracking the print. They would also stop when they came to a word of which they were unsure: "B . . . uh, what's this word?" Sulzby found that children in this category sometimes refused to read because they knew that they would not be able to do so with word-for-word accuracy. This behavior was in contrast to that of children in the other categories, who told the story freely, without being aware of the need to attend to print.

Sulzby cautions that children's emergent storybook reading behaviors must be viewed holistically and that, during the same reading event, children's reading may shift from one category to another and back again. These categories are meant to be descriptive of a "central tendency" in children's storybook reading, with the understanding that the boundaries between categories are not fixed.

As you have seen, Sulzby discovered that young children's early efforts to read storybooks began with the idea of telling the story, not dealing with print. This finding is consistent with the point made in Chapter 1, in connection with research by Denny Taylor (1983), that children become literate by attending first to the *uses* of print, not to print itself. In other words, the process of learning to read does not begin with sounds and letters but with an understanding of the reasons that people read. In the case of picture story-books, the usual reason is to enjoy a good story.

Additional insights into children's early understandings of how print works come from research conducted by Emilia Ferreiro and Ana Teberosky (1982), who studied Spanish-speaking children. In one task, children were shown a picture with a one-word text beneath it. In some cases there was a direct match between the entire picture and the word: a picture of a boat with the word *sailboat* (*velero*) beneath it. In other cases text described only part of the picture: for example, the profile of a man smoking a pipe with the word *pipe* (*pipa*) beneath it. When asked, "Show me where there is something to read," some children pointed to the picture rather than to the printed word. They also guessed that the second item was *man* not *pipe,* because they were attending only to the picture.

Even after children have started attending to print, their understandings of how print works are still evolving. Ferreiro and Teberosky believed that children's understandings of how print works might follow the progression described below:

1. Picture and print are not differentiated. The text is entirely predictable from the illustration. The text represents the same elements as the picture. Picture and print constitute a unit which cannot be separated. [That is, the child sees the illustration of the sailboat together with the word printed beneath as "one picture."]
2. The print is differentiated from the picture. The text is treated as a

unit independent of its graphic characteristics. The text represents either the name of the illustrated object or a sentence associated with the illustration, but in both cases the interpretation is attributed to the text as a unit. [The child thinks of the word *sailboat* as a whole without distinguishing the individual letters *s-a-i-l-b-o-a-t*.]

3. An initial consideration of graphic properties of print emerges. The text continues to be predictable from the illustration. [Now the child may notice that *sailboat* begins with an *s* and has other letters as well.]

4. Children search for a one-to-one correspondence between graphic and sound segments. [The child attends to the initial consonant *s* in *sailboat* and knows that the word begins with an *sss* sound.] (p. 65; words in brackets added)

Research by Ferreiro and Teberosky (1982), Clay (1975), and others shows that children's writing development also undergoes a process involving the shaping and reshaping of understandings of print. Figure 2.2 gives an overview of this process. Often, children begin writing with letterlike forms or scribbles that capture the characteristics of the writing system in their community (Harste, Woodward, & Burke, 1984). The scribbles of young children exposed to English look different from the scribbles of children exposed to Arabic or Hebrew, which use writing systems with different characteristics.

Many children then progress to writing strings of letters. While they produce recognizable letters, children are writing these letters without any thought to letter-sound relationships. For example, a child may write a string of letters such as *RXJXO* and tell the teacher that it says "I went to my grandma's house."

Later, children begin to write using a single letter to represent a syllable or whole word. For example, "I went to my grandma's house" is now written: *I W T M GM H.* This type of writing uses what is called *invented spelling* or *inventive spelling*—spellings that children have invented by applying their current understandings of writing and letter-sound relationships. Invented spelling is an easily recognized behavior in emergent literacy.

Gradually, as children's understandings evolve, they learn to add other letters, such as medial and final consonants and later, vowels. Eventually they spell by attempting to represent all the sounds they hear in a word. They also learn to spell common words, such as *the* and *is,* which they have seen many times in print. Research suggests that improvement in spelling is fostered not by spelling tests but by wide reading that exposes children again and again to the conventional spellings of many words. In support of the constructivist perspective, research also suggests that children who have the opportunity to invent their own spellings of words eventually become better spellers than those who lack this opportunity (Ehri, 1987). The reason for this finding seems to be that children who use invented

Category	Example
1. Children reproduce the features of the writing system of their culture.	*(handwritten script)*
2. Children use a number of different letters or letter-like forms to represent words. Letters do not correspond to the sounds of the words.	*(handwritten letter-like forms)*
3. Children use a letter to stand for each syllable in a word (syllabic hypothesis). Letters correspond to the sounds of words (usually, the beginning sound).	*(handwritten letters)*
4. Children use more than one letter to represent a syllable. They are beginning to analyze words beyond the level of the syllable.	*(handwritten letters)*
5. Children use letters to represent all the sounds they hear in a word (alphabetic hypothesis).	*grovm house*

(Adapted from Ferreiro & Teberosky, 1982)

FIGURE 2.2
Categories of Writing

spelling must construct their own understandings of how the English spelling system works, while children who are taught to spell through rote memorization do not always develop these understandings.

Teachers will find it useful to have an understanding of children's reading and writing development, as revealed in the research of Sulzby, Ferreiro, and Teberosky, and others who have studied emergent literacy. However, research also suggests that the literacy learning of individual children does not proceed in a lockstep manner, by a clear progression from one stage to the next. Rather, children may skip over some steps, move back to a step they appeared to have passed, or show behavior that reflects the characteristics of two stages at once. As shown in research by Donald Graves (1983), Anne Dyson (1989), and others, learning to read and write is a highly individual process. There is no one set way that children go about learning, and thus there is no set sequence of skills that needs to be taught to all children. While teachers should have a sense of how learning to read and write go *in general,* they must also engage in what Yetta Goodman (1985) describes as "kidwatching" to understand the literacy learning needs of particular children at particular moments in time.

The concept of emergent literacy has important practical implications for teachers working in kindergarten, first-grade, and even second-grade classrooms. William Teale (1987) suggests that the following kinds of instructional practices are supported by research on emergent literacy.

Use literacy to organize the classroom's daily activities. For example, have children look at a chart to find the names of those who are to be helpers that day. Have a child read classmates' names and take attendance. Have children sign up for the centers they would like to go to.

Give children lots of opportunities for dramatic play and creative expression, and make literacy a part of these activities. For example, put paper and pencil in the home center so children can play at taking phone messages and making shopping lists. Turn the home center into a restaurant and have children prepare menus and take orders. Encourage children to write labels for their block structures, as Hally Simmons did with her students. Give children sentence strips so they can write a sentence to go with their paintings.

Hold a daily writers' workshop, even in kindergarten, and encourage children to draw and to write about topics of their own choosing. Accept drawing, strings of letters, and invented spelling as valid forms of representation and successive approximation.

Read storybooks to children. Encourage children to respond to literature by discussing their feelings (see Chapter 3), raising questions, and making comments. Let children retell or act out the story. Give children the opportunity to reread favorite storybooks on their own. Accept and support the children's reading behaviors, which may include commenting and telling the story in their own words.

Use a mixture of teacher-led and child-centered activities. The morning message, reading storybooks aloud, and shared reading (see Key Concepts 2 and 3) are examples of teacher-led activities that usually include systematic instruction to promote children's understandings of literacy. Writing on self-selected topics, rereading favorite storybooks in the library center, and dramatic play in the home center are examples of child-centered activities that allow children to explore and make discoveries about literacy.

Involve parents in their children's literacy learning. Conduct workshops with parents to explain the concept of emergent literacy. Workshops help parents better understand the work their children bring home. For example, parents often benefit from learning about invented spelling. Ask parents what they have observed about their children's emergent literacy at home. Send books home and encourage parents to read with their children. (For more information on involving parents, see Chapter 8.)

Research on emergent literacy supports the view that children need to construct their own understandings of literacy. As Teale and others suggest, children's understandings are extended when they have the opportunity both for systematic, teacher-led instruction and for discovery through use of the full processes of reading and writing. In the next key concept, we explore how teachers of young children may achieve a balance between these two types of activities in their classrooms.

KINDERGARTEN AND FIRST-GRADE STUDENTS SHOULD LEARN ABOUT LITERACY IN A CLASSROOM COMMUNITY WITH MEANINGFUL CONTEXTS FOR SYSTEMATIC INSTRUCTION, INFORMAL INSTRUCTION, AND OPPORTUNITIES FOR DISCOVERY.

BALANCING INSTRUCTION AND DISCOVERY

As implied in the earlier description of Hally Simmons' classroom, we recommend that teachers promote kindergarten children's literacy through a variety of activities that provide a *meaningful context* for literacy learning. In a meaningful context children understand the reasons for reading and writing and so are motivated to participate actively and to try their best. For example, in the writers' workshop Hally Simmons' students understood that they were trying through drawing and writing to communicate ideas they felt important. At the home center they understood that they were trying to enact scenes of family life, including uses of reading and writing.

These meaningful contexts involve children in whole-to-part learning, as discussed in Chapter 1. For example, once children are involved in the full process of writing in the writers' workshop, they will be interested in learning letter sounds as a means for putting their words down on paper. In the opposite approach, part-to-whole learning, letter-sound lessons occur first. In this event children's learning may be slowed if they are not aware of the reasons for learning letter sounds, which may appear as an end in themselves rather than as a means for engaging in real reading and writing. We turn now to activities that use whole-to-part learning to build new understandings of literacy, beginning with systematic instruction provided through teacher-directed lessons.

Systematic Instruction

We use the phrase *systematic instruction* to describe lessons that teachers plan and conduct as part of their overall program for promoting children's literacy. Hally's morning message is an example.

First, she made the morning message a part of the daily routine, so this instruction occurred as a regular, planned part of the classroom literacy program. Hally did not have to worry about teaching the children a new routine, because the procedures for the lesson had already become familiar to them. Every morning, she composed a different message for the children to read and study under her guidance, and she could count on being able to teach new skills during this time.

Second, Hally demonstrated a purposeful use of literacy. In this case, she showed that writing could be used to communicate a message. This demonstration and communication placed the activity in a meaningful context for the children. Other purposeful uses of literacy that teachers might demonstrate include reading a story for enjoyment, reading a book or a magazine article to gain information, writing a letter, or writing about a personal experience. As mentioned in Chapter 1, this approach is consistent with the idea that children need to learn about the functions of literacy before they learn about the forms of literacy.

Third, over time, Hally covered a variety of skills in the lessons, moving in general from the skills children were likely to master more easily to those that were more difficult. For example, early in the year, Hally often used the same words in two or more sentences (Today is . . .), to give herself the chance to teach the children such concepts about print as matching words. (Refer to Key Concept 3 for further information on concepts about print.) She also worked with the children on beginning sounds (in the example, the sound of *s*). As the year continued, Hally wrote longer messages intended to call the children's attention to more advanced skills, such as punctuation (the use of periods and question marks) and word families (spelling patterns such as *-at* and *-in*).

Hally did not have a list of skills that she taught in a set order. Rather, as an experienced teacher, she worked from her knowledge of emergent literacy and her sense of the concepts that the children would eventually need to know. She also observed what the children were noticing about the message and took her cues from them. For example, when it became easy for many of the children to spot identical words in the message (such as noticing that *is* appeared in both the second and third sentences), Hally knew that she no longer needed to teach the concept of matching words and could move on to another skill. In the example, although she knew the children would be able to grasp the strategy only over time, Hally began teaching them to use a combination of beginning sounds and context (the meaning of the sentence) to figure out the word *snack*. (We will have more to say about these and other word-identification strategies in Key Concept 4.)

Teachers like Hally, who follow the process approach to writing, provide systematic instruction through mini-lessons that occur as part of the writers' workshop. Hally always started the writers' workshop with a mini-lesson. The children's own writing provided the meaningful context for instruction, and the content of the mini-lessons was determined by needs the children showed in their writing. In our example, Hally noticed that a number of children, including Carlton, were ready to begin using initial consonants to label their drawings. Thus, she made labeling using initial consonants the subject of the day's mini-lesson. Another form of systematic instruction, shared reading, is the subject of Key Concept 3.

Informal Instruction

We use the phrase *informal instruction* to describe instruction that is not planned by the teacher in advance but occurs because children have the need or interest to learn a skill at that particular time. These occurrences are called *teachable moments.*

A teachable moment occurred during the writers' workshop when Hally was conferring with Marco. Marco had drawn a picture of his brother and wanted to label his drawing, as Carlton had done. This interaction gave Hally the opportunity to teach Marco about labeling. Hally helped Marco say the word *brother* slowly, listening for the beginning sound. Then she showed him how he could write a *B* to stand for *brother.* Hally explained to Marco that he could label his drawings by saying the word slowly, listening for the beginning sound, and then writing the letter for the sound he heard. This whole interaction with Marco took less than two minutes.

This brief lesson occurred not because Hally had planned it but because of Marco's interest. Like Hally, teachers can make the most of teachable moments by centering their instruction on the child's immediate interest. However, instruction is not just a matter of helping children get on with the task but of teaching them *general strategies* that can be used to deal with problems of that type. In our example, Hally did not just show Marco how he could write a *B* for *brother.* Instead, she used the occasion to teach Marco a strategy for labeling (saying the word slowly, listening for the beginning sound, and then writing the letter).

Obviously, Hally could not plan this informal instruction in advance but had to respond to teachable moments as they occurred. However, Hally made teachable moments more likely by planning to have the children engage in a variety of meaningful literacy activities, such as reading the morning message or writing personal narratives during the writers' workshop. Carefully designed learning centers, such as those described next, also create teachable moments and the occasion for informal instruction.

Centers and Opportunities for Discovery

Learning centers are areas in the classroom dedicated to a particular type of activity and designed to allow children to explore, make discoveries, and learn on their own or with their peers. Hally Simmons' classroom had a library center, a message center, and others described earlier. There was usually time for the children to go to three of the centers every day. Hally allowed the children to choose the centers they wanted to attend, but she encouraged them to get around to all the centers during a week.

At the beginning of the school year, Hally circulated around the room, providing informal instruction and making sure the children were productively engaged at each center. She often carried a clipboard so she could take notes about the children's academic and social behaviors. For example, by observing the children in the library center, she could tell if they were retelling stories in their own oral language or the language of books, and if they were attending to print. She could also identify the children who were already enthusiastic about books, as well as those who would need help to become interested. Hally added these notes about the children to their portfolios (for more information about portfolios and ongoing assessment, refer to Chapter 7).

Hally's library center was in the corner of her classroom (for more information on classroom libraries, see Morrow & Weinstein, 1986). This center had shelves on three sides filled with books and a rug and cushions on the floor. Four children could fit comfortably in the area. There was also a rack displaying books written and published by children in Hally's class the previous year. Later, Hally would replace these books with those published by this year's class.

Hally introduced the library center to the children on the second day of school. She had them discuss what they already knew about libraries and explained that the purpose of the library center was to enjoy reading books either alone, with a partner, or with a small group. Then she selected four children to show the rest of the class how to look through the books, pick one out, and make themselves comfortable on the rug to read. Through this demonstration, the children understood why only four children would be allowed in the center at a time. Hally then guided the children through the process of putting the books back on the shelves. Later that day and for the next few days, Hally had the class evaluate events in the library center, both the good things and the problems.

In short, Hally had the responsibility of seeing that the children made the most of the opportunities for discovery presented by the centers. Her job was not only to arrange furniture and equip each center with supplies but also to teach the children how to make good use of the centers. She engaged the children in demonstrations of appropriate behavior at each center, including how to clean up and put materials away when they were finished. Hally introduced the centers one at a time, and she presented the children with a new center only when she was certain they knew what to do at the previously introduced center (see also Routman, 1991).

The message center, like the library center, was also designed specifically to promote literacy. This center consisted of a table with four chairs next to a large cork board with the label "Message Board." In this center students were to compose messages for classmates or the teacher and post them on the message board. Supplies at the center included slips of paper, pencils, and crayons; colored paper, paste, and scissors for making greeting cards; and letter stamps and ink pads.

Children's literacy learning can be promoted through their participation in other centers, such as a home center and blocks center, that encourage *symbolic play*. In symbolic play children may use one object to represent another, or they may transform the situation, for example, by saying that an area will now be a doctor's office. Research suggests that engaging in symbolic play helps children develop skills related to literacy (Pellegrini & Galda, 1993). For example, in symbolic play children learn that one thing may be used to represent another (a cardboard box may become a boat). The idea of representation becomes important in writing, where letters and words are used to represent objects and ideas.

At the home center, in addition to articles of clothing, dolls, a toy telephone, and dishes, there was a cookbook, a telephone book, a message pad, and pencils. As they acted out scenes of family life, the children played at following recipes in the cookbook, looking up phone numbers, and writing messages and shopping lists. As the year progressed, Hally would introduce new props in this center and help the children transform it into a grocery store, a restaurant, and a doctor's office. In each of these new settings, the children would have the chance to experiment with literacy as part of their play.

The science center consisted of a table with four chairs. Objects on the table changed every week or two. Right now there were jars with bugs that children could study through a magnifying glass. Paper, pencils, and crayons were kept in a bin at the science center so that children could record their observations. For more information on learning centers for young children, refer to Raines and Canady (1990) and Fisher (1991).

A teachable moment, when Hally could provide informal instruction, occurred the first day the science center was open. Lateesha and Bronson were examining the ladybugs, and Lateesha noticed that there were two kinds: blue ones and orange ones. She and Bronson decided to draw a picture of the two kinds of ladybugs. Hally got Lateesha and Bronson a large sheet of colored paper so they could make a poster with their pictures. The children wanted to write the words *blue ladybug* and *orange ladybug* under their drawings. Hally wrote the word *ladybug* for them and showed them where the words *blue* and *orange* appeared on a chart with color words. She explained to the children that they could sometimes find the words they wanted by looking at the charts posted around the room. Then she left them to copy the words over on their own. As in our earlier example of informal instruction, Hally did not stop at helping the children accomplish the immediate task before them, but sought to introduce a general strategy that they could use in the future.

Teachers should try to provide children with all three kinds of learning opportunities: systematic instruction, informal instruction, and discovery at learning centers. These learning opportunities are not mutually exclusive but tend to occur together. When children are engaged in discovery, either during group or individual projects or at learning centers, the teacher can provide informal instruction during teachable moments. Both systematic and informal instruction may occur during lessons such as the morning message, as seen in the example when Hally responded to the children's observations. Thus, a combination of the three types of learning opportunities serves to strengthen children's literacy learning.

KEY CONCEPT **3**

STUDENTS IN KINDERGARTEN AND FIRST GRADE SHOULD PARTICIPATE IN SHARED READING, WITH INSTRUCTION MOVING FROM WHOLE (THE STORY) TO PART (THE WORDS AND LETTERS).

SHARED READING

Shared reading is an instructional approach that attempts to bring the benefits of family storybook reading to the classroom. Research by Gordon Wells (1986) and others suggests that early experience with storybooks is the single best predictor of children's academic success at the elementary school level. In Wells' study, the most successful students were those who had been read to at home on many occasions before entering school. When they first entered school, children differed tremendously in terms of their previous experiences with storybooks, ranging from those who had never once been read to at home to those who had engaged in storybook reading on thousands of occasions.

What many American teachers, including Hally Simmons, call shared reading derives from the *shared book experience* developed by New Zealand educator Don Holdaway (1979), who had the idea of using big books to bring the benefits of family storybook reading into the classroom. By enlarging both the illustrations and print in a book, Holdaway made it possible for all of the children in the class to see the pages, just as they would if they were seated on the lap of a parent at home. Holdaway's approach works well for children regardless of their home experiences with storybook reading. Shared reading brings the benefits of home storybook reading to children who have had few or no experiences of this sort at home, while it builds on and extends the experiences of children who have been read to at home on many occasions.

Today, teachers can purchase big books and do not need to make their own. Little books with the same text are also available. Through shared reading, the classroom teacher can read and reread texts to children, and children are eventually able to read these texts on their own. Shared reading boosts children's learning to read by giving them the chance to:

Enjoy stories and participate by chiming in

Comprehend story elements, such as characters, setting, problem, and solution

Become familiar with concepts about print, such as that words are read from left to right

Learn to use word-identification strategies.

In short, shared reading can be a valuable instructional approach in kindergarten and first-grade classes.

Holdaway uses the term *discovery* to describe children's first experiences with the big book in shared reading. In the discovery phase the teacher's main goal is "to provide an enjoyable story experience to all children," a goal that he emphasizes "should not be sacrificed to any other purpose" (p. 71). With a new big book, the teacher might give a brief introduction by showing the children its cover and asking them a few open-ended questions, such as what they think the story will be about. She then reads the book aloud, pointing to the words as she reads and pausing at certain times to encourage the children to chime in.

Here is Holdaway's description of a typical first reading:

Now we bring out our first enlarged book—a version of 'The Three Billy Goats Gruff'. We choose this partly because of the strongly emotional language of the repetitive section which may draw the children into prediction and participation even on the first reading. The children are delighted with the enormous book and many keep their eyes glued on it as we use a pointer to follow the story as we read. Sure enough, on the second occasion of the 'Trip, trap!' and the 'Who's that tripping over my bridge?' some of the children chime in, encouraged by the invitational cues we give off. They are delighted in the closing couplet, 'Snip, snap, snout, This tale's told out', and want to say it for themselves. We compare the idiom with 'This story's run out,' and return to the original. We didn't expect this interest—youngsters are full of surprises. However, the children are obviously ready to dramatize the story and we have a first run at this to give them a little 'global involvement'— and it is very easy to improvise a bridge. We can see that there is a lot more running time in this story in many kinds of activities. (p. 66)

Kindergarten children participate in the shared reading of a big book. Big books with predictable language and enlarged text help teachers develop children's reading ability in a meaningful and enjoyable way.

In other words, the discovery phase of shared reading develops children's enthusiasm and serves as the springboard for a variety of other activities involving the story.

After the initial reading, the teacher might ask the children how the story made them feel or what part they liked best. Then the story is read over again. The second and subsequent readings of the story may follow different approaches, so that the children can be actively involved in the reading in different ways. Possibilities for rereading include (Wright Group, 1990):

Pointing clearly and definitely to each word, so that the children can track the print

Having the children use hand motions to act out the story as they read

Breaking the story into parts that are read by different groups of children

Having each group read a certain character's part, using a voice appropriate for that character

According to Holdaway, the second phase of shared reading involves *exploration*. During this phase the teacher rereads the big book aloud to the children, usually at their request. Gradually, the children's participation in the reading increases, as they become more and more familiar and comfortable with the text.

During the exploration phase of shared reading, the teacher uses her demonstrations of reading to teach or reinforce *concepts about print*. Concepts about print are basic understandings about print that emergent readers need to understand in order to read. According to Clay (1985), these concepts include:

Identifying the front of the book
Knowing that print and not pictures carry the message
Reading the left-hand page before the right-hand one
Reading words on a line moving from left to right
Reading a higher line before a lower line
Knowing where the first and last part of the story are
Knowing the difference between a letter and a word
Recognizing punctuation

The teacher can assess children's knowledge of concepts about print by asking questions during the reading, for example:

"Which page do I read first?"
"Where do I start reading on this page?"
"How many words do you see on this page?"

Children can also take turns using a ruler to point to the words as the teacher reads them.

The big book, as well as little-book versions of it, are left propped on the chalk rail or placed in the library center so the children can read the story on their own, in pairs, or in small groups, as they choose. If the text is simple enough, many children will eventually commit it to memory.

Included in the exploration phase are lessons that help the children become aware of the language, words, and letters in the book. To conduct these lessons, many teachers use pocket charts, sentence strips, word cards, and pictures taken from the text. For example, the story *The Little Red Hen* contains the following lines:

"Not I," said the dog.
"Not I," said the cat.
"Not I, said the pig.

The teacher might put each of these lines on its own sentence strip and ask the children to place the strips in the pocket chart in the same order that they appear in the book. This activity leads naturally to a discussion of how the words in the sentences are alike except for the last words: *dog, cat,* and *pig.* The teacher can write these animal words on the board and work with the children on beginning consonant sounds. Or the children might decide that they need to refer to the big book to check on the order of the sentences.

In a later lesson the teacher might cut the sentence strips apart and have the children reassemble the word cards as sentences. This activity leads naturally into a discussion of the words *Not, I, said,* and *the.* Children may be asked to talk about the first letter in the words, the number of letters in each word, and how they can tell the words apart. (For many other ideas for using sentence strips and word cards, refer to McCracken and McCracken, 1986.)

Holdaway suggests two types of *masking* activities to call children's attention to the features of print on pages of the big book. In the first activity the teacher uses a cardboard mask, as shown in Figure 2.3. The mask is held up over a page of the big book to mask or cover a particular word in the text. The strip of cardboard in the center of the mask is then pulled to the right to reveal the details of print that the teacher wants the children to notice. For example, suppose the teacher wants the children to focus on the word *groan.* She starts by covering the entire word and asking the children about the first letter they expect to see, then the second letter, and then the third one. She reveals the letters one at a time as the children make their guesses.

With the second type of masking activity, the teacher writes the text on an overhead transparency and places it within a frame, as shown in Figure 2.4. The cardboard strips are pulled to the right to reveal the letters and words in the text. For example, the teacher might ask the children, "If the first word is *Not,* what letters do you expect to see? Why?"

Pocket-chart and masking activities play an important part in shared reading. Through these activities, teachers can take advantage of the children's familiarity with the text to develop word-identification skills. In shared reading, memorization of the text is an advantage. If children know what words they expect to see on a page, the teacher can use pocket-chart and masking activities to help them to think about the letters they should anticipate. Word-identification skills are thus taught in a meaningful context, that of rereading a familiar and well-loved story.

The third phase of shared reading centers on what Holdaway calls *independent experience and expression.* One of the teacher's purposes during this phase is to provide opportunities for children to reread the story and to develop the ability to monitor and correct their own reading. As children reread the book on their own, the

FIGURE 2.3
Masking Words in a Big Book
Source: After Holdaway, 1979, p. 76.

teacher will watch for signs that they are growing in confidence and in the skills of using print.

A second purpose is to "encourage expressive activities using the interests and the language arising from the book so that children will identify more fully with the story and internalize the language as a permanent part of their competence" (Holdaway, 1979, p. 72). Often, children may be interested in acting out the story. For example, they may make hand puppets of the dog, cat, pig, and Little Red Hen and act out the story using their puppets.

Text reproductions and *text innovations* are other activities that encourage children to internalize the language patterns of the story. A text reproduction is just that. The teacher or the children copy the text of the story onto large sheets of paper, and the children draw their own illustrations for the story. Children enjoy reading and rereading their own big book, and it is put in the library center for the whole class to enjoy.

FIGURE 2.4
Masking Words with an Overhead Transparency
Source: After Holdaway, 1979, p. 75.

In a text innovation, the children invent their own version of the story using the language patterns of the original text. For example, suppose the children have been reading *The Little Red Hen.* The teacher tells them that they will be writing their own version of the story and asks who they would like the main character to be. The children brainstorm ideas and decide that their main character will be the Big Brown Bear. Then they brainstorm ideas for the other characters, the problem in the story, and so on. In this case the children might decide that the other characters will be a deer, a snake, and a raccoon, and that the bear wanted their help in packing a picnic basket.

With text innovations the teacher can give the children a chance to use their imaginations. The children might want to substitute the names of dinosaurs, use their own names in the story, change the setting or events in the story, and so on. As they develop the text innovation, they are applying many vocabulary and comprehension skills in a meaningful context and often in a playful and creative manner.

Art and music activities also fit nicely with shared reading. Children may make paintings and then write about their favorite part of the story. Or they may work together on murals depicting scenes in the story. The rhythmic language in some big books makes it possible for the text to be sung, or for the children to use rhythm instruments to keep the beat as the story is being read.

Using shared reading in first grade is much like using this approach in kindergarten, with a few critical differences. First, most first graders are ready to deal with somewhat more complex text, so the big books used for shared reading will have more words per page. Second, during the exploration phase of shared reading in first grade, the teacher will cover different skills. In kindergarten the emphasis is usually on concepts about print, prediction using the meaning of the sentence, and beginning consonant sounds. In first grade, children's use of beginning consonant sounds and the meaning of the sentence are reinforced, and new skills are addressed: consonants in the final and middle positions, blends and digraphs, and word families. These skills are explained further under Key Concept 4.

The text of big books designed for shared reading often differs from the text of picture storybooks, and therein lie both the advantages and disadvantages of big books and shared reading as an instructional approach. Some big books do not tell a story at all, or if they do, the story is very simple. Big books work best when the text has lots of rhyme, rhythm, and repetition, as in such favorites as *Mrs. Wishy-Washy* by Joy Cowley (1990). (Big books with text that will not hold children's interest should not be used for shared reading.) The advantage of big books is that their simplified text and strong picture-text match can serve very well to introduce children to print and help them feel comfortable with the process of reading.

In contrast, picture storybooks often have varied sentences and rich vocabulary, and they present complex plots and introduce themes and ideas rarely found in big books. These books are generally too difficult for kindergarten and first-grade children to read on their own, and so are better handled as teacher read-alouds. An example is *Sylvester and the Magic Pebble* by William Steig (1969). Good picture storybooks provide the substance for discussion, interpretation, and higher-level thinking about text that big books generally do not provide. Thus, the reading aloud of picture storybooks and discussion about these books are necessary if children are to develop strategies for comprehending texts beyond the most simple. In short, while shared reading has many benefits, teachers in kindergarten and first-grade classes need to be sure that this instructional approach is balanced with the reading aloud of picture storybooks.

KEY CONCEPT 4

STUDENTS IN KINDERGARTEN AND FIRST GRADE SHOULD LEARN TO USE A COMBINATION OF CUE SYSTEMS, INCLUDING SPELLING-TO-SOUND REGULARITIES, SO THEY WILL BE ABLE TO IDENTIFY WORDS ACCURATELY.

WORD IDENTIFICATION

In this key concept we tackle the topic of word identification. One of the chief responsibilities of Hally Simmons, Joan Lyons (whom you'll meet later in this book), and other kindergarten and first-grade teachers is to teach children to identify words quickly and accurately when reading connected text. In the primary grades word identification should start to become an almost automatic, effortless process for children, as it is for skilled readers. The less effort readers must devote to word identification, the more effort they can devote to comprehension and interpretation. Even in the primary grades, children need to understand that word identification is not an end in itself but part of the process of constructing meaning from and coming to understand the text.

Marie Clay (1985) discusses the different types of cues that children should be able to use when reading words. The first cue system is that of sense and meaning, also called *semantics.* When children come upon an unknown word, they should ask themselves what would make sense in that spot. For example, consider the following sentence:

The cat ran after the _____.

The child should be able to guess from the sense or meaning of the sentence that the unknown word is *mouse, rat,* or *ball* or anything else that a cat might chase.

The second cue system involves grammar and structure or *syntax.* Children have an intuitive sense of the structure of their own language. They can tell if a sentence or phrase "sounds right." For example, in the sentence above, suppose that the child guesses on the basis of the first letter that the unknown word is *me.* By reading the sentence over, "The cat ran after the me," the child will realize that one would not say such a sentence in English.

The third cue system is that of letters, also called *graphic* or *visual cues.* For example, if the child has guessed that the unknown word in the sentence above is *mouse,* the teacher might ask, "If that word is *mouse,* what letters do you expect to see?" If the child knows beginning sounds, he should answer that he expects to see an *m* at the beginning.

The goal of instruction in word identification is to help children use all three cue systems simultaneously. Often, children misread words because they are relying on only one or two of the cue systems. In this event, the teacher should ask the child a question that prompts use of the neglected cue system.

In the following example the teacher has the child reread and use different cue systems to correct an earlier error.

> *T:* You almost got that page right. There was something wrong with this line. See if you can find what was wrong.g
>
> *Ch:* (Child silently rereads, checking) I said Lizard but it's Lizard's.
>
> *T:* How did you know?
>
> *Ch:* 'Cause it's got an *s.*
>
> *T:* Is there any other way we could know? (Search further)
>
> *Ch:* (Child reruns in whisper) It's funny to say "Lizard dinner"! It has to be Lizard's dinner like Peter's dinner, doesn't it?
>
> *T:* (Reinforcing the searching) Yes. That was good. You found two ways to check on that tricky new word. (Clay, 1985, p. 74)

In this example the child first makes use of letters or visual cues, noticing that the word has an *s* and is actually *Lizard's,* not *Lizard.* After the teacher asks, "Is there any other way we could know?" the child makes use of structure and grammar, realizing that the word *Lizard* should be in possessive form for the sentence to be a proper one in standard English.

Clay (1985, p. 3) suggests that teachers use the following questions to prompt children to use the various cue systems. To prompt the use of sense and meaning, ask:

> *You said _____. Does that make sense?*

To prompt the use of structure and grammar, ask:

> *You said _____. Does that sound right?* or
> *Can you say it that way?*

To prompt the use of letters, ask:

Does that look right?

The general question "What's wrong?" can be asked in any situation.

Clay emphasizes the importance of teaching children to *cross check,* or use two or more cue systems to check the identity of the unknown word. Cross checking is essential because using just one cue system generally does not narrow down the possibilities sufficiently. For example, if only sense is used, many words might legitimately fit into the sentence, as suggested in the cat sentence above. If the child uses only letters and sounds, especially only the first letter, she may again come up with a number of different possibilities, including *man, me,* and *mother.* Cross checking by using at least two cue systems leads to accuracy, while an overreliance on one cue system leads children to make miscues or errors when reading. According to Clay, evidence that children are cross checking comes when they are observed to *self-correct* or correct reading errors on their own. For more information on analyzing children's oral reading using an approach called running records, refer to Clay (1985).

Word identification, including phonics, is perhaps the most hotly debated topic in the field of reading (see, for example, Adams et al., 1991). Our position is that most children can benefit from *phonics* (systematic instruction in letter-sound relationships) but it must always be seen as just one part of reading instruction and as serving the larger purpose of reading for meaning.

Actually, we prefer the term *spelling-to-sound regularities* to *letter-sound relationships,* because spelling patterns are a more reliable guide to pronunciation than individual letters. While consonant sounds are generally quite consistent in English, vowel sounds are not. For this reason, it is better to teach children about spelling patterns or word families such as *-at, -ain,* or *-ane* than to teach individual vowel sounds.

Research on emergent literacy and how children construct their own understandings of the English spelling system, as discussed in Key Concept 1 of this chapter, is relatively recent. Many people are not yet familiar with this research and continue to hold to an earlier, simplistic view of "phonics first" and "phonics only" as the key to learning to read. They believe that constructivist educational philosophies, such as whole language, do not pay enough attention to phonics (refer to Weaver [1990] for a whole-language analysis of phonics). The approach we take here is one that we believe captures the best of both worlds. First, we suggest that teachers give children plenty of opportunity to write and to use invented spelling. When children attempt to spell words, they are applying an understanding of phonics. Writing provides much more effective practice than the empty exercises often provided by worksheets. Second, we suggest that teachers give children systematic instruction in spelling-to-sound regularities. This instruction should be presented in the context of writing, shared reading, and other activities that make spelling-to-sound regularities meaningful to children. Perhaps the most important argument against traditional "spit and grunt" phonics instruction is that it gives children a misleading picture of what reading is all about. As established in Chapter 1, reading is about constructing meaning from text, not about "sounding out" words. "Spit and grunt" phonics instruction handicaps children by promoting an overreliance on only one strategy for identifying words: using visual cues. As Clay's work suggested, children need to learn to use all three cue systems, including meaning and structure, to be effective, accurate readers.

How Adults Use Letters to Identify Words

Before providing further information about teaching word identification, we will discuss how skilled readers identify words and how children go about learning to identify words. Apparently, skilled readers make use of two mechanisms (Rayner & Pollatsek, 1989). One, which we will call the *automatic recognition system,* allows word pronunciations and their meanings to be recognized directly and automatically. Most common words—including pronouns such as *she,* articles such as *the,* and frequently read nouns and verbs— are recognized in this way. These are often called *sight words,* and they make up what is referred to as the reader's *sight vocabulary.* In the sentence you just read, for example, automatic recognition probably occurred for the words *these, are, and, is,* and others.

Although you knew the remaining words in the sentence, such as *words, called,* and *referred,* they are not nearly so high in frequency, and you probably recognized them by the second mechanism, the *pattern-based system.* While slower, this mechanism provides a way of recognizing less common words and words never before seen. With this mechanism, words are recognized through letter patterns or clusters, analogies to known words, and rules. Thus, you might recognize *sap* and *cap* because of the *-ap* pattern. Or you might pronounce *might* and *bight* based on the *-ight* pattern. You would not make the unsophisticated guess of "big-hit" for *bight* because you know that *-ight* operates as a letter pattern or cluster and has a predictable pronunciation. You can make these judgments without conscious thought about the process because of your extensive knowledge of common words, rules, and letter patterns.

In summary, then, we can say that two systems are used when skilled readers identify words. An automatic recognition system allows high-frequency words to be "looked up" and identified instantly after the eyes fixate on them. A slower, pattern-based system enables readers to recognize most other words using knowledge of similarly spelled words and rules for analyzing words according to letter patterns.

How Children Develop Word-Reading Strategies

When children begin reading, they have neither a large store of sight words nor an understanding of letter pattern regularity. Because they do not know how to use the visual cue system, children are dependent on the cue systems of sense and structure. Typical four-year-old children recognize few words out of context except perhaps their first name and common sign and label words such as STOP, MILK, or M&M'S. Even these words are usually recognized imperfectly. When Masonheimer, Drum, and Ehri (1984) substituted XEPSI for PEPSI, they found that children did not notice the change but still called the word *Pepsi*. Gough, Juel, and Griffith (1986) even found children at this age paying more attention to a thumbprint on a card containing a word than to the letters!

Although children at this early phase of reading make little use of the visual cue system, unique letter cues are often noticed and used to remember words (for instance, *monkey* might be remembered because there seems to be a tail at the end). Children will know some words on food packages and in sentences that they have learned but usually will not be able to identify these words elsewhere, apart from these familiar contexts.

By the end of first grade, however, most children have acquired skills for recognizing many high-frequency words directly and are in the process of developing an understanding of the pattern-based system by making use of spelling-to-sound regularities. As a result, they make increasing use of the two word-identification mechanisms and they have less need to rely on pictures and the surrounding text context (Simon & Leu, 1987).

How do these changes occur? As discussed earlier, before children become aware that language can be analyzed into words and letter patterns, they scribble and explore books, listen to stories, and attempt to read and write following their own logic. They see letters and some words repeatedly in the same context. When looking at an alphabet book with parents, they might see the word *apple* accompanied by the letter *A* and a picture of an apple. Parents might help them recognize and print their first name. At breakfast there might be Special K cereal with an oversized *K* on the box. On outings, they might visit a McDonald's restaurant and see the sign with the golden arches. Early experiences with environmental print in conjunction with letter recognition and letter naming apparently provide the groundwork for word identification (Ehri, 1987). For example, a young child might say that she knows a particular word because it begins like her name, or she might use letters from her name to write other words. This is the foundation for word identification: the understanding that words are meaningful and can be recognized in context, that letters have names and are connected to words that begin with the same sound. From this foundation, children can move toward analyzing words into sounds.

Children must have an awareness of *phonemes* (the different sounds that can be heard within words) in order to understand spelling-to-sound regularities (Ehri, 1987). Most letters are represented by one phoneme (but not *x;* listen to its sound in *box*). Here are examples of words than contain three phonemes: *c-a-n, m-i-ne, b-a-ll, th-a-t, th-r-ee.* Children must be able to hear phonemes within words in order to be good readers, because hearing phonemes enables them to separate words into sounds and associate sounds with particular letters and letter patterns.

Most children develop phonemic awareness through literacy experiences at home. Alphabet books and rhymes help children hear beginning and ending phonemes. In fact, Maclean, Bryant, and Bradley (1987) determined that English children's knowledge of nursery rhymes at age three was strongly related to phonemic awareness and early reading performance. Knowledge not just of nursery rhymes but of any rhymes, as well as participation in rhyming activities, would likely have the same effect.

Early on, children are not aware of phonemes in words. They are more likely to be aware of syllables (*ba-by, el-e-phant*). Then they become aware that most one-syllable words have two parts, an *onset* and a *rime* (Trieman, 1985). The onset is the initial consonant portion of the syllable (*m* in *mask, spr* in *spring*), missing in words such as *and.* The rime includes the vowel and ending consonants (*ask* in *mask, ing* in *spring*). Trieman found that young children analyzed spoken words into onsets and rimes before they identified phonemes.

After children hear syllables and onset/rime segments, they begin to distinguish phonemes. The easiest and first-recognized phonemes are usually initial consonants, followed by final consonants, and then sounds in the middle of the word. At this time children might play word-sound games. Glenda Bissex (1980), for example, reported her son's discovery that he could remove *l* from *please* and have the word *peas.* Children may spontaneously notice and try to write rhyming words and words that begin with the same sound. In these ways, they start to understand the common spelling-to-sound regularities in English. They begin to recognize words in print by sounding out at least the first letter. Eventually, they figure out new words based on their knowledge of letter patterns in known words, and they can pronounce and spell many words on their own.

As children build their stores of known printed words and begin to get a sense of letter patterns, spelling-to-sound regularities are noticed. Words containing commonly occurring rimes (*met, ride, bait, dear*) become easier to learn and remember than words with uncommon rimes such as *noise, aisle, friend, choir*. Such knowledge of spelling-to-sound regularities begins to be used for word identification in about second grade (Adams, 1990), and by fourth grade is extended to recognition of syllable boundaries in multisyllable words. For example, children can correctly predict that *har-dball* is not appropriate because *-dball* cannot be a syllable in English.

In brief, by the end of first grade, many children are using both word-identification mechanisms (the automatic recognition system and the pattern-based system) to read less complex words fluently, and some use the pattern-based system to identify longer and more complex words. Most children recognize at least half of high-frequency words immediately and make good use of letter patterns and known, similar words to figure out many other words by a process of decoding by analogy or comparing and contrasting the unknown word to known words (a point to be discussed in more detail below). By the end of third or fourth grade, then, only uncommon, multisyllable words are difficult to identify (Adams et al., 1980). As children read widely and meaningfully, even these words become accessible, as discussed in Chapter 5.

Practical Implications

Children need to see, hear, and attempt to read words in a wide variety of contexts so they can learn to apply different word-identification strategies. They need opportunities to figure out words, partly by analyzing sounds in words and partly by checking their sense in context. Attending to meaning and sentence-structure cues as well as letter cues will enable them to connect word identification with text comprehension and to use a combination of cue systems as part of the whole act of constructing meaning from text.

Text understanding, not word identification, is the main goal of reading. Teachers in the primary grades want to ensure a balance between word-identification and comprehension activities (Resnick, 1979) and provide opportunities to integrate word study with text reading (Clay, 1979). While there are occasions when one or the other is emphasized for a teaching point, we advise that to the greatest possible extent words be taught in context, and word analysis be kept within the framework of meaningful texts. The use of sentence strips, word cards, and masking as part of shared reading, as described in Key Concept 3, are approaches that meet this criterion.

Keep in mind that instruction in word identification can occur during writing as well as during reading. As discussed earlier, writing allows children to construct and then read their own words. In a sense, writing then reverses the process because it requires children to take apart the words that they hear, while reading involves putting the letters together into sound clusters. Inventing their own spellings allows children to construct and test hypotheses about how the sounds they hear can be represented by letters. When children invent their own spellings, they are in essence teaching themselves about spelling-to-sound regularities.

Teaching About Consonants

As implied in the description above, children's learning of word identification is likely to be fostered by all three types of activities described in Key Concept 2: systematic instruction by the teacher, informal instruction during teachable moments, and opportunities for discovery when the child is trying to read and write on his own. First, let us discuss systematic instruction.

As discussed at the beginning of this key concept, the overall goal is to help children use a combination of cue systems to identify words. If they have an overall familiarity with English, children will enter school with quite a bit of knowledge about the cue systems of meaning and structure. The most common approach for promoting the use of these cue systems is called the *cloze* procedure. In this approach, which may be done orally at first and then later with print, the teacher leaves out a word and has the children guess what the word will be. Earlier, we used the cloze procedure in the sentence, "The cat ran after the _____." An oral cloze procedure can be used quite naturally if the teacher pauses at certain points while reading aloud. If the lesson is to focus on the systems of sense and structure, the teacher can ask the children not only to suggest possible words but also to discuss the reasons behind their suggestions.

Once the children have started to attend to print and have developed basic concepts about print, such as those listed in Key Concept 3, they are ready to begin learning to use the visual cue system or letters and letter patterns. Because children first attend to the first letter in the word, it is natural to begin instruction with a focus on initial consonants and consonant sounds. These lessons are best taught as part of shared reading with words drawn from the story. For example, a story about a baby, which also includes the words *ball* and *boy*, provides the opportunity to teach the sound of *b*. Children can study the words for *baby, ball,* and *boy* and notice that they all start with the same letter. They can think of other words that also begin with the sound of *b,* and the teacher can write all these *b* words on a chart. Classmates' names are often a powerful link to letters and sounds, so if there are children whose names start with *B,* those names should definitely be added to the chart. The teacher should always conclude the lesson by reminding children that learning letters and sounds will help them to read books.

The teacher can move from teaching about consonant sounds in the initial position to consonants in the final position and then to consonants in the middle of words, in keeping with the way that children generally progress in their developing knowledge of consonant sounds. Be prepared for the fact that, when the children are learning about consonant sounds, they may start to concentrate so much on the visual cue system that they forget to attend to the cue systems of meaning and structure. This is the point at which a child might read the sentence "The cat ran after the mouse" as "The cat ran after the me." The teacher will want to praise the child for looking at the first letter of the word, but then ask one of Clay's questions: "You said, 'The cat ran after the me.' Does that sound right?"

In other words, the teacher's job is to help the child achieve a balanced use of all three cue systems during reading. If children are not doing so on their own, they should be prompted through questioning to use all three cue systems. Balanced use remains the goal, even though considerable instruction may be devoted to teaching children to make use of the visual cue system, the one of which they have the least knowledge.

After children have learned about individual consonant sounds, the teacher will probably want to call their attention to *blends* and *digraphs.* Blends are combinations of consonants, such as *bl, cr,* or *st,* in which the phonemes associated with the individual letters can be heard. *Digraphs* are pairs of letters, such as *ch, sh, th,* or *ck,* that represent only one phoneme.

Decoding Words by Analogy

Learning about consonants, blends, and digraphs will do much to help children deal with what we have called the onset or first part of the word. To help children deal with the rime or the rest of the word, teach them to read words by analogy. Reading words by analogy involves comparing and contrasting the unknown word to known words with similar letters and spelling patterns (Gaskins, Downer, & Gaskins, 1986; 1987).

For example, if the unknown word is *dish* and children know the words *dog* and *fish,* they should be able to figure out the unknown word through a reasoning process that goes something like this:

This word begins like *dog* and belongs to the same spelling pattern as *fish.* I know, the word must be *dish.*

The *-ish* spelling pattern might also be termed a word family or a *phonogram.* When working with students, teachers may use any of these terms, as long as the same term is used consistently so students get the idea.

Gaskins and colleagues recommend that instruction follow one of two patterns. If the teacher knows that the children probably do not know the necessary spelling pattern, the teacher may model the use of decoding by analogy.

> Sentence: I need to go *back* to work now.
> Write the sentence on the board. Read the sentence aloud saying "blank" for the unknown word. Think aloud for the children, saying something like: "The spelling pattern in the new word is *a-c-k.* I know a word with that spelling pattern—*sack.* If *s-a-c-k* is *sack,* then *b-a-c-k* must be *back.*

If the children are likely to know the spelling pattern, remind them of the strategy of decoding by analogy and let them work out the solution.

> Sentence: The *band* will play at the fair.
> Write the sentence on the board and ask, "What is the spelling pattern in the underlined word?" The children should respond with *a-n-d.* Ask, "Can you think of a word we have already learned that has that spelling pattern?" The children should think of the key word *and* or spot it on a chart. Ask, "If *a-n-d* is *and,* what is *b-a-n-d?*" The children should be able to say that the word is *band.*

The strategy of decoding by analogy can be applied to multisyllable words, once children understand how words may be divided into syllables. For further ideas about teaching children to work with multisyllable words, refer to Chapter 5.

Summary

In the first key concept we discussed emergent literacy and gave an overview of children's development as readers and writers in the early years. As research suggests, children are actively constructing their own understandings about how reading and writing work and so may read and write in ways that adults find surprising. The second key concept dealt with the importance of teachers providing meaningful contexts for children's school literacy learning. Within these meaningful contexts, teachers provide children with a combination of systematic instruction, informal instruction, and opportunities for discovery. In the third key concept we looked at an instructional approach called shared reading and recommended it as an effective means for teaching children concepts about print and word identification. The fourth key concept addressed the topic of word identification, emphasizing the goal of teaching children to use all three cue systems: sense, structure, and visual. We presented an overview of children's development of word-identification ability and suggested teaching methods that fit with children's changing understandings of words and letters. We emphasized that word identification should not be taught as an end in itself but in the service of reading for meaning.

◀ **ACTIVITIES**

Reflecting on Your Own Literacy

Think back to your earliest memories of reading. What do you remember about reading at home, before going to school? What happened when you went to school? How do you think you learned to read?

Applying What You Have Learned to the Classroom

Arrange to observe in a kindergarten or first-grade classroom. Make notes about the reading and writing the children are doing. What signs of emergent literacy do you see? What understandings about reading and writing do the children seem to have?

BIBLIOGRAPHY

References

Adams, M., et al. (1980). *A prototype test of decoding skills.* Bethesda, MD: National Institute of Child Health and Human Development.

Adams, M. J. (1990). *Beginning to read: Thinking and learning about print.* Cambridge, MA: MIT Press.

Adams, M. J., et al. (1991). *Beginning to read:* A critique by literacy professionals and a response by Marilyn Jager Adams. *The Reading Teacher, 44* (6), 370–395.

Bissex, G. (1980). *GNYS AT WRK: A child learns to write and read.* Cambridge, MA: Harvard University Press.

Britton, J. N. (1970). *Language and learning: The importance of speech in children's development.* Portsmouth, NH: Heinemann.

Clay, M. (1975). *What did I write? Beginning writing behavior.* Portsmouth, NH: Heinemann.

Clay, M. (1979). *Reading: The patterning of complex behavior.* Portsmouth, NH: Heinemann.

Clay, M. M. (1985). *The early detection of reading difficulties* (3rd ed.). Auckland, New Zealand: Heinemann.

Dyson, A. H. (1989). *Multiple worlds of child writers: Friends learning to write.* New York: Teachers College, Columbia University.

Ehri, L. C. (1987). Learning to read and spell words. *Journal of Reading Behavior, 19*(1), 5–31.

Ferreiro, E., & Teberosky, A. (1982). *Literacy before schooling.* Portsmouth, NH: Heinemann.

Fisher, B. (1991). *Joyful learning: A whole language kindergarten.* Portsmouth, NH: Heinemann.

Gaskins, I., Downer, M., & Gaskins, R. (1986). *Introduction to the Benchmark School word identification/vocabulary development program.* Media, PA: Benchmark Press.

Gaskins, I., et al. (1987). A metacognitive approach to phonics: Using what you know to decode what you don't know. *Remedial and Special Education, 9,* 36–41.

Goodman, Y. M. (1985). Kidwatching: Observing children in the classroom. In A. Jagger & M. T. Smith-Burke (Eds.), *Observing the language learner.* Newark, DE: International Reading Association, pp. 9–18.

Gough, P., Juel, C., & Griffith, P. (1986). Reading, spelling, and the orthographic-cipher. Paper presented at the Conference on Early Reading, Center for Cognitive Science, University of Texas, Austin.

Graves, D. (1983). *Writing: Teachers and children at work.* Exeter, NH: Heinemann.

Harste, J., Woodward, V., & Burke, C. (1984). *Language stories and literacy lessons.* Portsmouth, NH: Heinemann.

Holdaway, D. (1979). *The foundations of literacy.* Sydney, Australia: Ashton Scholastic (distributed in the United States by Heinemann).

Maclean, M., Bryant, P., & Bradley, L. (1987). Rhymes, nursery rhymes and reading in early childhood. *Merrill Palmer Quarterly 33,* 255–282.

Masonheimer, P., Drum, P., & Ehri, L. (1984). Does environmental print identification lead children into word reading? *Journal of Reading Behavior, 16,* 257–271.

McCracken, R. A., & McCracken, M. J. (1986). *Stories, songs, and poetry to teach reading and writing.* Chicago: American Library Association.

Morrow, L. M., & Weinstein, C. S. (1986). Encouraging voluntary reading: The impact of a literature program on children's use of library centers. *Reading Research Quarterly, 21*(3), 330–346.

Pellegrini, A. D., & Galda, L. (1993). Ten years after: A reexamination of symbolic play and literacy research. *Reading Research Quarterly, 28*(2), 163–175.

Raines, S. C., & Canady, R. J. (1990). *The whole language kindergarten.* New York: Teachers College Press.

Rayner, K., & Pollatsek, A. (1989). *The psychology of reading.* Englewood Cliffs, NJ: Prentice-Hall.

Resnick, L. B. (1979). Theories and prescriptions for early reading intervention. In L. B. Resnick & P. A. Weaver (Eds.), *Theory and practice of early reading* (Vol. 2). Hillsdale, NJ: Erlbaum Associates.

Routman, R. (1991). *Invitations: Changing as teachers and learners K–12.* Portsmouth, NH: Heinemann.

Simon, H., & Leu, D. (1987). The use of contextual and graphic information in word recognition by second-, fourth-, and sixth-grade readers. *Journal of Reading Behavior, 19,* 33–47.

Sulzby, E. (1985). Children's emergent reading of favorite storybooks: A developmental study. *Reading Research Quarterly, 20*(4), 458–481.

Taylor, D. (1983). *Family literacy: Young children learning to read and write.* Portsmouth, NH: Heinemann.

Teale, W. H. (1987). *Emergent literacy: Reading and writing development in early childhood.* In J. E. Readence & R. S. Baldwin (Eds.), *Research in literacy: Merging perspectives.* Thirty-sixth yearbook of the National Reading Conference. Rochester, NY: National Reading Conference, pp. 45–74.

Trieman, R. (1985). Onsets and rimes as units of spoken syllables: Evidence from children. *Journal of Experimental Psychology, 39,* 161–181.

Wells, G. (1986). *The meaning makers: Children learning language and using language to learn.* Portsmouth, NH: Heinemann.

Wright Group (1990). *The story box, Level 1, Teacher guide.* Bothell, WA: Wright Group.

Suggested Classroom Resources

Carle, E. (1969). *The Very Hungry Caterpillar.* Scranton, PA: Collins-World.

Cowley, J. (1990). *Mrs. Wishy-Washy.* Bothell, WA: Wright Group.

Gag, W. (1928). *Millions of Cats.* New York: Coward.

Greenfield, E. (1976). *First Pink Light.* New York: Crowell.

Steig, W. (1969). *Sylvester and the Magic Pebble.* New York: Simon & Schuster.

Further Readings

Department of Education, Wellington. (1985). *Reading in junior classes.* Wellington, New Zealand: Department of Education.

Mason, J. M., & Sinha, S. (1993). Emergent literacy in the early childhood years: Applying a Vygotskian model of learning and development. In B. Spodek (Ed.), *Handbook of research on the education of young children.* New York: Macmillian, pp . 137–150.

Routman, R. (1988). *Transitions: From literature to literacy.* Portsmouth, NH: Heinemann.

Strickland, D. S., & Morrow, L. M. (1989). Developing skills: An emergent literacy perspective. *The Reading Teacher, 43* (1), 82–83.

Strickland, D. S., & Morrow, L. M. (Eds.) (1989). *Emerging literacy: Helping young children learn to read and write.* Newark, DE: International Reading Association.

3 Reading and Writing in Response to Literature

From an interview with Mike, who had read *The High King* by Lloyd Alexander:

Interviewer: If you could be one of the characters from *The High King*, which would it be?

Mike: Either Gwydion or Taran. They seemed the most noble. It seemed like they shared the same ideas I have.

(Mike described the friendship between Gwydion and Taran. "Close friends," he said, "go all out to help each other. They are loving, understanding, selfless.")

Interviewer: Is it important to you in the books you read that there be some sort of good or noble idea?

Mike: Um-hmm. If you go to battle just because you feel like killing someone, that's just stupid.

Interviewer: What major point do you think Lloyd Alexander was trying to get across in this book?

Mike: I don't know. The point he got across to me was to care more about a million people, or three people, than one person—yourself.

(Cramer, 1984, p. 257)

◀ OVERVIEW

This chapter begins with a description of the readers' workshop in a fifth-grade classroom. In the first key concept, we discuss the characteristics of literature-based instruction and the reader's personal responses to literature and enjoyment of reading. In the second key concept, we identify different genres of children's literature and show how teachers can help students see the connections among works of literature. The third key concept outlines an approach teachers can use to guide students in discussions of literature. Finally, in the fourth key concept, we look at the use of literature response logs for involving students in writing in response to literature.

KEY CONCEPT 1: Students should have the opportunity to develop personal responses to literature and to read from an aesthetic stance within a classroom community.

KEY CONCEPT 2: Students should learn about different literary genres, story elements, and the relationships among literary works.

KEY CONCEPT 3: Students should receive active, systematic instruction in comprehension strategies.

KEY CONCEPT 4: Students should write in response to literature in order to make connections between reading and writing.

◀ **PERSPECTIVE**

Readers' Workshop in a Fifth-Grade Classroom

This Wednesday in October, during the readers' workshop, Jessie Michaels is introducing three new novels to her students. The novels are the basis for a thematic unit on the problems faced by young people growing up in different families. Jessie chose these novels because she thinks her students will be able to relate to the characters and the challenging situations they face. She would like her students to learn that many problems can be overcome through determination and the support of family and friends.

Jessie knows that the authors of these novels have also written many other books. She hopes students will like these books enough to seek out other works by these authors to read on their own. (The topic of students' voluntary reading is discussed in detail in Chapter 8.)

Jessie has already given brief book talks on two of the novels. *The Best Bad Thing* by Yoshiko Uchida (1983) tells what happens to Rinko Tsujimura when she must spend the summer helping Mrs. Hata, a recently widowed friend of her parents. *Have a Happy . . .* by Mildred Pitts Walter (1989) tells about Chris Dodd and the troubles his family must weather when his father is out of work. In addition, this novel describes the celebration of Kwanzaa in African-American families.

"The third novel in our new unit is *Dear Mr. Henshaw* by Beverly Cleary," Jessie says. "How many of you are familiar with other books by Beverly Cleary?" All the students raise their hands, and Jessie takes a few minutes to let them discuss books by Cleary read in earlier grades.

"Well," Jessie continues, "this book by Beverly Cleary may surprise you. Some of it is humorous but not in the same way as her books about Ramona and Henry. The main character in this book, Leigh Botts, has some serious problems to deal with. His parents are divorced, and he hardly gets to see his dad any more. Another thing about this book is the interesting way that it's written, not in chapters but in another way. I won't tell you what that is, but I think you'll figure it out when you take a look at the book."

Jessie puts three copies of each of the novels on a table near the library center so the students can take a look at them over the next two days. On Friday she will have them write down their first and second choices. Then she will divide the class into three groups, one reading each of the novels. The children will be grouped by interest in the novels, rather than by ability. However, because there is a wide range of reading ability among the students in the class, Jessie has chosen one book (*The Best Bad Thing*) that is quite challenging for many fifth graders, and another (*Dear Mr. Henshaw*) that is considerably easier.

At the start of the readers' workshop on Monday morning, Jessie announces the names of the students who will be reading each of the novels. She reminds the students about the routine they will be following for the readers' workshop, which lasts for an hour and 15 minutes each day.

"Our schedule will be the same as it was during our last thematic unit," Jessie tells the class. She explains that she will hold teacher-guided literature discussions with two groups a day. The third group will hold its own, student-guided discussion. Each group will meet with the teacher on two out of three days. (The terms *literature discussion groups* [Routman, 1991] and *literature circles* [Harste, Short, & Burke, 1988] are often used to describe either teacher-guided or student-guided discussions of novels and stories. The term *book club* refers to a student-guided discussion [McMahon, 1992].)

Jessie reminds the students that they will be writing in their literature response logs every day. When they are finished, they have a choice of activities: reading a book on their own or with a buddy, continuing work on a piece started during the writers' workshop, or working on their science reports.

Jessie meets briefly with the first group, to get them started on their writing. Some of the nine students in this group are among the most capable readers in the class, including Robyn, Mariko, Jorge, and Garnett. Jessie says, "Right now I want you to start making predictions about your new novel. Spend a few minutes writing about the title, *The Best Bad Thing.* How could there be a 'best' bad thing? What do you think will happen in the story?" She asks the students to take about 15 minutes to write and then to get together for a student-guided discussion of their answers. After the discussion, the students are to read chapter 1.

Jessie calls up the next group, which is reading *Dear Mr. Henshaw,* for a teacher-guided literature discussion. The students have read the first three or four pages of the novel, and Jessie asks about their reactions. Russell says he thinks the book is going to be funny because of what Leigh writes and the way he spells. Jessie asks what they have learned about Leigh so far, and the students indicate that Leigh has a dog, isn't a very good speller, and just seems like an ordinary boy.

Teacher: I agree, he doesn't seem special, he just seems like someone who might be in our class. And did you notice that this book isn't in chapters? What did you see instead?

Guillermo: He's writing letters to Mr. Henshaw.

Teacher: Um-hm, Leigh Botts is writing letters. And who is Mr. Henshaw? Tonya?

Tonya: He's an author, he wrote Leigh Botts' favorite book.

Teacher: And why would a student like Leigh, or like you for that matter, want to write to an author?

Russell and Darrah discuss their experience in an earlier grade with writing letters to their favorite authors.

Russell: It was so they would know you liked their books, and like if you had any questions.

Teacher: Okay, so that was why you and Darrah wrote letters to authors when you were in Ms. Meyer's class. As you continue reading, I'd like you to think about why Leigh is writing to Mr. Henshaw. As you noticed, he didn't just write one letter like you did, he wrote several.

Jessie has the students decide how many pages they will read before their next meeting. Then she asks them to write in their literature response logs about their feelings about the book so far, why they have those feelings, and their opinion of the main character, Leigh Botts. She hopes that the students will soon realize that Leigh is not writing to Mr. Henshaw for the same reasons that they wrote to their favorite authors, but because Leigh needs to communicate with someone about the problems in his life.

Jessie calls up the last group, which is reading *Have a Happy . . .* , for a teacher-guided discussion. The students have started reading chapter 1 but several have not yet finished it. Jessie begins the discussion by asking if any of the students are familiar with Kwanzaa. Sharita replies that her family has been celebrating that festival for several years now, and Jessie asks her to explain Kwanzaa to the other students. Sharita is familiar with the seven principles of Kwanzaa, such as *umoja* or unity and *imani* or faith. Edouard asks if celebrating Kwanzaa means you don't celebrate Christmas, and Sharita replies that her family celebrates both. Jessie tells the students that it will be interesting for Sharita to continue to share what she knows about Kwanzaa as the students get further into the story.

Jessie asks the students about the response they are having to the story so far. Myong comments that she has a cousin who was born on December 25, just like Chris, and that her cousin always feels that everyone is forgetting his birthday. Guillermo adds that he is planning to deliver newspapers to make money, just as Chris' friend Miles is doing. Jessie is pleased that the students are making connections between the novel and their own lives. However, these connections are to specific details and she would like to see if they have an overall sense of what is going on at the beginning of the novel.

> *Teacher:* Great, I can see that you're drawing on your own experiences as you're reading the novel. But now let me ask you about what's happening with Chris, the main character. What have we learned about Chris so far?
>
> *Edouard:* He has these two friends, Miles and Jamal, but they have bikes and he doesn't.
>
> *Tammy:* And there's no way he's gonna get a bike either, 'cause his daddy's out of work.
>
> *Teacher:* Right, that's definitely a problem for Chris. And are there any other problems?
>
> *Travis:* Yeah, he has a little sister to look after, and that's a *big* problem. I should know!

Jessie and the students laugh as Travis proceeds to explain, with considerable exaggeration, everything that he must do to look after his younger sister and brother after school. Jessie concludes the discussion by asking the students to finish chapter 1.

As with the second group, she asks this group to write in their literature response logs about their feelings about the book so far, why they have those feelings, and what they have learned about the main character, Chris Dodd, and his problems. Once the students have finished writing in their logs, she will begin the lessons by having them share what they have written.

When students are just starting a novel, Jessie establishes a pattern of having them write after they have finished each chapter. Occasionally Jessie has students first discuss what they have read and then write a reflection. When students are farther into the novels and want to move ahead more quickly, they may read several chapters before writing.

After school, Jessie takes a few minutes to write in her journal about the start of the new literature unit.

> The students seem excited about starting their new novels. I hope that they'll be able to empathize with the characters and their situations. My assessment of the responses some students gave today was

that they were too focused on little details. In my lessons I need to be sure they are getting the big picture of what is going on in each novel and making deeper connections between the novels and their own lives.

I feel the need to know more about how the student-led discussion groups are going. I don't want to join in on those discussions, because then the students will expect me to lead them. Perhaps I should try tape-recording their discussions.

Jessie knows that one of the sixth-grade teachers is also using student-led discussion groups, and she makes a mental note to ask this teacher's advice at their support group meeting next week.

KEY CONCEPT **1** STUDENTS SHOULD HAVE THE OPPORTUNITY TO DEVELOP PERSONAL RESPONSES TO LITERATURE AND TO READ FROM AN AESTHETIC STANCE WITHIN A CLASSROOM COMMUNITY.

RESPONDING TO LITERATURE

In the thematic unit on overcoming problems, Jessie Michaels is having her students read novels she believes they will enjoy. Although there are certain understandings she would like students to gain, Jessie does not want her students to become so wrapped up in the details of the novels that reading becomes laborious and boring. That is why Jessie does not emphasize details but tries to involve her students in the world of each novel and to have them explore the connections between the novels and their own lives.

Jessie Michaels is using *literature-based instruction,* in which teachers use children's literature as the basis for teaching students to read and to enjoy reading. Children's literature may be defined as "books that are not only read and enjoyed [by] but also that have been written for children and that meet high literary and artistic standards" (Sutherland & Arbuthnot, 1991, p. 5). A work used in literature-based instruction is authentic (just as the author wrote it, without changes in wording), and students read the full novel or story, not an excerpt.

Because it can take students weeks to finish reading a novel, Jessie is careful to select novels with depth, those that will hold her students' interest. Jessie wants her students to enjoy the works of such well-known authors as Beverly Cleary and Judy Blume. However, she is aware of the dangers of introducing her students only to literature written from a mainstream perspective, which does not show the diverse life experiences of groups in the United States today. To present students with a broader perspective, Jessie tries to include works of multicultural literature, particularly works written by authors of diverse cultural backgrounds. *The Best Bad Thing* and *Have a Happy* . . . are examples of multicultural literature, one depicting the experiences of Japanese-Americans and the other experiences of African-Americans.

Jessie knows that selecting motivating works of literature is just the first step in literature-based instruction. It is also important to have an idea of how instruction is to be approached. Jessie has learned that she must not just consider the text, but also the reader and the social situation for reading, as discussed in Chapter 1.

In literature-based instruction, the reader's personal response to the literature is foremost. Jessie Michaels addresses her students' personal responses to literature by having them write about and discuss their feelings about the novels, the connections between the novels and their own lives, and their interpretations of the theme. Jessie believes that her students' experience of reading and discussing novels will be more meaningful and enjoyable if she recognizes their personal responses to literature. She is trying to create a social situation for reading in which students know that their personal responses and interpretations will be accepted and valued by others.

The importance of the readers' personal response to the text and enjoyment of the reading experience is highlighted by Louise Rosenblatt (1978, 1991). She suggests that there are two ways of reading, or two stances that readers may adopt toward a text: the *aesthetic* and the *efferent.* In aesthetic reading, what is important is the lived-through experience of reading, or the reading experience itself. Aesthetic reading, or reading for the sheer enjoyment of reading, reaches its height when the reader becomes lost in a book. Teachers who emphasize aesthetic reading "create an environment where literature is appreciated for its artistic value: to amuse, to sadden, to thrill, to frighten, to inspire" (Zarrillo, 1991, p. 223).

In efferent reading, what is important is not the reading experience itself but what the reader can take away from the text. The term *efferent* comes from a Latin word meaning to carry away. We are reading to carry something away from the text when we read for specific information; for example, we read a biography to learn about Harry Truman or a manual to learn how to use a new software program.

Rosenblatt emphasizes that aesthetic and efferent reading should not be viewed in an either-or fashion.

> Instead of thinking of the *text* as either literary or informational, efferent or aesthetic, we should think of it as written for a particular *predominant* attitude or stance, efferent or aesthetic, on the part of the reader. We have ignored the fact that our reading is not all-of-one-piece. We read for information, but we are also conscious of emotions

Students in this fourth-grade class made models of their own cupboards, after reading the novel *The Indian in the Cupboard.* Art activities are an excellent means of encouraging students to respond to literature.

about it and feel pleasure when the words we call up arouse vivid images and are rhythmic to the inner ear. Or we experience a poem but are conscious of acquiring some information about, say, Greek warfare. To confuse matters even further, we can switch stances while reading. And we can read aesthetically something written mainly to inform or read efferently something written mainly to communicate experience. Our present purpose and past experiences, as well as the text, are factors in our choice of stance. (1991, p. 445)

The predominant stance of novels, such as those Jessie Michaels' students are reading, is the aesthetic. Jessie wants her students to take the stance of reading for the experience of reading and for the personal responses that the reading evokes. Here is an example from a discussion with the group reading the *The Best Bad Thing.* As you will see, Jessie finds that the situation described in the novel has evoked strong responses in the students.

The students have just finished reading the second chapter in the novel, in which her parents decide that Rinko should spend the last month of her summer vacation helping Mrs. Hata. Mrs. Hata, whose husband has just died, is struggling to run a farm and raise two young sons, Zenny and Abu.

Teacher: So who wants to start by sharing their reactions to the chapter? Kelly?

Kelly: (reads from her response journal) "I think it's really unfair for her parents to make Rinko go and help Mrs. Hata. They didn't ask Rinko, they just made her go, and she has to stay for the rest of her vacation. She won't get to see her friends and she won't have any fun. It's wrong for parents to make kids do things they really don't want to do."

Teacher: Okay, so you felt strongly about that. You could understand why Rinko was so reluctant to go and stay with Mrs. Hata and her two boys. How about someone else? Jorge?

Jorge: I wrote, "I would be very angry if I was Rinko and my parents made me go to help their friend for one whole month. Rinko's mom should go and let Rinko stay home because Rinko said she could do everything at home if her mom goes. And Rinko doesn't even know Mrs. Hata and Mrs. Hata might be crazy."

Teacher: Okay, your feelings about Rinko's problem were similar to Kelly's. Garnett, what did you want to say?

Garnett: My parents are always saying, "You'll thank me later!" I hate when they say that! They, like, think they know what's best for me, and Rinko's parents are the same way.

This discussion focuses on the aesthetic stance, because students are sharing their feelings about the text and its connection to their own lives. However, the discussion is also partly efferent, because students refer to specific information that they have "carried away" from the text. As Rosenblatt suggests, the line between aesthetic and efferent stances is easily crossed.

Jessie tries to respect her students' feelings and ideas. However, she also tries to expand their thinking by introducing other perspectives that have not yet occurred to them. In this case, Jessie told the group that she could understand their feelings that Rinko's parents were being unfair. However, she also shared her own point of view, that Rinko and her parents are part of a close-knit community of Japanese-American families who try to help one another through difficult times. She suggested that Mrs. Hata would probably try to help Rinko's family if they were the ones in trouble. Jessie felt that it was important for the students to understand this alternative point of view, although she did not expect them to agree with it. While respectful of her students' opinions, Jessie does not abandon her responsibility to introduce new ideas that may give students a different or deeper understanding of the novel.

Sometimes Jessie wants her students to read with an efferent stance and to carry something away from the text, even though they are reading a novel. For example, chapter 8 of *Have a Happy . . .* describes the first day of the Kwanzaa celebration at the home of Chris

Dodd's Uncle Ronald. Jessie asked the students not only to write about their feelings about this chapter and about how Chris was feeling, but also to write down three things that they had learned about Kwanzaa. During the discussion of chapter 8, she asked the students to share this information, as well as to tell what they thought Chris was feeling during the Kwanzaa ceremony.

Jessie realizes that there is a delicate balance between aesthetic and efferent reading. She is aware that there is a tendency for teachers to overemphasize efferent reading and to neglect aesthetic reading (Rosenblatt, 1991; Zarrillo, 1991). Rosenblatt (1980, p.393) provides the following suggestions about how teachers can maintain an aesthetic stance:

> Questions or comments should lead the reader back, to savor what was seen, heard, felt, thought, during the calling-forth of the poem or story from the text. What caught the interest most? What pleased, frightened, surprised? What troubled? What seemed wrong? What things in the child's own life paralleled those in the poem or story?

Similarly, Zarrillo (1991) suggests three levels of questioning that teachers can use to encourage an aesthetic stance toward the reading of literature. As shown in Figure 3.1, the questions at level one draw on students' free responses, those at level two have students relive the reading experience, and those at level three call for them to interpret the literature.

In short, literature-based instruction emphasizes the reading of literature from an aesthetic stance, although an efferent stance is occasionally adopted as well. Teachers encourage students' personal responses to literature and the making of connections between literature and students' own lives.

KEY CONCEPT **2** STUDENTS SHOULD LEARN ABOUT DIFFERENT LITERARY GENRES, STORY ELEMENTS, AND THE RELATIONSHIPS AMONG LITERARY WORKS.

CHIDREN'S LITERATURE

The term *genres* refers to different types of literature within the broad categories of fiction and nonfiction. For example, Jessie Michaels' students are reading novels of a genre that might be called modern fiction. The characters are portrayed in a realistic, well-rounded fashion and are not stereotyped. They face problems and situations that might well be encountered in the lives of many other young people.

Level One: Free Response (most conducive to aesthetic reading)
a. Write (or draw) whatever you want about what you just read.
b. Does anybody have anything they want to say about what you just read?

Level Two: Reliving the Reading Experience
2.1 Identifying vivid episodes
a. Did anything seem especially interesting? Annoying? Puzzling? Frightening? Weird? Funny? Sad?
2.2 Imaging and picturing
a. Pretend you (were doing something a character did).
b. Picture in your mind (an event or scenes in the book).
c. What would it feel like to (be a character in the book or participate in an event in the book)?
d. What would (a scene in the book) have looked like (from the perspective of one of the characters)?
2.3 Preference
a. What was your favorite (or least favorite) part of the book?

Level Three: Interpreting the Reading Experience
3.1 Personal associations
a. Have you ever experienced what (a character in the book) experienced?
b. Have you ever read a story (or seen a TV show or movie) where (event in the book) happened?
c. Have you ever known anyone like (a character in the book)?
3.2 Speculation
a. What do you think will happen (to the characters in the book) in the future?
b. What do you think would have happened if (an event in the book had been altered)?
c. What do you think would happen to (the book's characters in a different setting)?
3.3 Summative opinion
a. Did you like (enjoy) the (name of the book)?
b. What about the book led to your judgment?

FIGURE 3.1
Aesthetic Teaching: Questions and Prompts
Source: Zarrillo, 1991, p. 232.

Jessie is aware that there are no hard and fast rules about which genres or specific works of children's literature are best introduced and read at each grade level. Jessie knows that she must use her own professional judgment in deciding which genres and books to introduce to her students. She tries to introduce them to some genres they usually have not encountered in earlier grades. For example, because she teaches her students about American history, she introduces Native American tales, tall tales, and historical fiction.

Like other teachers committed to literature-based instruction, Jessie enjoys learning about new children's books through conversations with the school librarian and through reading the reviews in professional journals such as *Book Links, Language Arts, The New Advocate,* and *The Reading Teacher.* Because Jessie is concerned about the quality of literature her students read, she tries to familiarize herself with books that have won the Newbery Medal or Newbery honor awards, presented annually by the Children's Services Division of the American Library Association for the most distinguished contributions to children's literature published in the United States. The Caldecott Medal and honor awards are similarly given to the most distinguished picture books published in the United States.

Genres of Children's Literature

Teachers will find it useful to become familiar with high-quality books in several genres suitable for use at their grade levels. Zena Sutherland and May Arbuthnot (1991) divide children's literature into the following nine genres:

1. picture books
2. folktales
3. fables, myths, and epics
4. modern fantasy
5. poetry
6. modern fiction
7. historical fiction
8. biography
9. informational books

Drawing on the work of these authors, we briefly discuss the important characteristics of each genre. Several titles are listed as examples of each genre. Instructional suggestions, in addition to the use of teacher- and student-guided discussion, are provided.

PICTURE BOOKS. Picture books play an important part in the classroom reading program in the primary grades, particularly in kindergarten and first grade, although some of these books are often enjoyed by older students as well. A key here is the quality of the illustrations and whether they can attract and hold children's attention. Sutherland and Arbuthnot point out that picture books of lasting value play up two themes: love or reassurance and achievement.

Recent Caldecott Award books young children may especially enjoy include *Owl Moon,* written by Jane Yolen and illustrated by John Schoenherr (1987) and *Lon Po Po: A Red Riding Hood Story from*

China translated and illustrated by Ed Young (1989). With picture books that tell a story, teachers might help children attend to the emotional response of the characters and their problems.

With Mother Goose, ABC, counting, and concept books, you can point out the games that are played with language or illustrations. B. G. Hennessy's *A, B, C, D, Tummy, Toes, Hands, Knees* (1989), illustrated by Wendy Watson, is an example of a delightful naming book. Read these books aloud to kindergarten and first-grade students and then place them in the classroom library area. Encourage the children to read the books on their own or with other children. Many of these books will become classroom favorites, to be read aloud to the children over and over again.

FOLKTALES. Today children are the main audience for folktales, which are part of a heritage based in oral tradition. According to Sutherland and Arbuthnot, qualities of folktales children find appealing are that they are filled with action, convey a clear sense of right and wrong, often include rhyme and repetition, and end in a satisfying way.

Excellent collections of the folktales of many different cultures are now available, and you may wish to introduce your students to folktales from African, Native American, and Asian groups, as well as to American tall tales and traditional European tales. Collections of folktales reflecting America's multicultural heritage include *The People Could Fly: American Black Folktales* retold by Virginia Hamilton (1985), *The Rainbow People* by Laurence Yep (1989), and *Tonweya and the Eagles and Other Lakota Tales* by Rosebud Yellow Robe (1979). Because most of the tales were meant to be told, rather than read silently, they lend themselves well to reading aloud, story telling, puppetry, and creative dramatics.

FABLES, MYTHS, AND EPICS. Fables, myths, and epics, like tales, have their source in folklore and are also important parts of the child's literary heritage. They are more moral in nature. Fables, such as those by Aesop, present straightforward, simple lessons. Tom Paxton, a noted folksinger, is the author of *Belling the Cat and Other Aesop's Fables* (1990), an updated and humorous retelling of these familiar fables.

Myths often provided explanations for troubling or little-understood aspects of the human condition, such as disease or the changing of the seasons. Myths can be highly complex and symbolic, but older children may find the stories both fascinating and inspiring. *In the Beginning: Creation Stories from Around the World* by Virginia Hamilton (1989) is an example of a collection of myths written for children. Twelve classics are retold for children by Mary Pope Osborne (1989) in *Favorite Greek Myths.*

MODERN FANTASY. According to Sutherland and Arbuthnot, fantasy "is the art form many modern writers have chosen to . . . lay out for children the realities of life—not in a physical or social sense, but in a psychological sense" (p. 226). Modern fantasy encompasses everything from Beatrix Potter's story of Peter Rabbit to the elegant and elaborate novels of Lewis Carroll, J. R. R. Tolkien, Ursula Le Guin, and Madeleine L'Engle. Favorites with students include L'Engle's *A Wrinkle in Time* (1962), *Mrs. Frisby and the Rats of NIMH* by Robert O'Brien (1971), *Jumanji* by Chris Van Allsburg (1981), and *The Whipping Boy* by Sid Fleischman (1986).

These books, which present imaginary worlds and events that could not really happen, can appeal to children for the same reasons as folktales, fables, myths, and epics. When reading such books, children experience a sense of adventure and escape and can come to understand different ways of approaching life's problems.

Books you feel the class as a whole will find appealing may be read aloud, one chapter a day. A brief discussion, including reactions and predictions, may follow each day's reading. When the novel has been completed, interested children may be encouraged to read other works by the same author.

POETRY. Poetry plays on emotions, triggers insight, and develops an appreciation for the beauty and power of language. Sutherland and Arbuthnot suggest that children enjoy the "singing quality" of poetry, its story elements, humor, and appeal to the senses. The following collections by individual poets are likely to win many children over to poetry: *Joyful Noise: Poems of Two Voices* by Paul Fleischman (1989), *Honey I Love and Other Love Poems* and *Nathaniel Talking* by Eloise Greenfield (1978, 1989), *Ride a Purple Pelican* by Jack Prelutsky (1986), and *A Light in the Attic* and *Where the Sidewalk Ends* by Shel Silverstein (1981, 1974).

Here are some guidelines for the use of poetry:

Do read poetry aloud often.
Do provide a variety of poems in records, books, and tapes.
Do make several anthologies available to children.
Do select contemporary poetry along with older material.
Do help children avoid sing-song reading aloud.
Do choose poems with comprehensive subject matter.
Do encourage the writing of poetry.
Do choose poems that have action or humor.
Do try choral readings. (Sutherland & Arbuthnot, 1991, p. 227)

Poetry can be read in connection with other literature. Jessie Michaels selects poems with themes similar to those students are encountering in their novels. For example, she introduced the class to poems by Langston Hughes (1959) dealing with pride and African-

American heritage, when her students were reading *Have a Happy . . .* by Mildred Pitts Walter.

MODERN FICTION. This realistic form of fiction, according to Sutherland and Arbuthnot, introduces children to the lives of families past and present, to worlds similar to or very different from their own. As shown earlier in this chapter, Jessie Michaels' students read three works of modern fiction. While some modern fiction, such as mysteries or humorous books, is written largely to entertain, other books explore deeper themes, such as being different or alone, and touch on controversial topics. An example of the former is *Herbie Jones and the Monster Ball* by Suzy Kline (1988), while an example of the latter is *Scorpions* by Walter Dean Myers (1988), which deals with issues of gangs and violence in an inner-city setting. Other well-known authors of modern fiction for children include Judy Blume, Betsy Byars, Beverly Cleary, Virginia Hamilton, Lois Lowry, Nicholasa Mohr, Katherine Paterson, Gary Paulsen, Gary Soto, and Laurence Yep.

In considering which of the vast array of books of this genre to introduce to the class or to recommend to individual children, Sutherland and Arbuthnot propose these guidelines:

> If these books center on children's basic needs; if they give them increased insight into their own personal problems and social relationships; if they show that people are more alike than different, more akin to each other than alien; if they convince young readers that they can do something about their lives—have fun and adventures and get things done without any magic other than their own earnest efforts—then they are worthwhile books (p. 333).

HISTORICAL FICTION. Historical fiction for children introduces characters, often children themselves, in an authentic setting of the past. For example, *Roll of Thunder, Hear My Cry* and *Let the Circle Be Unbroken* by Mildred Taylor (1976, 1981) describe events in the life of Cassie Logan and her family, portraying both the racist environment of the early decades of the twentieth century and the strong family ties that enabled African-American families like the Logans to survive.

According to Sutherland and Arbuthnot, historical fiction should show life in an accurate and honest way because children generally do not have the background knowledge to evaluate the material critically. In true historical fiction, the picture painted of the historical period helps the reader to understand the events in the story. This is likely to make historical events much more interesting to students. Because of this possibility, historical fiction can serve as a bridge to informational text, particularly in social studies.

Help children to identify the important historical events in the story. For example, the Holocaust is the background for *Number the Stars* by Lois Lowry (1989), and *Journey to Topaz* by Yoshiko Uchida (1975) depicts the internment of Japanese-Americans during World

War II. Guide students to trace the story line and to separate important ideas in the text from incidental details simply used to add a bit of color. Encourage them to seek out other books on the same historical period to verify information or to learn more.

BIOGRAPHY. A good biography, or account of someone's life, will be historically accurate and treat its subject as an individual, not merely as the ideal or representative of a group. Jean Fritz, perhaps the best-known author of biographies for children, has written about famous American leaders such as James Madison (*The Great Little Madison,* 1989). A touch of humor enlivens some of her books about patriots of the American Revolution, including *Why Don't You Get a Horse, Sam Adams?* (1974). Another outstanding writer of biographies for children is Russell Freedman, author of *Lincoln: A Photobiography* (1988), winner of the Newbery Medal, and *Franklin Delano Roosevelt* (1990). Sutherland and Arbuthnot recommend that biography and historical fiction be used to reinforce each other, because both give children a sense of what it was like to "be there" in another time and place.

INFORMATIONAL BOOKS. Informational books for children cover a huge number of topics, and books can be found to match the natural curiosity of every child to learn more about something. Joanna Cole has written many science books for children, including a series in which science topics are explained while a class journeys with their teacher on a magic school bus (for example, *The Magic School Bus: Inside the Earth,* 1987). Patricia Lauber, another well-known author of science books, has written about such high-interest topics as dinosaurs (*Dinosaurs Walked Here and Other Stories Fossils Tell,* 1987) and volcanoes (*Volcano: The Eruption and Healing of Mount St. Helens,* 1986). The genre of informational books is discussed further in Chapter 4.

Teaching Literature

Glenna Davis Sloan (1991), drawing on the work of Northrop Frye, suggests that teachers should show students that works of literature are related to one another, just like members of a large extended family. Literature is not a miscellaneous collection of individual books with no connection to one another. Works of literature may be related by genre, as discussed above, or by other elements. The term *intertextuality* refers to the relationships or links that may be found among different books or texts.

In the case of fiction, Sloan suggests that teachers should help students recognize that literature should be approached more with feeling and imagination than with reason. Teachers should emphasize divergent thinking, in which students are encouraged to come up with different interpretations, for example of a character's motivation or the theme of the story.

Teachers can highlight for students the elements that are found in every story: characters, setting, plot, conflict or problem, solution, point of view, language (including dialogue), and theme. Students can come to appreciate both the elements shared by many stories and the unique features of each story. Helping students to prepare a story matrix, such as that shown in Figure 3.2, is one means of helping them to see common story elements. The teacher puts the blank matrix on a sheet of chart paper, then elicits from students the information needed to fill in the cells.

Jessie Michaels had a whole-class lesson based on a story matrix after her students had finished reading the three novels. Each group supplied information for the novel they had read. This gave students a chance to discuss similarities and differences in the characters, settings, problems, themes, and so on. For example, students recognized that there was a difference in the circumstances of the main characters: Chris and Rinko were helped through the support of family and friends, while Leigh at times could turn only to his mother. They found a similarity in the main characters' ability to keep trying and eventually to see good results from what started as a bad situation.

Sloan suggests that teachers may wish to use questions such as the following (pp. 119–124) to heighten students' awareness of both shared and unique features of particular literary works. The alternative questions in brackets may be used with younger children.

Type of Story

- Every storyteller constructs a make-believe world that may be very like our own or entirely different from it. What signs and signals indicate whether a story will be more fanciful than realistic? [Is this a real story or a make-believe story? How can you tell?]
- If the world created by the author is far different from the one we know, how does the author make the story seem possible and believable?

Setting and Plot

- Where and when does the story take place? How do you know? If the story took place somewhere else or in a different time, how would it be changed?

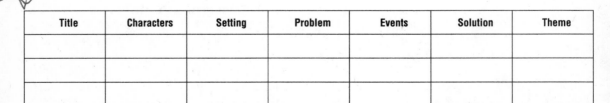

Title	Characters	Setting	Problem	Events	Solution	Theme

FIGURE 3.2
A Story Matrix

- What incident, problem, conflict, or situation gets the story started? [What is the problem in this story? How does the problem get solved?]
- What does the author do to create suspense, to make you want to read on to find out what happens? Is what happens made credible and plausible? How?
- Trace the main events of the story. Is it possible to change their order? Leave any of them out? Why or why not? [What happened first? Then what happened?]
- Suppose you thought of a different ending for the story. How would the rest of the story have to be changed to fit the new ending?
- Did the story end as you expected it to? What clues did the author offer to prepare you to expect this ending? [Did you think the story would end this way? How did you know?]

Characters

- Who is the main character in the story? What kind of person is this character? How do you know? Do you sympathize with the character? Why? Do you recognize here any character types that you know from other stories?
- Do any characters change in the course of the story? If so, how are they different in the end? What changed them? Does the change seem believable?

Point of View

- Who tells the story? Is it told in the first person—I? Is it the omniscient viewpoint of the all-knowing author, who uses third person—he, she, they? Is it limited omniscient point of view, where, although the story is told in the third person, it concentrates on the thoughts and feelings of the central character?

Mood or Tone

- Does the story as a whole create a definite mood or feeling? How is it created? Does the mood or tone change during the course of the story? How does the author signal this change?
- Did you have strong feelings throughout the story?
- What did the author do to make you feel strongly?

Style

- Does the style of writing fit the subject? Do the characters speak naturally and in keeping with their setting? Is the language rich in imagery and in memorable ways of expressing ideas? Does it flow rhythmically when it is read aloud?

Theme

- What is the idea *behind* the story that gives point to the whole? [What do you think the author wanted you to learn from this story? What is the author's message?]

Making Connections

- Is this story, though different in content, like any other story you have read or watched in its form and structure? [Does this story re-

mind you of any other story? Why? How is it the same? How is it different?]
- Think of all the characters in the story. Are any of them the same or similar to characters in other stories, cartoons, comics, movies?

By introducing students to different genres of literature, teachers show them the tremendous variety in the world of books, and make it more likely that students will learn about the kinds of books they will enjoy reading on their own. Through questioning and discussion, teachers can give students a sense of the connections among works of literature, as well as a deeper understanding of particular works.

KEY CONCEPT 3   STUDENTS SHOULD RECEIVE ACTIVE, SYSTEMATIC INSTRUCTION IN COMPREHENSION STRATEGIES, INCLUDING TEACHER ASSESSMENT OF THE EFFECTIVENESS OF INSTRUCTION.

INSTRUCTION IN COMPREHENSION STRATEGIES

In the first key concept we discussed the importance of aesthetic responses and children's personal feelings and interpretations of literature. In the present key concept we discuss what teachers can do to foster students' ability to grasp the common understandings many readers might have about a text, as well as to arrive at personal interpretations of the text.

Back in Chapter 1 we described the teacher's role as that of moving students forward through what Vygotsky called the zone of proximal development. In this key concept you will learn about the experience-text-relationship (ETR) approach, which can be used as the basis for teacher-guided discussion that promotes students' comprehension of novels and stories.

Promoting Discussion

In lessons following the ETR framework, the teacher must actively involve students in discussion of the story. Hearing students' responses allows the teacher to determine the kind of comprehension activities they can carry out on their own and the ones they need help with. Here are some guidelines to follow when you want your students to participate actively in a discussion.

1. Aim for a balance between teacher talk and student talk. Create numerous opportunities for students to respond.

For a discussion to be successful in improving students' comprehension ability, there must be a balance between teacher talk and student talk. If the teacher does most of the talking, there will be little opportunity for the give-and-take required to improve students' comprehension ability.

2. In general, elicit answers from students rather than telling them the answers.

Effective teachers consistently try to draw answers from students during comprehension discussions (Au & Kawakami, 1984). They almost never tell the answer, instead pushing the children to come up with the right answer themselves. They do, however, ask leading questions that make it possible for the children eventually to succeed. Rather than simply repeating their original question, they paraphrase it or break it into two or more easier questions for the children to answer. Then they help the children put the pieces together to answer the original, more difficult question. At a deeper level, effective teachers are not concerned just with right or wrong answers but with guiding children through a process of sound reasoning about text ideas.

3. Use lessons as an opportunity to build students' independence and to promote voluntary reading.

During teacher-guided discussions, students can be encouraged to ask their own questions about the text, rather than always answering the teacher's questions. Eventually, we want students to be able to raise and answer their own questions while reading on their own.

Books read for guided discussion may provide a springboard for voluntary reading. If students enjoy books of a particular genre, they may look for other books in that genre to read on their own. If students enjoy reading the work of a particular author, they may be inspired to seek out other books by that same author. For example, Jessie Michaels is trying to promote voluntary reading by kindling students' interest in three authors (Beverly Cleary, Yoshiko Uchida, and Mildred Pitts Walter).

Experience-Text-Relationship (ETR) Approach

The purpose of this approach (Au, 1979) is to give students a general strategy for text comprehension, including the use of background knowledge. Basically, lessons involve the teacher leading the students in the discussion of text and text-related topics. At the same time, the teacher models for the students the process an expert reader goes through in trying to construct meaning from text. Through repeated experiences in ETR lessons, the students should be able to use this overall approach independently.

PLANNING. Start by choosing the piece of literature you want students to read. Preview the story and identify its central theme, as well as important or interesting points you want the children to grasp. Decide in what way the central theme or important points might be connected to the children's own background experiences. Of course, this requires knowledge of your students as well as of the text.

While previewing the story, look for natural breaks, so that you can divide the story into segments for silent reading. If the story is likely to be easy for the children, the segments can be longer. If the story is likely to be challenging for them, the segments should be shorter.

As you have seen, Jessie Michaels selected three novels for her students to read. She chose these novels because they shared a common theme of overcoming problems through perseverance. Jessie knew that many of her students had already experienced similar problems in their own lives, including their parents' separation or divorce and financial difficulties caused by a parent being out of work.

Jessie decided that she would have her students begin by reading the novels one chapter at a time. This would allow her to introduce background information, for example about Kwanzaa or Japanese-American history, to enhance the students' understanding of the world of the novels (E phase). Jessie provided her students with guided discussion lessons until they were about halfway through the novels (T phase). Then she let the groups finish reading the novels on their own and hold their own discussions. When each group was finished, she held a final small-group lesson to discuss students' responses to the novel as a whole and their interpretations of the theme of the novel (R phase).

EXPERIENCE OR E PHASE. Begin the lesson by finding out about the students' background experiences related to the theme or topic of the text (for information about the importance of background or prior knowledge, refer back to Chapter 1). From a general beginning, move the discussion closer to the story about to be read. For example, you might show the students one of the illustrations, refer students to the title of the story, or describe an incident early in the story. Make sure students see the connection to the background knowledge activated earlier. You may want students to make predictions about the story, and have them read to see if their predictions are correct.

At the beginning of this chapter, you saw how Jessie Michaels had students talk about their background knowledge relevant to the novels they were starting to read. For example, she asked the group reading *Have a Happy . . .* to discuss the problems that Chris was experiencing and how these problems might be like their own.

TEXT OR T PHASE. When the students have finished reading each portion of the text, have them talk about their feelings and ideas. For example, if they made predictions, have them discuss whether their predictions were confirmed by the text. Ask them about the characters and their motivation, the setting, and the plot. Have them discuss the problem in the story and how they think the problem will be solved. Ask them if they came across any interesting language in the text.

As the students finished each new chapter (or section, in the case of *Dear Mr. Henshaw,* which does not have chapters), Jessie Michaels held ETR lessons to explore their responses to the novels and to monitor their comprehension. For example, here is a lesson that occurred after students had finished reading chapter 4 of *Have a Happy. . . .* Jessie asked the students to begin by sharing the writing they had done in their literature response logs about this chapter (a detailed description of the use of literature response logs is given in Key Concept 4).

Teacher: Who would like to begin? Vanessa?

Vanessa: I wrote about my feelings about this chapter. (reads from literature response log) "This chapter made me feel sad. Chris was waiting for his father to come home. But when he finally did, he didn't have a job. Chris is feeling scared because his father said they might have to move. If my dad lost his job and we had to move, I would feel scared too. I would be thinking about missing my grandma and my cousins and my friends."

Teacher: You know, Vanessa, I had the same feelings when I was reading the chapter.

Myong: And you have to go to a new school, and you won't know anybody there.

Teacher: Is that what you wrote, Myong?

Myong: Yes, because it was so hard when I had to move here two years ago.

Teacher: So you could understand why Chris was scared.

The group spent some time discussing Chris' feelings, and Jessie could tell from the discussion that the students had a good understanding of events in the chapter. She decided to see if there were any points that were puzzling them.

Teacher: Does anyone have any questions they wanted to bring up to the group?

Edouard: Yeah, I got one. (reads from literature response log) "Why does Uncle Ronald keep asking Chris about the animals? He should know that Chris is feeling bad and leave Chris alone."

Tammy: Yeah, it's like, Uncle Ronald should be cheering Chris up and letting Chris have some fun, but instead he's just pushing him to finish making some dumb animals. Like, it's like he's so selfish.

Teacher: Um-hm, it does seem that way. Chase?

Chase: If I was Chris, I would say, forget it. You want animals, you make 'em yourself! I'm outta here!

Teacher: Okay, but why do you think having the animals is so important to Uncle Ronald?

Sharita: Well, maybe he doesn't really care about the animals but he wants Chris to be doing something, instead of just feeling all depressed and all.

Jessie concluded the lesson by having the students make predictions about what might happen in chapter 5. Then the students returned to their seats to begin reading that chapter.

If students are likely to have difficulty reading the text on their own, the teacher can try a number of different approaches. One approach is to have the students read a part of the text silently, perhaps just a page or two, during their small-group lesson. Periods of silent reading alternate with periods of discussion. Points the students do not understand, or words they cannot figure out, can be discussed on the spot.

Another approach is to have students read the text in pairs. For example, a struggling reader can be paired up with another student who reads more fluently. As you saw in Chapter 1, this is an approach used by Susan Meyer. Jessie Michaels does not have her students read in pairs, but students know those in their group who will be able to give them help.

RELATIONSHIP OR R PHASE. When students have finished reading the novel, help them to draw relationships between the story and their own lives. The making of personal connections to the text helps students to see that reading can be meaningful in their own lives (this is an aspect of ownership of literacy; see Chapter 1). Ask students about the theme or author's message and how the message might be important in their own lives. Here are some questions that teachers can ask to help students explore the theme of the story and make personal connections to the text.

Theme

In your opinion, what is the theme or author's message?

Why do you think the author wrote this story?

What do you think the author wanted us to learn?

Personal Connections

What connections do you see between this story and your own life?

How could you apply the theme or author's message in your own life?

How is [main character] similar to you? How is [main character] different from you?

When the group had finished reading *Have a Happy* . . . , Jessie asked them to write about their reactions to the novel as a whole and about the theme of the story. Then she held a literature discussion.

Teacher: Travis, do you want to start?

Travis: (reads from his literature response log) "I liked this novel because I liked reading about Chris and how his family celebrated Kwanzaa. I was happy when Chris' father got a job at the end of the story."

Teacher: I'm glad you liked this story. And what did you write about the author's message?

Travis: I wrote, "The author is telling us to not worry because things will always work out okay."

Teacher: Okay, I think I understand, but can you explain your idea a little bit more?

Travis: Like, Chris was getting mad at his sister and he was worrying and all, like he was making himself crazy.

Sharita: I wrote something different. (reads from literature response log) "I think the author's message is to keep on trying. Because if Chris gave up or if his father gave up, they wouldn't have the jobs." You can't say, don't worry, because people are going to worry anyway!

Travis: Yeah, but I'm saying, why do you worry if there's nothing you can do about it?

Jessie let the students debate about the theme. She encouraged students to explain and support their interpretations. She concluded the lesson by having students discuss the relationships they saw between the story and their own lives.

Teacher: So let me ask you one last thing. What are some connections you see between this story and your own life? Spencer?

Spencer: (reads from literature response log) "The connection to my own life is that people in my family are always helping each other out. Just like people in Chris' family, like his Uncle Ronald." Like when my grandma's house needed painting, we all went over there to help.

Teacher: That's a good connection. In the book and in your life, you learned that it's easier to get something done if people help one another.

Using the combination of literature response logs and guided discussion lessons allows teachers to engage in ongoing assessment of students' comprehension of a story. During lessons, teachers can monitor the questions students raise as well as their responses to questions. From students' questions and responses, teachers can identify those who are making good progress in learning to comprehend a story, and those who need greater guidance or support. Teachers can gain similar assessment information by monitoring the writing in students' literature response logs.

For example, Jessie Michaels discovered that several students in the group reading *Dear Mr. Henshaw* were having difficulty understanding the events in Leigh Botts' life, which are only gradually revealed in his letters. To help these students, Jessie conducted a lesson in which she introduced the idea of *flashbacks,* when the author breaks the normal order of events to describe something that happened earlier. The students were able to recognize that Leigh's description of Christmas dinner the year before was an example of a flashback. Jessie set up a chart with two columns, as shown below, and the students were able to provide the following information for each column:

Leigh's Life Before the Divorce	*Leigh's Life After the Divorce*
lived with mother and father	lives with mother only
lived in mobile home	lives in small house
had a dog named Bandit	doesn't have a pet
was happy	is sad (trouble at school, misses his dad)

Jessie asked students to be alert for flashbacks as they read. In later lessons, the students suggested information to be added to the chart as they learned more about what Leigh's life was like before and after his parents' divorce.

As this example shows, by assessing students' responses during discussions and the writing in their literature response logs, teachers can identify areas in which instruction is required. Once these areas are identified, teachers can provide instruction, introducing new concepts such as flashbacks, and showing students comprehension strategies (in this case, reorganizing information in chronological order).

By using the ETR approach, teachers can help students to understand literature, both in terms of their own personal responses and in terms of the common understandings many readers are likely to have about a text. Teachers use discussions to guide students through the process of constructing meaning from text. Students are constructing meaning when they draw on background knowledge, when they identify and interpret elements such as the characters' motivation, and when they make connections between the text and their own lives. Teachers can engage in ongoing assessment of students' comprehension through continuous monitoring of their oral and written responses to text. Assessment allows teachers to provide instruction to strengthen students' comprehension ability.

KEY CONCEPT 4   STUDENTS SHOULD WRITE IN RESPONSE TO LITERATURE IN ORDER TO MAKE CONNECTIONS BETWEEN READING AND WRITING.

WRITING IN RESPONSE TO LITERATURE

As you have seen, Jessie Michaels has her fifth graders write about the novels they are reading. Every day, students record their reactions to the stories in their literature response logs. Literature response logs are also called reading response logs, literature logs, reading logs, or reading journals (Routman, 1991). A literature response log is a notebook in which students record their written responses to literature. Jessie has her students use spiral-bound notebooks, but students in some other upper-grade classes use three-ring binders.

During the first quarter of the school year, Jessie gradually introduced her students to various possibilities for writing in response to literature. For example, here is how she introduced the idea of diary entries.

Teacher: Today you'll learn a new format for writing in your literature response logs. This new format is called a diary entry. Who knows what that is?

Robyn: A diary is like a private journal where you write what's happening in your life.

Teacher: Thanks, Robyn. That's right, a diary is like a kind of private journal. Usually, the writer is the only one who reads it, so it shows the writer's true feelings. So let's say that I'm reading *The Best Bad Thing* and I come to the part you just read, where Rinko feels her parents are forcing her to go and stay with Mrs. Hata. I decide to put myself in Rinko's place and write what she might have written in her diary. I start by writing, Dear Diary. (writes these words on chart paper) Now tell me about what you think Rinko might write in her diary.

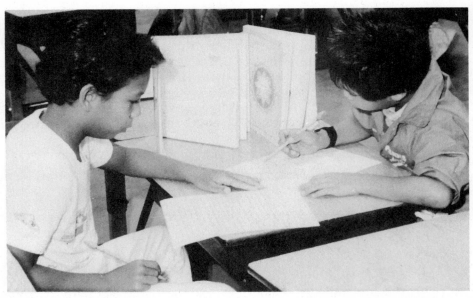

Students in this second-grade class engage in open-ended writing about the story they have just read. Activities like this simultaneously improve both reading and writing ability.

Garnett: She might write how she thinks her parents are so unfair.

Teacher: Good, but try to say it again in the words that Rinko would write.

Garnett: I think my parents are so unfair.

Teacher: (writes down Garnett's words) Okay, what else could she write?

As each new format was introduced, Jessie asked all of the students to try it. Frequently, Jessie found that she needed to demonstrate a new format to students for three or four days in a row before she could be sure they all understood it. She had students who did a good job with a particular format share their writing with the class. Then she and the students discussed the strengths of the writing that had been shared. Finally, Jessie posted copies of excellent examples of students' work on the bulletin board.

It took quite some time for Jessie to introduce the students to a variety of formats, because she found it best to introduce only one new format a week. Eventually, students had a menu of ideas they could choose from when writing in response to literature.

Most of the time, Jessie allowed her students to choose what they would write about. She kept a list on chart paper of ideas for writing in response to literature. From time to time, Jessie or the students would think of other ideas for writing, so the list grew as the year progressed. Here is the list of formats that Jessie's students used in October:

Feelings

Example: This chapter made me feel sad. Chris was waiting for his father to come home. But when he finally did, he didn't have a job. Chris is feeling scared because his father said they might have to move . . .

Favorite Part

Example: My favorite part of this chapter is when Chris opens the door and finds out he is having a surprise birthday party. It is funny to see someone's face when they are surprised . . .

Character I Like

Example: I like Uncle Ronald because he is helping Chris and his family. And he is the one who knows about Kwanzaa . . .

Character I Dislike

Example: I dislike Beth because she is such a pest just like my sister . . .

Interesting Language

Example: This chapter had lots of African words like *kanzu, bendera, dashiki* . . .

Diary Entry

Example: Dear Diary,
I am feeling terrible because Beth broke all the decorations for the Christmas tree. It was her fault but everybody got mad at me . . .

Connection to Another Book

Example: This book is like *Out from This Place* because both are about how black people have to stick together and help one another to survive . . .

Connection to My Own Life

Example: The connection to my own life is that people in my family are always helping each other out. Just like people in Chris' family, like his Uncle Ronald . . .

Every day, Jessie's students also write down any questions they have about the part of the novel they have just finished reading. For example, you saw how Edouard came up with the question, "Why does Uncle Ronald keep asking Chris about the animals?" Jessie often uses the students' own questions as the basis for group discussion. However, she does not hesitate to introduce questions of her own if there are points she wants to call to the students' attention.

Jessie does not always let students choose the kind of writing they will do in response to literature. Sometimes, if she wants the group's discussion to have a certain focus, she assigns students a question or two to write about. For example, when she wanted to have a group discussion about the author's message and relationships between the novel and students' own lives, she had students answer the following questions:

What is the author's message?
What connections do you see between the novel and your own life?

By using literature response logs, teachers establish a connection between reading and writing. Logs can be used flexibly, at times for allowing students choice and at times for directing students' attention to particular aspects of the text.

SUMMARY

At the start of this chapter, you saw an example of a readers' workshop in Jessie Michaels' fifth-grade classroom. Each of the three groups in her class was reading a different novel. The groups engaged in three major activities: teacher-led discussion lessons, student discussions, and writing in response to literature.

You learned in the first key concept about the nature of literature-based instruction and that literature is usually read from an aesthetic stance. Ideas for maintaining an aesthetic stance in literature discussions were presented. In the second key concept you were introduced to nine genres of children's literature. You also learned about different story elements that might be discussed with students and about the importance of helping students to see the connections among different works of literature.

In the third key concept you read about the experience-text-relationship approach, which can be used to guide students in discussions of novels or stories. You saw how teachers can use students' oral and written responses in the process of ongoing assessment and to guide instruction. The topic of the fourth key concept was making connections between reading and writing through the use of literature response logs. Teachers introduce students to different formats for writing in response to literature, then often allow students to choose the format they wish to use. One theme that cuts across this chapter is the need for a balance between activities centering on teacher-directed instruction and those emphasizing student choice and open-ended responding.

◀ ACTIVITIES

Reflecting on Your Own Literacy

Think about a favorite work of literature, among all those you have read while attending school. Write a brief description of this literary work. Why do you like it so much? What do you think a teacher can do to help students appreciate and enjoy literature?

Applying What You Have Learned to the Classroom

Find a children's book that you would like to use to teach following the experience-text-relationship approach, as described in Key Concept 3. What theme would you try to develop if teaching with this book? What connections would you try to make between the book and the students' own background experiences?

BIBLIOGRAPHY

References

Au, K. H. (1979). Using the experience-text-relationship method with minority children. *Reading Teacher, 32*(6), 677–679.

Au, K. H., & Kawakami, A. J. (1984). Vygotskian perspectives on discussion processes in small group reading lessons. In P. L. Peterson, L. C. Wilkinson, & M. Hallinan (Eds.), *The social context of instruction: Group organization and group processes.* New York: Academic Press.

Cramer, B. B. (1984). Bequest of wings: Three readers and special books. *Language Arts, 61*(3), 253–260.

Harste, J. C., & Short, K. G., with Burke, C., & contributing teacher researchers (1988). *Creating classrooms for authors: The reading-writing connnection.* Portsmouth, NH: Heinemann.

McMahon, S. I. (1992). Book club: A case study of a group of fifth graders as they participate in a literature-based reading program. *Reading Research Quarterly, 27*(4), 292–294.

Rosenblatt, L. (1978). *The reader, the text, the poem: The transactional theory of the literary work.* Carbondale, IL: Southern Illinois University Press.

Rosenblatt, L. (1980). What facts does this poem teach you? *Language Arts, 57*(4), 386–394.

Rosenblatt, L. (1991). Literature—S.O.S! *Language Arts, 68*(6), 444–448.

Routman, R. (1991). *Invitations: Changing as teachers and learners K–12.* Portsmouth, NH: Heinemann.

Sloan, G. D. (1991). *The child as critic: Teaching literature in elementary and middle school* (3rd ed.). New York: Teachers College Press.

Sutherland, Z., & Arbuthnot, M. H. (1991). *Children and books* (8th ed.). Glenview, IL: Scott, Foresman.

Zarrillo, J. (1991). Theory becomes practice: Aesthetic teaching with literature. *The New Advocate, 4*(4), 221–234.

Suggested Classroom Resources

Cole, J. (1987). *The magic school bus: Inside the earth.* Illustrated by B. Degan. New York: Scholastic.

Fleischman, P. (1989). *Joyful noise: Poems for two voices.* New York: Harper.

Fleischman, S. (1986). *The whipping boy.* New York: Greenwillow.

Freedman, R. (1990). *Franklin Delano Roosevelt.* Boston: Clarion.

Freedman, R. (1988). *Lincoln: A photobiography.* Boston: Clarion.

Fritz, J. (1974). *Why don't you get a horse, Sam Adams?* Illustrated by T. S. Hyman. New York: Coward, McCann.

Fritz, J. (1989). *The great little Madison.* New York: Putnam.

Greenfield, E. (1978). *Honey, I love and other love poems.* New York: Harper Trophy.

Greenfield, E. (1989). *Nathaniel talking.* New York: Black Butterfly Children's Books.

Hamilton, V. (1985). *The people could fly: American black folktales.* Illustrated by L. and D. Dillon. New York: Knopf.

Hamilton, V. (1989). *In the beginning: Creation stories from around the world.* Orlando, FL: Harcourt.

Hennessy, D. G. (1989). *A, B, C, D, tummy, toes, hands, knees.* New York: Viking Kestrel.

Hughes, L. (1959). *Selected poems of Langston Hughes.* New York: Knopf.

Kline, S. (1988). *Hervie Jones and the monster ball.* Illustrated by R. Williams. New York: Putnam.

Lauber, P. (1986). *Dinosaurs walked here and other stories fossils tell.* New York: Bradbury.

Lauber, P. (1986). *Volcano: The eruption and healing of Mount St. Helens.* New York: Bradbury.

L'Engle, M. (1962). *A wrinkle in time.* New York: Farrar, Straus & Giroux.

Lowry, L. (1989). *Number the stars.* Boston: Houghton Mifflin.

Myers, W. D. (1988). *Scorpions.* New York: Harper & Row.

O'Brien, R. C. (1971). *Mrs. Frisby and the rats of NIMH.* New York: Atheneum.

Osborne, M. P. (1989). *Favorite Greek myths.* New York: Scholastic.

Paxton, T. (1990). *Belling the cat and other Aesop's fables.* New York: Morrow.

Prelutsky, J. (1986). *Ride a purple pelican.* Illustrated by G. Williams. New York: Greenwillow.

Silverstein, S. (1974). *Where the sidewalk ends.* New York: Harper & Row.

Silverstein, S. (1981). *A light in the attic.* New York: Harper & Row.

Taylor, M. (1976). *Roll of thunder, hear my cry.* New York: Dial.
Taylor, M. (1981). *Let the circle be unbroken.* New York: Dial.
Uchida, Y. (1975). *Journey to Topaz.* New York: Scribner.
Uchida, Y. (1983). *The best bad thing.* New York: Atheneum.
Van Allsburg, C. (1981). *Jumanji.* Boston: Houghton Mifflin.
Walter, M. P. (1989). *Have a happy . . .* New York: Morrow.
Yellow Robe, R. (1979). *Tonweya and the eagles and other Lakota tales.* Illustrated by J. Pinkney. New York: Dial.
Yep, L. (1989). *The rainbow people.* New York: Harper & Row.
Yolen, J. (1987). *Owl moon.* Illustrated by J. Schoenherr. New York: Philomel.
Young, E. (1989). *Lon Po Po: A Red Riding Hood story from China.* New York: Philomel.

Further Readings

Bishop, R. S. (1993). Multicultural literature for children: Making informed choices. In V. J. Harris (Ed.), *Teaching multicultural literature in grades K–8.* Norwood, MA: Christopher-Gordon, pp. 37–53.
Routman, R. (1988). *Transitions: From literature to literacy.* Portsmouth, NH: Heinemann.
Urzua, C. (1992). Faith in learners through literature studies. *Language Arts, 69* (7), 492–501.
Walmsley, S. A. (1992). Reflections on the state of elementary literature instruction. *Language Arts, 69* (7), 508–514.

4 READING COMPREHENSION OF NONFICTION AND REPORT WRITING

Here are four readers' recollections of books that triggered new interests:

[Reader A:] In the eighth grade, I thought I had found my life's work when we started to study electricity. I even remember trying to read some engineering books, and especially one on armature winding. I read the biography of Thomas Edison and dug into everything I could find on electricity. That was the first year I asked for books for Christmas.

[Reader B:] By my last two years my reading tastes had changed to mysteries and war. Strangely enough the war novels were usually documentary. I would spend hours following the blow by blow account of the fall of the Remagen Bridge. I mapped out troop movements of the Battle of the Bulge and of Rommel's Africa Corps. Here for once a major impact had been made upon me by literature. Largely through my reading, I decided to major in history in college.

[Reader C:] I think Madame Curie became my idol as a result of her biography. At the time I was very interested in science and thought I would one day become a doctor. Her biography was an appealing example. *Arrowsmith* was also about a scientist and therefore another of my favorites. (Hope I have the title right.)

[Reader D:] A very definite influence on my reading at this time was a growing interest in science. In the 10th grade I decided medicine was my field and I would become a great woman doctor. Of course, I read Elizabeth Blackwell over and over. Another favorite was *Microbe Hunters*. One of my other favorites was *Madame Curie,* a book I still enjoy. My burning desire to become a doctor faded during my junior year when my progress was blocked by a monster known as Chemistry, but my interest in scientific books remains with me, perhaps because I married a doctor. (Carlsen & Sherrill, 1988, pp. 80–81)

OVERVIEW

We begin by describing a research project in a third-grade classroom. The students are engaged in a process of reading and writing in order to investigate a topic about which they would like to learn more. As they become "experts" on their chosen topics, they share their learning with others.

We then discuss four concepts that support students' learning from informational text. In the first key concept we consider how the classroom community can support students in taking ownership of their learning. Next we discuss the kinds of informational text resources available to elementary age students. In the third key concept we present several approaches to nonfiction through which students can develop comprehension strategies. Finally, we show how reading and writing come together as students develop their own research reports and projects.

KEY CONCEPT 1: Students should learn from informational text within a classroom community where ownership of one's own learning is valued.

KEY CONCEPT 2: Students should use a variety of informational text resources and develop an understanding of how these texts can serve their purposes for learning.

KEY CONCEPT 3: Students should develop strategies for the comprehension of informational texts.

KEY CONCEPT 4: Students should be involved in research projects integrating reading and writing.

◀ PERSPECTIVE

Research Report Writing in a Third-Grade Classroom

Joyce Souza takes a few minutes to stand back and observe her third graders' involvement during their writers' workshop. On this day in February the children are busily engaged in their second research project, this one focused on birds. The project evolved from students' interest during a larger unit of study on animals and the theme of interdependence, which correlates with the school district's third-grade science and social studies curriculum. Joyce has planned that the students will engage in three group-focused research projects during the second half of the school year. Two projects, in which students choose an animal to research, closely follow one another. The children will decide on a third project in the spring to correlate with another unit of study.

The classroom library is well stocked with a variety of books and references. Throughout her 12 years of teaching, Joyce has been building a good personal collection of fiction and nonfiction titles that, along with books from the school and community libraries, are continually rotated through the classroom library. One area of the classroom library now features trade books, textbooks, reference books, magazines, posters, and tapes with information about birds. The students go in and out of this area as they choose, browse through, and return books related to their topics. This display will grow throughout the project. Joyce reminds herself to encourage the students to look for materials outside school that they can bring in to share. She also notes that Camela needs help with materials. Camela chose the bird of paradise and has been able to find only one resource.

Joyce observes how well these ethnically mixed, urban children have evolved into a classroom community and the level of enthusiasm they have for learning about "their birds." Joyce highly values and nurtures this learning environment. She regularly shares her own curiosity as she wonders with the students, "Why do you think that happened?" "How can we learn more?" She expresses her enthusiasm and caring when she exclaims, "Isn't that interesting! I didn't know that." Her sincere reflections and delight in discovery provide positive models for the children's own thinking and attitudes about learning.

Joyce uses the class list she carries on a clipboard to record some of her observations. Chantelle, who is investigating pelicans, took her book to Josh's table and said, "Do you want this book next? It's got good information about penguins, too." Joyce is pleased that Chantelle knows of other students' topics and thinks to recommend resources that they may find helpful. Joyce also notes that Sui-lyn couldn't wait to share with Boyd, a classmate respected for his strength and humor, that her book says penguins regurgitate fish to feed their babies. "That means 'throw up,' you know." Sui-lyn was rewarded with the expected reaction from Boyd. Joyce thought, "Well, OK. I *do* want them to share. This shows ownership."

"Look, Mrs. Souza," says Chantelle. "Remember? I knew that pelicans eat fish but I wanted to know if they could hold lots of fish in their bills. This book tells about it right here." Chantelle and many of the other children feel quite comfortable with the K-W-L approach (to be discussed later in this chapter) in which they first write what they already *K*now about their topics, what they *W*ant to find out, and then, as they research their topics, what they *L*earn. Joyce has modeled this approach and provided many opportunities for students to practice using it throughout the year.

As they engage in their bird research, the students will have many occasions to independently orchestrate strategies that they have practiced with Joyce's support. During their first research project, in which they chose a mammal to investigate, much of their attention was given to the research process itself. Now that the children have had some experience with the process, Joyce expects that their depth of learning will be greater as a result of this second project. She is also confident that the children will need less support from her than they needed during their first project.

Yesterday, when they began their study of birds, Joyce showed her own use of the K-W-L strategy along with how she thinks about selecting a topic. After the students, as a group, developed a lengthy list of birds from which they might choose, Joyce said, "As we were listing all these birds, I have been thinking about one I'd like to know more about. I thought maybe I'd choose to research the wren, because at home we have a wren house outside our kitchen window. I like to watch the birds go in and out as they build their nests, and I like to hear them sing, but I wonder where they go in the winter. I wonder how long the babies stay with their parents. Then I thought maybe I'd choose a parakeet, because Petey lives in his cage in our family room. I'm curious about where parakeets live in their natural habitat—when they're not someone's pets. But when Jermaine said, 'roadrunner,' I decided 'That's my bird!' I used to love roadrunner cartoons, and I realize I never thought about them being real birds. Do they really run fast like the cartoon character? Can they fly? Where do they live?" Through modeling, Joyce shared her own process for deciding on a topic for a research report.

Next, she used an overhead transparency to record what she knew. She wrote, "They have long legs. I think they can run very fast. I think they live in deserts." Then she completed part W of the strategy, listing what types of information she would like to learn (see Figure 4.4).

After Joyce's demonstration, most children were able to choose a topic and begin a K-W-L sheet of their own. Karl, Jamal, and Dede had difficulty getting started, and Joyce recalled that they had needed help to begin the mammal project too. Joyce asked these three students to meet with her in the conference corner. After discussion, Karl and Jamal decided to investigate robins and Joyce suggested they get started by working together to write what they already know. Dede chose the pelican, and Chantelle agreed to help Dede begin her research.

At the end of that day's writers' workshop, Joyce suggested that the students pair up to share the information and questions they had written on their K-W-L sheets. After talking with a partner, the students gathered together in their large-group meeting spot on the carpet. Joyce asked, "Who had a helpful conference? Does anyone have something to share?"

Many children talked of their experiences. "Boyd wrote, 'How high does the eagle fly?' and that made me wonder, How high can a condor fly?" Jermaine said.

"Good," Joyce responded. "Hearing someone else's questions can make you think of new questions about your own topic."

Now, during the second day of their bird research, the children are working on step L, writing what they are learning from their resources. Most of the children read independently. Sui-lyn and Josh have paired up to read a book about penguins. Two other boys are listening to a tape as they follow along in a book about herons. Joyce observes the students' note-taking strategies. The children have been helped through guided practice to take notes after listening to information and after reading from informational texts themselves. She notes how the students are managing on their own. Some of the children, like Josh and Sui-lyn, read, record the information they find interesting, then read some more. Some students like Jamal and Karl have been reading but have not yet written any notes. Chantelle, Dede, and Ryan have gone to the conference area to share their new information with one another.

Before the work period comes to a close, Joyce asks Josh and Sui-lyn if they are willing to share their notes with the class. They agree. Then Joyce asks, "What are some important things to remember when we take notes?"

"Just write the important things," Boyd offers.

"Don't write all the words. Like, if you're writing about a condor, you don't have to say 'condor' every time," Matt suggests.

"Put the ideas in your own words," says Camela. "Tell the interesting things you learned."

"Good," replies Joyce. "Let's take some time for our notes now. I noticed that Josh and Sui-lyn were taking good notes as they were reading. They have agreed to share."

Josh and Sui-lyn read their notes about penguins from their K-W-L forms:

"Smallest is 1 foot high"
"Largest is 4 feet"
"Spiky tongue helps them hold fish"
"Vomits up digested fish"

"Now," Joyce says, "let's spend ten minutes writing our notes. Let's make sure we get down all that important and interesting information we've learned. Then we'll take some time to reread what we have written. Finally, we will meet as a large group to share."

As the students write, Joyce adds notes to her own form about the roadrunner. She has made a commitment to work through a project of her own along with the children. She planned to do that with the mammal research, and though she had begun, she did not continue her own project.

Later, when the group gathers together Joyce asks, "Who'd like to share something from their notes that's especially interesting?" Several children volunteer.

Matt reads about the condor: "lays eggs in caves; wings 8–10 feet; called scavenger—eat dead animals."

Randi reads, "An ostrich is a very big bird and can weigh up to 300 pounds."

The group is impressed with Randi's information, but they think she could have recorded it in fewer words. They suggest, "Weigh up to 300 pounds. Remember, you don't have to say 'ostrich' all the time."

When Joyce asks for problems or concerns, Camela says that she is having difficulty finding information about the bird of paradise. She decides to visit the school library during recess to see if the librarian can help her. Ryan thinks he has a book at home about tropical birds to share with Camela. Joyce suggests that they all help one another by looking for resources outside school to add to their classroom library. The children respond with excited, "I've got. . . " and "I know I can bring. . . ."

Finally, Joyce reminds the children that after they "fill themselves full" with information, they will be sharing what they have learned by writing a report, just as they did when they studied mammals. They will have conferences, write drafts, revise, edit, and publish as they do regularly during writers' workshop. She reminds them to think of the different ways their classmates shared their mammal reports. Chantelle made a pop-up book. Boyd wrote his report from an elephant's perspective, as if the elephant were telling a story about himself. Joyce continues, "We also know of different ways other authors have written nonfiction. Let's think how Dorothy Patent chooses to tell about turkeys as you listen to a chapter from our read-aloud today. Some of you might like to try her ideas."

Joyce often chooses nonfiction selections as read-alouds and for book talks, purposely choosing different styles and formats. She has been pleased to note an increase in the number of beautifully illustrated and well-written informational books appropriate for young children. She knows that in addition to providing information, the books can provide models for the children's own writing. Today she reads from *Wild Turkey, Tame Turkey* (Patent, 1989). After reading, Joyce helps the students note how the author chose to write her book in the structure of comparison and contrast. She thinks some of the children may want to try using a similar structure once they begin drafting their bird reports.

After a brief discussion of Patent's writing style, two students read aloud a poem from *I Am Phoenix: Poems for Two Voices* (Fleischman, 1985). Several of the children have been enjoying this poetry about birds. Then the children move into readers' workshop, where their three small discussion groups are exploring the themes of interdependence and environmental preservation. One group is reading *One Day in the Woods* (George, 1988), another, *Saving the Peregrine Falcon* (Arnold, 1985), and the third, *Peeping in the Shell: A Whooping Crane Is Hatched* (McNulty, 1986).

At the end of the school day, Joyce writes some thoughts about their current research project in her teaching journal.

> I know it's important that the kids see me as a writer. When I write, I can better understand how to help them. I *will* complete my own research project along with them this time. Maybe my report will include a poem about a roadrunner. I surprised myself with the poem I wrote during writers' workshop last month. I'd like to try again!
>
> These kids seem to be doing so much better with their projects than the kids last year. I'm glad I've been consistent in my instruction since September. Also, I see that the literature links are paying off!
>
> Many students are quite independent—and they are good resources for others. I need to follow up with Jamal, Karl, and Dede. They will need extra support in working through the research process—and they'll need support in reading some of the information they'll want. Maybe Dede and Chantelle can work together to complete one joint project. I'm not quite sure what will best help the boys. I'll check with them at the beginning of tomorrow's writers' workshop to see what they need.
>
> I think everyone could benefit from more discussion about note taking. I want to allow plenty of time for the kids to share each day. I know it's important for them to see what others are doing. Then more of them are willing to try out new things for themselves.

Joyce thinks ahead to her grade-level meeting on Thursday with fellow teachers, Susan and Lucia. The three of them have been keeping teaching journals since September and meeting regularly to share with one another. Joyce is glad that Susan thought of starting a support group. The group provides a way that they can learn and share together in much the same way that their students work together in the classroom. The writing they do in their teaching journals helps them reflect on what is important in their classrooms. Sharing with one another provides a social context in which they can extend and revise their thinking.

The students in all three classrooms are now involved with reading from informational texts. Susan's students are in the midst of their first research project and Lucia has been systematically teaching note-taking strategies, building upon ideas from a professional article the three teachers read and discussed earlier. Joyce is eager to hear how things are going in their classrooms. She wonders, too, what they are doing to support their less independent students like Dede, Karl, and Jamal. She makes a note to ask.

OWNERSHIP OF LEARNING

Authenticity

Joyce Souza believes that if students are to be interested and involved in learning from informational texts, they need to be engaged in authentic activities. During her first three years of teaching, Joyce worked with fifth graders. She remembers assigning chapters from the social studies text. "Read; then write your answers to the questions at the end of the chapter. Your papers are due to me by the end of the week." She realizes now that such assignments are not enough. In order for students to be active learners, they must be involved in reading and writing for a range of real purposes. She feels that her third graders are benefitting from her increased knowledge about literacy learning.

When students read informational books, formulate their own questions, take notes, and write research reports, they engage in the

These third graders explore a thematic unit by researching topics of their own choosing. Charts hung across the classroom remind students of what they have learned about the writing process and different forms of literacy.

same kinds of authentic activities in which all researchers engage. This process of inquiry is as useful for student learners as it is for adult researchers.

Role of Ownership

Joyce Souza is aware of how essential the classroom community is in supporting students' developing sense of ownership. She believes that fostering of third graders' ownership of learning will affect the value they place on their literate abilities and the choices they make throughout their lives.

There are many elements of ownership that make up a classroom community. We will discuss some that were apparent in our third-grade example.

MAKING CHOICES. Choice is one element of ownership that is clearly evident as the students work on their research projects. Joyce Souza organizes the classroom to encourage student choice, and she makes instructional decisions that allow students to have input into what and how they will learn. Though the school district's curriculum determines their study of animals and interdependence, Joyce's students have options in selecting their topics. They also choose how to write and present their final reports. When the students prepared their mammal reports, Chantelle chose to design a pop-up book, and Boyd decided to create Eli the Elephant to share his information as a reader's theater presentation.

When students are given choices, their interest and involvement in learning are heightened. Students can select the materials that they consider important and relevant, and they can select strategies that they determine to be helpful to their learning. Students can choose what to write and how to write it in order to remember, share, and reflect upon their topics. When students have choices, they often take ownership for extending their learning in ways their teachers might never think to suggest.

SETTING OWN PURPOSES. Learners take ownership when they set their own purposes for reading and writing. Joyce Souza fosters this feature of ownership when she encourages the children to form their own questions about their topics. When students set purposes for reading and writing they use literacy to seek specific information that they are curious about.

Often students use reading and writing for purposes they initiate on their own. Children can organize the classroom library in ways they find useful. In this third-grade classroom, some of the girls organized the resource collection in alphabetical order by names of birds. They placed all the general reference books together and made a section for materials that did not fit their two other categories. They began a notebook in which their classmates could write notes to ask for help in locating information about their topics. Three other students put their printing and illustrating talents to use in a sign they made for the resource collection: "Information about Birds—Right Here, Dudes!"

SHARING. Joyce Souza understands that a willingness to share is essential to developing ownership. She models this frequently as she shares her own questions and joy in learning, and she encourages the children to share and respond to one another's ideas. Joyce realizes that in her early days of teaching, when she taught by handing out assignments, she was regarded as the holder of all answers and the maker of all decisions. She also remembers being frustrated that her fifth graders were overly dependent on her. They seemed always to be asking, "Is this right?" "Is this what you want?"

"No wonder," she now thinks. She had not viewed her classroom as a community in which students could learn by sharing their ideas about reading and writing with one another.

Teachers who value student collaboration and sharing organize their classrooms in ways that allow students to meet and discuss information informally as well as in more structured ways. They ask questions such as "Who learned something new or interesting from your partner?" "Did your sharing make you ask some new questions?" Jane Hansen describes such a climate as a response system that sets a tone in which everyone is always wondering about something (1987, p. 149). As students make their knowledge and questions public, they share as a community of learners aware of one another's interests, problems, and concerns—a community in which they are responsible for supporting each other's learning.

RECOGNIZING INTERESTS OF OTHERS. Joyce Souza recognizes that a more sophisticated form of sharing includes an awareness of the interests of others. She often models her awareness when she recommends new books to students in the class. "When I saw this book, I thought of Beth. I know that Beth has been enjoying many *Nate the Great* books. I thought she might like to try another mystery, *The Case of the Invisible Dog*" (Hilidick, 1977).

As the students pursued their bird research, Joyce encouraged them to be aware of information that might be helpful to others. When Chantelle recommended a book to Josh with information about penguins because she knew of his research focus, and when on another day Sunni brought in a newspaper article about condors for Matt and Jermaine, they were displaying their ownership of literacy.

CONNECTING READING AND WRITING. Ownership of literacy is enhanced when students are involved in making connections between reading and writing. We saw how Joyce Souza suggested connections between her students' research report writing and the compare/contrast structure Dorothy Patent used to write *Wild Turkey, Tame Turkey.* Also, because these third graders had written poetry of their own, they could bring greater appreciation and understanding to their exploration of poems about birds. On other occasions the students examined different text structures used by published authors such as problem/solution, description, and sequence, and they experimented with these structures in their own writing.

When students see themselves as writers as well as readers, they come to view texts differently. They begin to "read as writers" (Smith, 1983, p. 562), making connections between the texts they read and the texts they write. They bring a different perspective to their reading and their thinking about reading because they understand what it means to be an author.

ASSESSING ONE'S LEARNING. Ownership is also shown through students' ability to assess their own learning. When students set personal learning goals, it is possible for them to monitor and revise the expectations they have set for themselves. In Joyce Souza's classroom, use of the K-W-L strategy supports students in this process. The children set their own goals or purposes for reading when they wrote questions about their birds. They monitored their success in learning as they found answers to their questions. The students were able to assess their growth in learning by comparing the amount of information they knew about their topics before and after their research.

Lucy Calkins (1990, p. 209) suggests that students who continually plan and monitor their progress become deliberate students of their subjects. All researchers must continually look backward and forward, asking, "What am I learning?" "What do I need to learn?" and "How can I learn this?" Bette Bosma suggests that students reflect upon their learning by asking themselves, "What do I know?" "What questions do I still have?" "Are there things I don't understand from my reading?" (Bosma, in Freeman & Person, 1992, p. 52).

As the students in Joyce Souza's class concluded their bird research, Joyce suggested, "Think about the research you did for your mammal project. Now that you have finished your bird research, I wonder if you've learned more about being a researcher. Take a few minutes to think and write about your thoughts. Then we'll meet together to share our ideas." While the K-W-L forms helped the students assess their increase in *knowledge,* Joyce's inquiry asked them to assess the *process* in which they engaged as researchers.

Bette Bosma describes how a sixth-grade teacher involved her students in assessing both the knowledge and process components of their learning. As they worked through a unit of study, they wrote weekly reports in which they reflected upon:

1. Process—students noted their understanding of the material, their vocabulary needs, and their rate of progress toward self-developed goals.
2. Knowledge—students prepared a progress report about what they learned.
3. Presentation—students stated their plans for presenting their new information to the class, or they presented a plan for evaluating their final presentation (Freeman & Person, 1992, p. 52).

We have seen how learning from informational text can be supported within a classroom community in which authentic learning activities and ownership of literacy are valued. Students who participate in such a community are likely to become thoughtful learners, capable of informing themselves, who will come to understand their lives and their world (McGinley & Madigan, 1990).

KEY CONCEPT **2**   STUDENTS SHOULD USE A VARIETY OF INFORMATIONAL TEXT RESOURCES AND DEVELOP AN UNDERSTANDING OF HOW THESE TEXTS CAN SERVE THEIR PURPOSES FOR LEARNING.

INFORMATIONAL LITERATURE

We saw that the children in Joyce Souza's third-grade classroom used many kinds of texts as they investigated birds during the readers' and writers' workshops. They listened to nonfiction and poetry that was read aloud. They independently read and discussed their responses to literature selections within their small discussion groups. They used a variety of print resources such as picture books, single-title books, series books, reference books, and textbooks as they carried out their own research. Joyce knows that children learn to read by reading. Therefore, if her students are to learn to read for information, they must have many opportunities to engage with a variety of informational texts.

This is very different from Joyce's approach when she first began teaching. Then she relied exclusively on textbooks for content learning in areas such as science and social studies, in much the same way that she used a basal for reading instruction. Now, during their readers' workshop her students use literature almost exclusively when they read for information as well as when they read for pleasure.

One advantage to using a variety of literature instead of a single textbook is that all children, regardless of prior knowledge or reading ability, can experience success as learners. Often many students find it difficult to construct meaning from textbooks. Some textbooks are poorly organized, or they present concepts with such density that even skilled readers have difficulty selecting pertinent information. Also, the textbook narrator usually speaks with a distant, rational, and authoritarian voice. It is difficult for students to be involved and critical readers of such texts (Freeman & Person, 1992, p. 48).

Joyce has noted an increase in the number and quality of informational books written for elementary-grade students, and her observations are confirmed by the National Council of Teachers of English's Committee on Using Nonfiction in the Elementary Language Arts Classroom. They suggest that this is largely the result of teachers' increased use of picture books and fiction rather than basal programs for reading instruction in their elementary classrooms. Now that teachers are recognizing the instructional potential for quality literature, nonfiction is beginning to receive the same attention as fiction (Freeman & Person, 1992, p. vii).

Joyce Souza recognizes that content information is often gained from literature that is not traditionally classified as informational text. As the students enjoyed poetry about birds, they also noted some new information. In their reading of fiction throughout the year, they often comment on what they are learning. For example, when one literature group read and responded to the novel *Sarah, Plain and Tall* (MacLachlan, 1985), part of their discussion included information they had learned about that time in history.

Though readers can certainly learn content from texts other than those classified as informational, it will be helpful for your students to learn to distinguish between the genres of fiction and nonfiction. Though "fiction" and "nonfiction" represent the long-accepted Dewey decimal classification of books, we have adopted the National Council of Teachers of English's Committee's decision to use the terms *informational books* and *nonfiction* interchangeably. These terms designate books in the Dewey decimal classification that have numerical or biographical designation, excepting poetry and folklore (1992, vii). Other texts that your students will find helpful in their search for information are reference books. We will examine several types of reference books and informational books and consider how they might support elementary students' learning of content information.

Nonfiction Resources

Textbooks, encyclopedias, dictionaries, and thesauruses are kinds of reference books often used by students. They can be used to locate specific details prompted by students' reading, by their discussions, and as a result of their own research interests. The glossaries and indexes of these references are often helpful resources for the sort of specific information students seek.

Classroom libraries usually offer a variety of other resources that are readily accessible to students. Within the genre of nonfiction or informational books, series books are one type that is popular with elementary-grade children. A series of several books will often focus on a specific area of study such as "plants and animals of the desert" or "community workers." Nature Watch Books (Carolrhoda, 1986) and Where Animals Live Books (Putnam's, 1987) are examples.

Although many of these books are written to a formula and the author's voice is seldom heard, children find series books helpful resources for their research. The books are usually organized in a way that allows students easy access to facts and information through pictures and text. In addition, they often present information through graphs, charts, timelines, glossaries, and bibliographies (Freeman & Person, 1992, p. 27). You will probably want to include selected series books for your classroom library. When students begin their research projects, they often turn to these books first. Their format is familiar so that most students know what to expect and can use them with independence.

Because of the limitations of series books you will want to seek other literature to read aloud and for your students to read and discuss during readers' workshop. For these purposes, teachers usually choose from what are termed single or nonseries titles. The best of these books "are personalized by the author's deep-seated interest in his or her subject. Hours of research, thoughtful writing, well-chosen graphics, and careful balance between fact and narrative result in books that can be truly termed literature" (Freeman & Person, 1992, p. 28).

Hearing and reading quality nonfiction allow students to build on their current information and extend their knowledge of the subject. It also stimulates them to further research (Freeman & Person, 1992, p. 29). When students explore books such as *Wild Turkey, Tame Turkey* and *Peeping in the Shell: A Whooping Crane Is Hatched,* they come to understand how quality literature can support their learning in content areas.

Myra Zarnowski (1990) encourages a similar approach to support students' learning of history. She suggests that biographies be used to build upon and extend students' knowledge and understanding of historical events. Zarnowski points out that when teachers use textbooks, they should only "serve as a basis for further inquiry—inquiry that makes use of the growing body of high-quality nonfiction literature for children" (p. 15). To better understand the people and events that shaped, for example, America's history, Zarnowski suggests an in-depth study of influential figures of the times through the reading of biographies. When students engage in such a study, they come to develop a more balanced view of the leaders of that day and a more complete understanding of the times in which they lived (p. 16).

Instructional Purposes

When Joyce Souza chooses a book to read aloud, she usually selects one that is too difficult for most of her students to read on their own. The read-alouds serve to extend students' background experiences and expand their knowledge of vocabulary and sentence patterns. They also expose students to authors and types of books that they are not likely to have encountered in their own reading (Freeman & Person, 1992, p. 78).

When Joyce selects nonfiction titles for her students' literature discussion groups, she considers the children's background knowledge, interests, and concerns. She is also attentive to the book's potential for evoking thought and discussion.

Sylvia Vardell and Kathleen Copeland point out that when students tune in to nonfiction, they want to talk about it. "When students exchange responses to ideas read or heard, they are exposed to viewpoints that could reaffirm, challenge, or extend their own understanding." Furthermore, students "encounter new vocabulary and information that they would not meet through daily conversations or through reading only fiction" (Vardell & Copeland, in Freeman & Person, 1992, p. 77). Good nonfiction engages students with new concepts and motivates them to ask their own questions, a sure indication of their learning. As students hear, read, reflect upon, and discuss informational literature, they come to understand how this genre can contribute to their knowledge and understanding of the world.

Certainly a major goal of reading nonfiction is to gain information. Children's author Russell Freedman suggests that "the basic purpose of nonfiction is to inform, to instruct, [and] hopefully to enlighten" (Freeman & Person, 1992, p. 3). When readers approach text to gain specific information they are adopting what Rosenblatt (1978) terms an *efferent stance*. You learned in Chapter 3 that when we read in an efferent mode, we read the text as nonliterature. As students search trade books, textbooks, and encyclopedias to answer their questions and to learn more about their topics, their reading is primarily efferent. Their main focus is on the information and knowledge that remains after the reading.

But Joyce Souza has an additional goal for her students' understanding of this genre: making personal connections to the information and to the literary text as well. The effective nonfiction book must do more than offer facts. As Freedman notes, it "must animate its subject, infuse it with life. It must create a vivid and believable world that the reader will enter willingly and leave only with reluctance. A good nonfiction book should be a pleasure to read. It should be just as compelling as a good story. After all, there's a story to everything" (Freeman & Person, 1992, p. 3). Readers who are able to appreciate the author's research and craft, who can experience the writing as literature, are taking an *aesthetic stance.*

When Joyce Souza and her students shared poetry selections from *I Am Phoenix: Poems for Two Voices* (Fleischman, 1985), they took both an aesthetic and an efferent approach as they explored the world of birds through the pleasures of their sounds and songs. When Joyce suggested that they consider Dorothy Patent's approach to writing as she read aloud from *Wild Turkey, Tame Turkey,* she was asking that they appreciate the person behind the writing. This person, or author, has views about her subject and has made decisions to present the information in specific ways. When we ask students to respond to an author's opinions, attitudes, and writing style, we are inviting them to adopt an aesthetic stance toward their reading.

Evaluation of Books

Students' understanding of the genre of nonfiction and its contribution to their learning can be heightened by their reflection and evaluation. You might ask your students to assess how authors and texts contributed to their understanding, learning, and appreciation of the topics they investigate. Bosma presents a form (see Figure 4.1) that is useful for student evaluation (Freeman & Person, 1992, p. 54). It asks students to consider the book's content as well as how the text supported their learning.

KEY CONCEPT **3**   STUDENTS SHOULD DEVELOP STRATEGIES FOR THE COMPREHENSION OF INFORMATIONAL TEXTS.

COMPREHENDING INFORMATIONAL TEXT

In earlier chapters we discussed the importance of knowledgeable others to students' literacy development. Joyce Souza serves as a knowledgeable other in the classroom as she shares strategies, provides opportunities for learning, and nurtures an enthusiasm for

	Title		
Author			
Subject			

+ Good   ✔ OK   − Poor

Format (What it looks like)

1. Is the print easy to read?

2. Are binding and paper of good quality?

3. Are the table of contents and index easy to use?

Quality of content (What's in it)

4. Is the information up-to-date for the time the book was published?

5. Are statements supported with facts?

6. Does the information given match what you expected to find in the book?

Author's style (How the book is written)

7. Does the author write in clear language?

8. Does the author explain with enough detail?

9. Is the information well organized?

Illustrations (Drawings, charts, photographs)

10. Do they help your understanding of the text?

11. Do the pictures make you want to read the book?

FIGURE 4.1
Student Evaluation of Information Books
Source: Freeman & Person, 1992.

wanting to learn. We noted several occasions when Joyce provided scaffolding for processes that students could later use on their own.

Freeman and Person (1992, p. 46) state that "a common goal of teachers in all subject areas is to teach the content in such a way that students gain knowledge and interest and become independent learners." In this section we will explore some specific ways teachers might do this, as they guide students' reading and comprehension of informational text and as they support students' in synthesizing and organizing text information.

We present four frameworks that teachers have found useful for reading comprehension lessons:

1. Concept-text-application approach, or CTA
2. Directed reading-thinking approach, or DRTA
3. K-W-L approach
4. Estimate, read, respond, question, or ERRQ

All begin with students' background knowledge about the topic, and all are methods of actively involving students in thinking about expository texts.

CTA is an appropriate choice if you are working with children who are likely to need considerable guidance while reading and extra help with concepts central to understanding of the text. It is a good overarching framework to use when trying to give students a general understanding of how to approach content-area texts. DRTA can be used at all grade levels to develop students' ability to make and test predictions while reading. Used together, CTA lessons and DRTA lessons can provide students with a solid foundation for comprehending informational texts. After students have this foundation, the teacher may want to move on to K-W-L and ERRQ. They differ from the other two frameworks in providing a way of transferring responsibility for comprehension from the teacher over to the students.

Concept-Text-Application Approach

The concept-text-application (CTA) approach developed by Jo Ann Wong and Kathryn Au (1985) is a framework for organizing lessons to improve comprehension of informational text and can be used with students from the second grade on up. It takes students through prereading, guided reading, and postreading phases of instruction.

The CTA method is based on the idea that effective reading instruction starts by building on children's background knowledge. It proceeds with guided discussion of nonfiction trade books, or passages from content-area textbooks or children's magazines. Joyce Souza often uses this approach with literature discussion groups within her readers' workshop.

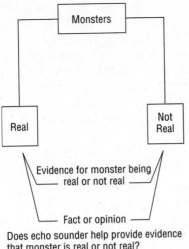

FIGURE 4.2
Do You Believe in Monsters? A Teacher's Plan
Source: Wong & Au, 1985. Reprinted by permission of the authors and the International Reading Association.

The CTA method is designed to complement the ETR method for teaching comprehension of stories, as described in Chapter 3. It too incorporates three different phases. The concept assessment/development or C phase is a prereading discussion during which the teacher brings out what students already know about the topic. Unfamiliar concepts and vocabulary necessary for understanding the text may be introduced during this phase. During the text or T phase, purposes for reading are set and guided reading and discussion of the text takes place. Finally, during the application or A phase, the students are encouraged to put to use the new information learned.

PLANNING. First, preview the text and identify the main idea or central theme you wish to focus on. If necessary, do some background reading on the topic. Second, reread the text and work out the visual structure to be developed with the children during the lesson. For example, Figure 4.2 shows the visual structure used by a teacher to plan a second-grade lesson based on "The Monster of Loch Ness" (Shogren, 1978). When making up the structure, you may also wish to note vocabulary to be covered. Then plan the application or follow-up activity. In the example, the teacher decided to have the children conduct a survey of their classmates.

CONCEPT ASSESSMENT/DEVELOPMENT. Build on the children's interest at the very start of the lesson. In this example, the group began by discussing their own beliefs about monsters. Then move on to more fo-

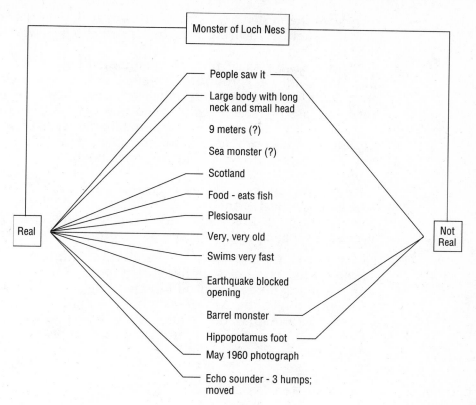

FIGURE 4.3
Completed Visual Structure on the Loch Ness Monster
Source: Wong & Au, 1985. Reprinted by permission of the authors and the International Reading Association.

cused questions to identify key concepts and vocabulary unfamiliar to the children. For example, in this lesson the children had to be taught that *loch* is the Scottish word for lake.

TEXT. After assessing background knowledge and developing important concepts and vocabulary, move into guided reading of the text. Work with the children to set a purpose (usually, a question to be answered) for reading each segment. Have them read the segment and then discuss the information covered. Continue alternating periods of silent reading and discussion until the text has been completed.

After the first segment is discussed, lay out the framework for the visual structure. During each discussion period, continue to add to it. Figure 4.3 shows the visual structure completed in this manner for the lessons on the Loch Ness monster. The items in the structure were those mentioned by the children, and the lines were drawn after the children decided whether each item supported the view that the monster was "real" or "not real." The teacher used this visual structure to bring out the central theme: whether the monster was real.

Watch during the T phase for signs that you should help the children build up background knowledge and fit new text information with what has already been understood. For instance, in the sample series of lessons, the teacher found that the children did not understand how an echo sounder worked. She had to explain this to them because the text provided little information on this point. Then she led them to see how an echo sounder might be used to locate the monster.

After the entire text has been read, ask the children to summarize and synthesize the information. During this process, encourage them to refer to the visual structure. Students may use individual notebooks, called learning logs, to record what they learned.

APPLICATION. In our example, several of the students expressed their views on the issue of whether the monster was real. The children's application extended to a poll of their classmates to see how many of them thought the Loch Ness monster was real. They then made a bar graph to display the results. Some students went on to investigate other "monsters" of nature such as Bigfoot and the Abominable Snowman.

Directed Reading-Thinking Activity

Stauffer's (1969) directed reading-thinking activity (DRTA) encourages active involvement by having students generate hypotheses about text and then check on the accuracy of their predictions. The DRTA can be used with virtually any kind of reading material. As Spiegel (1981) points out, it is especially useful when students already have the necessary vocabulary and background knowledge. There are many variations to the basic DRTA concept. Here is the one we prefer:

Step 1: Ask children to make predictions based on the selection's title or illustrations, or ask them to share what they already know about the topic. They may do this by first writing in their learning logs and then discussing their ideas with a partner. As students share their thinking with the larger group, write their predictions and other ideas on the board.

Step 2: Point out to the children that they will be reading to see if the text verifies the information on the board. Have them read a portion of the text silently.

Step 3: Reopen the discussion by having the students review the list of predictions and ideas on the board, telling which were verified. Point out to the children that there are several possibilities.

The idea could be:

- Verified by the text (in which case, a student can read the relevant sentence aloud)
- Disproved by the text (again, a child might read the relevant sentence aloud)
- Only partially verified or disproved, with more information being required to make a definite decision about whether the idea is right or wrong
- Shown to be only partially right or wrong, but definitely requiring revision on the basis of text information
- Not mentioned.

Items in the list are rewritten, marked as true, crossed off if false, and so on. New hypotheses may also be added. Thus, the list should become a running record of important text information.

Step 4: Alternate periods of silent reading and discussion until the whole text has been read. Students may continue to use their learning logs to mark their initial predictions, record new information, and add new hypotheses of their own. In all cases, the emphasis is on the quality of the reasoning students are doing, rather than just the correctness of their initial hypotheses.

K-W-L

You saw how some of Joyce Souza's students used the K-W-L approach during their research on birds. Joyce has used this approach, developed by Donna Ogle (1986), as the framework for several literature group discussions throughout the school year.

K-W-L is based on the idea that teachers should begin discussions of nonfiction by honoring what students already know about

1. K—What we know	W—What we want to find out	L—What we learned and still need to learn

2. Categories of information we expect to use

A.	E.
B.	F.
C.	G.
D.	

FIGURE 4.4
K-W-L Strategy Sheet

the topic and by helping them decide what else they would like to learn about it. The letters *K, W,* and *L* stand for the three basic steps in the procedure: assessing what I *K*now, determining what I *W*ant to know, and recalling what I *L*earned through reading. Each student uses a worksheet, shown in Figure 4.4, to record ideas as the lessons progress.

STEP K, WHAT I KNOW. You will be working with students' prior knowledge at two levels. Start by having the students brainstorm, to come up with ideas they already have about the topic. On chart paper, record the ideas the students share. Be sure to center brainstorming on a concept specific enough to link directly to the information students will encounter in their reading. For example, if the students are going to be reading about sea turtles, the teacher should ask, "What do you know about sea turtles?" not "What do you know about animals that live in the sea?"

When students volunteer ideas, help them become aware of areas of uncertainty and areas they would like to know more about. Ogle suggests asking questions such as "Where did you learn that?" and "How could you prove that?" Questions like these prompt students to think about their own sources of information and whether their ideas are sound or speculative.

In the second part of brainstorming, you will involve students in thinking about the general categories of information they are likely to find in the text. Begin by telling students that they should now think about the kinds of information they will probably be reading. Have them look at the list of ideas generated during the discussion, and ask if any of the ideas go together in a general category.

In the beginning, you may need to model this step. For example, with the topic of sea turtle, Ogle suggests that the teacher might say, "I see three different pieces of information about how turtles look. Description or looks is certainly one category of information I would expect this article to include" (p. 566). The teacher would then write this category ("how sea turtles look") under the Categories of Information heading, modeling what students will do later on their own worksheets. The teacher will then have students refer to the list to come up with other categories of their own.

STEP W, WHAT DO I WANT TO LEARN? As you take students through the two levels of brainstorming, you will find that they are coming up with questions. You will want to highlight for students areas of conflict or uncertainty and areas where nothing is yet known. These areas and questions provide purposes for reading that grow out of students' own interests.

Step W can be combined as an individual and a group activity. In addition to recording on the group chart, ask students to write on their worksheets the questions they most want to pursue. This gives each student a chance to set personal purposes for reading.

STEP L, WHAT I LEARNED. After students have finished reading, ask them to write down what they learned. Have them refer to their questions to decide whether the text provided the relevant information. If it did not, you might suggest they do other reading to find the answers.

Estimate, Read, Respond, Question (ERRQ)

ERRQ is based on an approach developed by Dorothy Watson (cited in Cairney, 1990). It requires students to actively engage with text in order to link new information with their background knowledge. It requires them to engage in a recursive process of reading, writing, and talking.

Step 1: Ask students to scan the text. Look at subheadings, illustrations, and diagrams, and read the first few sentences of several sections. Estimate what the text will be about by writing brief comments in note form.

Step 2: Have students read the whole text straight through. While reading they should consider ideas or images it brings to mind, previous texts, ideas that are difficult to understand or agree with, and so on.

Step 3: Ask students to respond to the text in some way. This is the time for them to share the thoughts they had while reading. It is often helpful for students to first write in their learning logs and then to share with someone else.

Step 4: Have students question themselves in some way. Their self-questioning might relate to the content of the text and deal with such questions as: "What was it about?" "What was its 'big idea'?" "What am I still puzzled about?" "What do I have trouble accepting?" Their questions can be written in their learning logs and later shared with other members of their literature discussion group.

These four instructional frameworks provide guidance as students read to learn from informational texts. They help to provide the scaffolding that supports students' growth toward independence.

Student learning is also supported by skills and strategies for recording and merging what they have learned. We will now consider four ways in which teachers can guide students to synthesize and organize content text information: learning logs, diagrams, note taking, and summarizing. All are ways in which students can structure their learning through writing.

Learning Logs

Learning logs are a form of the literature response log discussed in Chapter 3. Students use learning logs to communicate their understandings about a unit or a topic of study. In the comprehension frameworks discussed earlier, you saw ways in which learning logs might be used by students. Lucy Calkins (1986) suggests that learning logs be used to:

1. Ask questions. As an example, Calkins suggests that prior to studying the Civil War students could record questions they have about the war. After reading, the students will look back at their questions to note which were answered and which now seem irrelevant, and to add new questions.

Teachers can support students' asking of more probing and appropriate questions by asking them to think about their questions. Which was their best? What makes one question better than another? Students might then meet in groups to compare their questions and select a single important question to bring to the larger class discussion.

2. Make guesses. Calkins points out that in science making guesses is called forming hypotheses. In reading, it is prediction. Using the Civil War example, she suggests that students be asked to write what they imagine might have caused the war. "Pretend to be an expert on the topic and make up some causes for the war." After writing a version of their own, students will read differently because they have made an investment in the topic.

Students should be encouraged to reflect on their guesses. Were they wild guesses, or did they have some basis in prior knowledge or text clues?

3. Organize information. Calkins emphasizes that learning takes place when students are helped to organize information on their own. She suggests that children use their learning logs to create systems of organization. One way they can do this is to write down the details about their topic of study and then come up with ways to categorize their information. Or, after gathering information on a topic, the teacher can help them rethink and reread the information, shaping it into categories, searching for a line of argument or an organizing vision. They then could use their learning logs to take notes on the patterns they create.

Calkins reminds us that our purpose in using learning logs is not only to nudge students to think but also to teach them habits of thought. Our support will encourage students to ask questions, make guesses, and organize as they read to learn on their own (pp. 264–270).

Even early-elementary grade children can use learning logs for some of the same purposes that Calkins discussed. When Joan Lyons' first-graders studied zoo animals, they shared both fiction and nonfiction books and materials, and the children expressed their learning in a variety of ways. Shelly, for example, used drawing and invented spelling to record and reflect upon her understanding of giraffes (see Figure 4.5). She asks a question, "Do giraffes drink?" She makes guesses about the giraffe's eating habits and she orga-

the graffe is eating Food,
the graffe has Spoochs
the graffe is Big.
the graffe has a Log neck
Like a Danasor.
I Want to No iF a graffe
Drinks Do a graffe Drinkss,

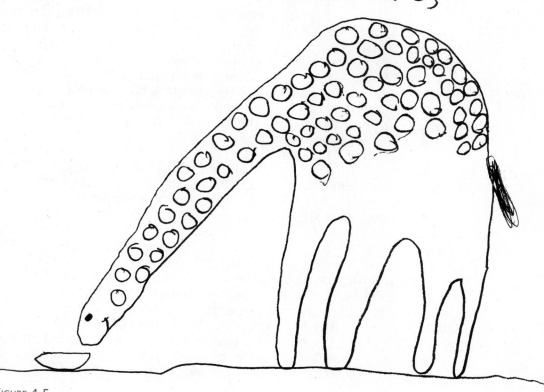

FIGURE 4.5
Drawing and Invented Spelling in a Learning Log

nizes by integrating her knowledge and understanding: "The giraffe has a long neck like a dinosaur."

Diagrams

Students can be helped to develop diagrams that display text information and the relationships among pieces of information. Diagrams—often referred to as structured overviews (Herber, 1978), maps, webs, or timelines—are forms of visual structures or visual displays and are useful means for students to organize information. Concepts, vocabulary (see Chapter 5), main ideas, facts, and details can all be explored through diagrams.

Trevor Cairney (1990) suggests that teachers model the use of a variety of diagrams for a variety of purposes. As teachers share a diagram, it is important that they point out that this is their own personal representation, and that the children might choose to organize the information differently.

You saw how a diagram was used to organize information in our CTA description (Figure 4.3). Webs are good diagrams for organizing information in the form of main ideas and supporting details. Students can be helped to construct a web after reading informational text and recording information in their learning logs. You might start by asking students what they think the main idea is. After discussion, the students should come to a consensus on one main idea to head their web, which the teacher writes on chart paper. The next step is to organize and categorize the students' information (Cairney, 1990, p.70). Cairney emphasizes that teachers must provide students with a great deal of guided practice in using diagrams before they become independent. One child's web is shown in Figure 4.6. You will note that the main idea is at the top of the web, followed by three categories of information that support the main idea.

Timelines are useful diagrams for displaying and organizing historical events. Myra Zarnowski (1990) suggests that intermediate-grade students focus their research on the life of a historical subject. The information they gather can be organized into a timeline that spans the years of their subject's life (see Figure 4.7).

In a fifth-grade classroom described by Zarnowski, the students studied Martin Luther King and chronicled civil rights events during his life. To guide her students, this teacher posted a timeline on a large bulletin board. After each day's research, the students and teacher discussed new information and added it to their timelines (p. 65).

Note Taking

Students need opportunities to take notes for a variety of purposes. You saw earlier how Joyce Souza's students used note taking as a

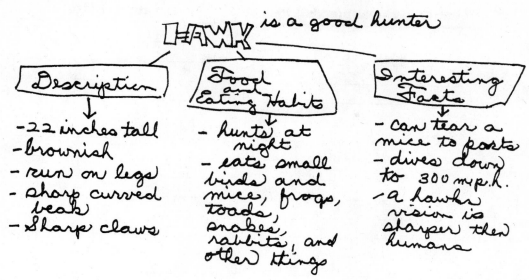

FIGURE 4.6
One Child's Semantic Web for Hawk

part of their research on birds. You also saw the attention Joyce gave to guiding her students with the process. She knows that although note taking is a very important skill for students, it is also very difficult to learn.

Donald Graves (1989, p. 92) defines a note as "an abstract of a text written or spoken by another person. It can be an idea that comes in the midst of thinking about a subject. We jot it down, not in complete sentences but in a few words that stand for the whole idea." He believes that even first and second graders are able to do it.

When introducing children to this skill, Graves suggests that teachers begin by demonstrating their own process. They should show students how they select the most important facts, write them down, and then use the notes to talk about what they have learned. As students later practice on their own, the teacher should circulate among them asking, "Tell me what idea that information stands for" (p. 93). You can see that the purpose for taking notes is not simply to record information, but to think and learn about the topic.

Some teachers have found that children are more thoughtful and reflective when they record their notes after, rather than during, reading. This method also avoids the direct copying from text that is so common when students write content reports. Third-grade teacher

Events in the Subject's Life		Events in History
_____	1900	_____
_____		_____
_____	1901	_____
_____		_____
_____	1902	_____
_____		_____
_____	1903	_____
_____		_____
_____	1904	_____
_____		_____
_____	1905	_____
_____	1906	_____
_____		_____
_____	1907	_____
_____		_____
_____	1908	_____

FIGURE 4.7
A Timeline Format for a Life-and-Times Biography.

Donna Maxim gives her students many opportunities to take notes in this way. She asks that they write questions about their topics, read for short periods (ten minutes), close their books, and then make notes in their learning logs of the answers they found. Though her students find this difficult at first, they learn to recognize important facts, take meaningful notes, and record facts quickly and easily (Atwell, 1990, p. 6).

Summarizing

When students summarize, they arrive at a condensed version of important text information. They begin by analyzing the text and then restate the ideas in their own words. The key to effective use of summarizing is to make sure that the students actually reorder and reword text information.

Students who have been regularly engaged in recording and organizing information in learning logs, diagrams, and notes will have developed some strategies helpful to shaping information into summaries. Cairney (1990) suggests that teachers begin by showing and reading several summaries to their students. Next, the teacher should demonstrate how a summary is written (p. 72). For example, the teacher whose students constructed the web about the hawk (see Figure 4.6) might use it to demonstrate summary writing. Through discussion a small group of students with their teacher would write a summary of three paragraphs, each with a topic sentence and supporting details, based on the structure of the web. Students will find it helpful to talk through the organization of their ideas. They might begin by working with partners to orally retell everything they learned about each category. Using the category headers, the teacher then guides students to compose topic sentences followed by summaries of the important information.

Summarizing is a difficult task, even for college students, so teachers should not expect elementary students to master this writing technique. They will need regular guidance and pratice in order to gain independence. The goal is to give students experience with summarizing, not to have them produce perfect summaries.

KEY CONCEPT **4**

STUDENTS SHOULD BE INVOLVED IN RESEARCH PROJECTS INTEGRATING READING AND WRITING.

RESEARCH PROJECTS

At the beginning of this chapter, we presented a description of report writing in Joyce Souza's third-grade classroom. We saw how Joyce actively involved students in a number of different ways with their study of birds. We know that students learn more when they must become involved with reading and writing in ways that require them to think actively about the material. When students are reading for specific purposes, especially those they set for themselves, they generally make more of an effort to read carefully and accurately.

We know too that students learn from writing. Writing helps them think more deeply about their topics. Through writing they can clarify information for themselves as they reflect on it in a personal way. If the writing is to be shared with others, they must also be sure it will speak clearly to their audience.

It follows, then, that writing research reports, based on a number of different texts, is a powerful way of learning. Unfortunately, many students have not found it to be so. Calkins (1986) shares a conversation with nine-year-old Debbie.

> "When my teacher told us to write a report, I got goosebumps and butterflies in my stomach and everything. I knew this time would come because all the kids write real reports in fourth grade, but when it was here I didn't know what to do, I was so scared. On Saturday I went to the library like my sister used to do, and I got the encyclopedia and put down the facts: people, places, dates, Indians, wars. Then I wrote it up" (p. 273).

Fortunately, given what we now know about heightening children's interest in reading and writing and about the writing process, we are able to help them approach report writing with strategies, interest, and a sense of purpose.

Joyce Souza followed an approach to report writing similar to one described by John Beach (1983); it is consistent with a process approach to writing and with the idea that students should take control of their own reading and writing activities. The approach is based on the premise that students will learn more when they are personally involved in their writing tasks. Specifically, they should be writing about a topic they find interesting and addressing their writing to an audience they think important—in this case, their classmates.

Here is an overview of Beach's approach. The teacher opens the unit with an activity to stimulate interest in the subject. Students engage in discussion and then choose a specific topic they wish to explore further. Next the teacher takes students through focusing activities. Students generate questions about their topics, then revise their questions with the help of peers. Further focusing takes place as students organize their reports, search for facts, and take notes. Then they write their reports, following a process approach to writing.

Let us examine the activities in which Joyce Souza's students engaged within this framework.

Activities to Stimulate Interest

As a part of their science and social studies curriculum, Joyce's students had been studying animals and their interdependency and conservation over several months. Joyce decided to focus on mammals for her students' first research project. She talked with the students about a topic for a second report, and they brainstormed a list

After researching her topic, this third grader
decided to display what she learned about
traditional Hawaiian villages by creating a model
and presenting her report on large index cards. Other
students chose different forms to share their research.

of possibilities. During a recent field trip to the zoo, the aviary had
been of special interest, so the group decided to investigate birds.

Next, Joyce helped the students generate a list of all the birds
they knew. She then gave students time to explore the materials that
were available in the classroom. The children then wrote their
names on the list next to the bird they wanted to research, or added
another bird to the list along with their name.

Joyce talked with the students about the form their reports
might take. She shared the reports of former students, reminded
them about the kinds of reports they wrote in the mammal project,
and asked them to recall the formats and styles of professional authors. The idea here is to give students a clear picture of the kinds of
information they will be gathering and ideas for how they might
want their published reports to look.

To maintain interest throughout the researching process, Joyce
and the students contributed new information to the library area.
They read and discussed birds in fiction and nonfiction. And Joyce

brought her pet, Petey, to the classroom so the students could make firsthand observational notes.

Activities to Focus Students on the Report

After students had chosen their topics, Joyce focused their attention on the purpose of the report, their audience, and their researching plan. Students used their K-W-L sheets to write down all the questions they had about their bird. They shared their questions in pairs and with the larger group. Through their sharing, they learned of effective questions and "borrowed" ideas from one another.

When children have questions in mind before reading, their focus is clearer as they search for specific information. Note taking is easier, and their questions help them distinguish between relevant and irrelevant information. Also, their questions serve to remind them of the interests of their audience.

After Joyce's students had questions in mind and were in the midst of gathering information, she began a series of discussions focused on organization. The children came to recognize that many of their questions related to the bird's appearance. They later distinguished other categories: family life, interesting facts, geographical location, habitat, and diet.

Joyce had been working with her students on paragraphing, and she recognized that this would be a logical time to focus on this skill. She demonstrated the use of webs as a way of organizing information by categories, and showed the students how each category could become a paragraph in their report.

As the children continued to gather information, Joyce provided instruction as needed. She helped students learn more about note taking from their peers and from her own demonstrations. As children used encyclopedias and other references, they discussed effective use of glossaries, indexes, diagrams, and maps.

Report-Writing Activities

Joyce's students are well acquainted with the writing process. During their writers' workshop they have written several personal narratives and many of their published pieces are a part of the classroom library. Now that they are writing research reports, Joyce helps them understand that they are engaged in the same process. She reminds them that just as they are experts on the personal information contained in their narrative pieces, now they are becoming experts by gathering information on their research topics.

As they take notes and write drafts of their reports, they confer to help one another. Joyce and the students model and discuss questions and suggestions that will help them improve their reports.

CONDOR

I already Know...	I want to Know.....	I learned that....
Fastest bird Biggest bird	Where do they live? What do they eat? What color? 12/12/91 Do they migrate How many types	live North America California Dead animal black while red egge every other year 2/11/91 Is a vulture A bird of prey Does not have Feather on head Almost extinct No habitat found in western hemisphere 8 types

I learned that....

wings open ten Feet long

Is a new world vulture
old world vulture found in Southern Europe

FIGURE 4.8
A Student's Research Report on Condors.

I chose the **Condor**

DESCRIPTION

SIZE 45 to 55 inches and 114 to 140 centermeters big A wing span of 8-10 feet long COLOR Black on the body one type has white underwings and red by the head	BODY COVERING Feathers	DISTINGUISHING FEATURES Bald head while underwings BEAK Poor hooked beak that is bad for carrying FEET prey
FAMILY LIFE AND REPRODUCTION Lays one egg every Other year almost extinct 30 more condors in the world or less sits on eggs 7 to 9 weeks	INTERESTING FACTS Habitat destroyed by man. A new world vultures old world vultures found in Southern Europe and Asia. Sits in pearches most of the day do not build nests lay eggs in holes, caves or among bolders Good flier glides long distances	
WHERE IN THE WORLD? North America	HOME/HABITAT Western Hemisphere temprate rigoins	FOOD AND EATING HABITS Scavengers eat fleash of dead cattle, sheep, ground squirrels deer

FIGURE 4.8 (continued))

My name is Crazy Condor
I like to sit in high
peaches and look for food. My
eating habits are dead animals. I
am a scavenger.
I look like a storm cloud because
I am mostly black and white. Around
my neck are ruffled feathers. My
head is orange and red. I am also
bald on the head. I am 45 to 55
inches and a 114 to 140 centimeters.
My wings are 8 to 10 feet long.
Our beeks are not very good for
carrying prey so we drag them into
caves.
I live in the Los Angeles zoo
and Sanfrancisco zoo.
My family likes to sit in high
peaches all day long and look
for food. My mom does not build
nest, are lay one egg in caves.
My parents lay one egg every year.
I have less than 30 friends left.
It takes 7 to 9 weeks for my brother
to hatch.

FIGURE 4.8 (continued))

When students' revisions are complete, their pieces are edited and then published.

Students in Joyce's class have a variety of options for publishing. Some decide to construct pop-up books and charts. They choose among formats: narratives, poems, and plays. Some examine their topics from an aesthetic as well as an efferent stance.

Figure 4.8 on pp. 137–139 shows the process of Matt's research on the condor, from question generation to published report.

If students are to gain independence in report writing, they should be guided through the process at least three or four times a year. After their first project, you should be able to reduce the amount of assistance given. Be sure to vary the types of topics or the form of the reports, to broaden students' report-writing ability.

Beach feels that two features of the approach contribute to its effectiveness:

> First, accepting children's concerns about a topic instead of imposing adult issues as report topics enables the teacher to utilize students' curiosity and motivation to aid in achieving the goal. And second, organizing ahead of time reduces the task to a size that is manageable for elementary school students (p. 220).

SUMMARY

In this chapter we looked at the development of students' learning from informational text. In the past this area of instruction has seemed challenging. Currently, with an increase in well-written non-fiction for elementary-age students and with our knowledge of the learning process, this area becomes more accessible and interesting to children. In Key Concept 1 you learned how teachers like Joyce Souza create a classroom community that supports students' learning of information. Within this community there is an enthusiasm for learning and each child's contribution is valued. In Key Concept 2 you saw the importance of making a variety of quality informational texts available to enhance students' knowledge and understanding of content. Teachers should guide and challenge students as together they explore the benefits and joys nonfiction holds for its readers.

In Key Concept 3 you learned ways teachers can guide students' reading and learning from informational texts. We discussed four frameworks for teaching comprehension: the content-text-application approach (CTA), the directed reading-thinking activity (DRTA), K-W-L, and the estimate, read, respond, question approach (ERRQ). All are designed to have students think critically about expository text by raising questions, applying what they have learned, or making predictions. You also saw how students' understanding and thinking about information are enhanced as they express their ideas in learning logs, take notes, use diagrams, and write summaries. Finally, in Key Concept 4 we examined the value of involving students in research report writing. When children can generate their own questions and set purposes for their reading and writing, they are more likely to become active, continual pursuers of information.

◀ ACTIVITIES

Reflecting on Your Own Literacy

For what purposes do you read for information in your daily life? Do you approach reading differently depending on your purpose? To answer these questions, keep a record for a week of your nonfiction reading. Include what you read and your reflections on how you read. Note when and why you connect writing with reading.

Applying What You Have Learned to the Classroom

Visit a children's library to examine the selection of informational texts. Locate single titles, series books, periodicals, and reference materials. Note the author's voice, point of view, and style. Choose a variety of texts on one topic and prepare a book talk to highlight the positive features of the materials you have selected.

BIBLIOGRAPHY

References

Atwell, N. (Ed.). (1990). *Coming to know: Writing to learn in the intermediate grades.* Portsmouth, NH: Heinemann.

Beach, J. D. (1983). Teaching students to write informational reports. *Elementary School Journal, 84*(2), 213–220.

Bosma, B. (1992). The voice of learning: Teacher, child, and text. In E. B. Freeman & D. G. Person (Eds.), *Using nonfiction trade books in the elementary school: From ants to zeppelins.* Urbana, IL: National Council of Teachers of English.

Cairney, T. H. (1990). *Teaching reading comprehension: Meaning makers at work.* Bristol, PA: Open University Press.

Calkins, L. M. (1986). *The art of teaching writing.* Portsmouth, NH: Heinemann.

Calkins, L. M. (1990). *Living between the lines.* Portsmouth, NH: Heinemann.

Carlsen, G. R., & Sherrill, A. (1988). *Voices of readers: How we come to love books.* Urbana, IL: National Council of Teachers of English.

Freedman, R. (1992). Fact or fiction. In E. B. Freeman & D. G. Person, (Eds.), *Using nonfiction trade books in the elementary school: From ants to zeppelins.* Urbana, IL: National Council of Teachers of English.

Freeman, E. B., & Person, D. G. (Eds.) (1992). *Using nonfiction trade books in the elementary classroom.* Urbana, IL: National Council of Teachers of English.

Graves, D. H. (1989). *Investigate nonfiction.* Portsmouth, NH: Heinemann.

Hansen, J. (1987). *When writers read.* Portsmouth, NH: Heinemann.

Herber, H. L. (1978). *Teaching reading in content areas* (2nd ed.). Englewood Cliffs, NJ: Prentice-Hall.

McGinley, W., & Madigan, D., (1990). The research "story": A forum for integrating reading, writing, and learning. *Language Arts, 67,* 474–483.

Ogle, D. M. (1986). K-W-L: A teaching model that develops active reading of expository text. *The Reading Teacher, 39*(6), 564–570.

Rosenblatt, L. (1978). *The reader, the text, the poem: The transactional theory of the literary work.* Carbondale, IL: Southern Illinois University Press.

Smith, F. (1983). Reading like a writer. *Language Arts, 60,* 558–567.

Spiegel, D. L. (1981). *Reading for pleasure: Guidelines.* Newark, DE: International Reading Association.

Stauffer, R. G. (1969). *Reading as a thinking process.* New York: Harper & Row.

Vardell, S. M., & Copeland, K. A. (1992). Reading aloud and responding to nonfiction: Let's talk about it. In E. B. Freeman & D. G. Person, (Eds.), *Using nonfiction trade books in the elementary school: From ants to zeppelins.* Urbana, IL: National Council of Teachers of English.

Wong, J. A., & Au, K. H. (1985). The concept-text-application approach: Helping elementary students comprehend expository text. *The Reading Teacher, 38*(7), 612–618.

Watson, D. (1985). Estimate, read, respond, question. In A. Crismore (Ed.), *Landscapes: A state-of-the-art assessment of reading comprehension research, 1974–1984.* Final report of US Department of Education funded project, USDEC-C-300-83-0130, Indiana University.

Zarnowski, M. (1990). *Learning about biographies: A reading-and-writing approach for children.* Urbana, IL: National Council of Teachers of English.

Suggested Classroom Resources

Arnold, C. (1985). *Saving the peregrine falcon.* Photographs by R. Hewett. Minneapolis, MN: Carolrhoda Books/Nature Watch Books.

Fleischman, P. (1985). *I am phoenix: Poems for two voices.* Illustrated by K. Nutt. New York: Harper & Row.

George, J. (1988). *One day in the woods.* Illustrated by G. Allen. New York: Thomas Y. Crowell.

Hilidick, E. (1977). *The case of the invisible dog.* New York: Macmillan.

MacLachlan, P. (1985). *Sarah, plain and tall.* New York: Harper & Row.

McNulty, F. (1986). *Peeping in the shell: A whooping crane is hatched.* Illustrated by I. Brady. New York: Harper & Row.

Patent, D. (1989). *Wild turkey, tame turkey.* New York: Clarion Books.

Shogren, M. (1978). The monster of Loch Ness. In R. B. Ruddell, M. Shogren, & A. L. Ryle, *Moon Magic.* Boston: Allyn & Bacon.

Nature Watch Books (1986). Minneapolis, MN: Carolrhoda Books.

Where Animals Live Books (1987). New York: G. P. Putnam's Sons.

Further Readings

Cudd, E. J. (1989). Research and report writing in the elementary grades. *The Reading Teacher, 42*(6), 268–269.

Giacobbe, M. E. (1986). Learning to write and writing to learn in the elementary school. In A. R. Perosky & D. Bartholomae (Eds.), *The teaching of writing.* Eighty-fifth yearbook of the National Society for the Study of Education. Chicago: National Society for the Study of Education, pp. 144–173.

Hess, M. L. (1989). All about hawks or Oliver's disaster: From facts to narrative. *Language Arts, 66*(3), 304–308.

Nelms, B. F. (1987). Response and responsibility: Reading, writing, and social studies. *Elementary School Journal, 87*(5), 571–589.

Pardo, L. S., & Raphael, T. E., (1991). Classroom organization for instruction in content areas. *The Reading Teacher, 44*(8), 556–565.

Wilde, J. (1993). Engaging and informing: Reconsidering the written report. Chapter 5 in *A door opens: Writing in fifth grade.* Portsmouth, NH: Heinemann.

Woolsey, D. P., & Burton, F. R. (1986). Blending literary and informational ways of knowing. *Language Arts, 63*(3), 273–280.

Videotapes

Grossberg, F., & Maxwell, J. *Teachers teaching writing: Flight.* Alexandria, VA: Association for Supervision Curriculum Development.

Pardo, L. (1991). *Literacy in content area instruction.* In the six-part series *Teaching reading: Strategies from successful classrooms.* Urbana-Champaign: Center for the Study of Reading, University of Illinois.

5 VOCABULARY DEVELOPMENT

Juan arrived in September from Venezuela, speaking no English but filled with joy at being in school. As I struggled during our first few weeks together to find out what he could and could not do (and found out that, according to my teacher's agenda, he could not do many things), Juan very graciously attempted to help me understand what he could do. He would tolerate a few minutes of my informal assessment activities and then use his one word of English: "Paint?" he would suggest cheerfully, and by that time I would agree. "Paint," for Juan, meant drawing, painting, modeling, or constructing, and it was his passion. As the weeks passed, I continued to be amazed by his talent and frustrated by his inability to learn the alphabet and basic readiness skills. However, Juan's own nonchalance about the process of learning to read and write was somewhat contagious, and I began to see that his art was presenting both what he had already learned at home and in school, and what he desired to learn. It soon became a catalogue of science information and science questions, and that information began to provide material for his involvement in reading and writing—and learning a new language. As Juan drew, we built a reading and speaking vocabulary from his pictures, and that vocabulary, together with his interest in representing science, also became the subject matter of his writing.

Juan was teaching me once again a lesson that I seem to have to relearn each year: When given the opportunity, listen to the children. They will show you what they know and how they learn best, and often that way is not the teacher's way. (Gallas, 1991, pp. 40–41)

◀ OVERVIEW

Children's vocabulary expands at an amazing rate in the early and middle school years, perhaps as many as 3,000 words a year (Nagy, Herman, & Anderson, 1985). New growth in vocabulary also undergoes a fascinating shift at around third or fourth grade, when students become proficient readers and enlarge their written vocabulary. Of course, writing, listening, and speaking all play a role in oral and written vocabulary development, but reading is a particularly important source. Regular and sustained reading increases children's reading vocabulary, which improves text understanding, making reading easier and boosting an interest in reading.

How does a teacher start to nurture this vocabulary-building cycle? Reading to children and engaging them in talk about poems, stories, and informational texts help to build their oral vocabularies, as noted in the first key concept. As children learn to read, their written vocabularies can be expanded enormously through word analysis, as described in the second key concept. The third key concept deals with how vocabulary may be expanded through text analysis strategies, while the fourth key concept describes how it may be encouraged through wide reading.

KEY CONCEPT 1: Students should expand their vocabulary knowledge through a diverse set of listening and oral language activities.

KEY CONCEPT 2: Students should learn to use structural analysis to expand their reading vocabulary.

KEY CONCEPT 3: Students should learn to combine word- and text-reading strategies to increase their general vocabulary knowledge.

KEY CONCEPT 4: Students should be motivated to attend to new vocabulary during wide reading at home and at school.

◀ PERSPECTIVE

Vocabulary Activities Across the Grades

All the teachers you have read about in earlier chapters foster vocabulary development, but the focus and procedures they use vary with their students' reading, writing, and language competencies. They are acute observers of their students' language use, and they listen for new language use, watch for its application to writing, and support and teach their students strategies that build vocabulary knowledge.

Hally Simmons (Chapter 2) maintains a sharp ear for the language her kindergartners use in their dramatic play, their conversations with one another, and their comments and questions to her. She hopes to hear them using book language—its rhythmic and alliterative lilt, interesting words, novel expressions, and clarifying terms. So, when she has read and reread a classic story, such as *Goldilocks and the Three Bears* (Brett, 1987), she encourages students to act out the story and ask questions of one another. They might mimic story characters with, "Who's been sitting in my chair?" or "Where's my porridge?" She often adds story retelling and story acting of their favorites to extend their opportunities for using book language. She watches for children to retell stories that they've heard, recollecting the story line and imagining the dialogue. She listens for them to sprinkle interesting new words in their comments and discussion questions that occur during and after a story is read. Rereading stories often helps children produce the new story vocabulary on their own.

During the shared reading of big books (as described in Chapter 2) Hally often explores opportunities for extending her students' use of language. For example, after reading *Yuk Soup* (Cowley, 1986), she asked the children to think of other words with the same meaning as *yuk* and she listed their ideas. Following the next day's reading of the story they talked about *yum,* the opposite of *yuk,* and generated a second, parallel list of synonyms (see Figure 5.1). Another day, Hally helped the children create an innovation of the story, which they entitled *Yum Soup.* In their version, delicious-tasting items were added to the pot in place of the disgusting things added in the original version.

First-grade teacher Joan Lyons continues these same kinds of activities in her classroom, and as her students read aloud she listens for problems in decoding, word meaning, and story understanding. She likes to look at the phrases her students construct in their early story and report writing to determine whether their words and expressions resemble the stories they have read or heard her read to them. Because rereading nourishes language mimicry in writing as well as in speech, she chooses books with interesting new words and unusual expressions that are well knit into the story line and illustrations. She also reads aloud the first few chapters from books in adventure series that are based upon a single set of characters. She relied on work by Dina Feitelson (1986), who found that reading these books to students every day enhanced their reading interest and achievement. Joan has noticed that as story language becomes more familiar, her students want to borrow the books to read at home, and then they become more able to extract ideas from the story language and plot to write their own episodes.

Yuk	Yum
awful	good
bad	delicious
icky	wonderful
terrible	great
horrible	super
nasty	
disgusting	

FIGURE 5.1
Building Vocabulary with Word Lists: Opposites

Joyce Souza's third graders (Chapter 4) are rather good independent readers, and are on the brink of amassing a written vocabulary at a tremendous rate. One of her goals, then, goes beyond expecting new vocabulary usage. She hopes her students will become fascinated with the structure and origins of the language. Word study helps. Learning that many new words contain prefixes and suffixes of familiar words (e.g., *jump* expands to *jumping, jumped, jumper, jumpy, jumpiness; pack* can become *repack, package, prepackage, unpack, packaged;* and so on) helps them recognize the meaningful connections between words in word families. So Joyce listens for good questions about language, praises her students' text and dictionary searches to find related words, and invites them to play word-family games and use newly read words in their writing.

Jessie Michaels and her fifth-grade students (Chapter 3) are becoming sophisticated users of language. As wordsmiths, she wants them to strive to find accurate wordings, clear statements, and evocative expressions. She appreciates their language jokes, analysis of advertisements and other double-meaning messages, and criticisms of unclear language in the expository texts they are reading. She wants her students to analyze language structures to understand how words and phrases are woven into texts to specify meanings and to evoke emotional responses. She listens for development of clear and concise expressions in their oral and written text summaries, apt and varied use of written language, and good questions about written language usage. She supports their keen interest and attention to precise language and effective communications.

The teachers have overlapping perspectives about vocabulary development, but the ways that they help students become more knowledgeable about words reflect the increasing demands that the language places on students as they become proficient readers and advance through the grades.

| KEY CONCEPT | 1 | STUDENTS SHOULD EXPAND THEIR VOCABULARY KNOWLEDGE THROUGH A DIVERSE SET OF LISTENING AND ORAL LANGUAGE ACTIVITIES. |

ACQUISITION OF VOCABULARY KNOWLEDGE

William Labov (1973) pointed out that words can be "slippery customers, and many scholars have been distressed by their tendency to shift their meanings and slide out from under any simple definition" (p. 341). Words tend to shift their meanings depending on the context, which makes effective vocabulary instruction difficult. To combat this problem, teachers often place vocabulary instruction within the text context and discuss word meanings as part of comprehension. In that way, students can be acquainted with new words by hearing or reading them in their meaningful and appropriate contexts.

This way of connecting vocabulary with comprehension underscores the close relationship between vocabulary, or knowledge of meanings, and reading comprehension (see, for example, Davis, 1944). One explanation is discussed as the *knowledge hypothesis* (Freebody & Anderson, 1983; Mezynski, 1983). According to this hypothesis, words we can read and understand indicate personal knowledge of the words as well as the reader's underlying concepts about the words. This sum of knowledge is represented by vocabulary and is what enables better comprehension. For example, it would be difficult to understand a story about an aunt and uncle if you lacked knowledge of kinship systems. All readers find texts with many new words more difficult to read, but if the concepts that underlie the text are familiar, readers can link the words conceptually and still comprehend the text.

Our teachers frequently use oral language and listening activities to promote the links between students' personal knowledge and their understanding of underlying concepts. Such activities allow students to gain familiarity and facility with new and related language, thus furthering their growth in both vocabulary and in comprehension.

Oral Language Activities

Hally Simmons, the kindergarten teacher, planned a trip to the farmers' market as part of a unit on foods we can grow, a topic connected with a health unit on nutrition. She prepared the children for the trip by creating a pictorial map of vegetables. She placed a picture of several vegetables on the chalkboard and printed the word VEGETABLES below the picture. She told students what it said and asked them to name vegetables they saw in the picture. As students named the vegetables and told what they knew about them, Hally wrote each name and drew a line back to the word VEGETABLES. She also showed the children individual pictures of the vegetables they named. If students named vegetables that were not in the center picture, she made a separate list and encouraged students to describe other vegetables they were familiar with.

The introduction helped her students elaborate their understandings, see the printed words with pictures, and describe and distinguish a variety of vegetables. When she made copies of the vegetable map for children to look at during the trip to the farmers' market, they recalled more of the names and were able to locate most of the vegetables at the market. Next she helped students pur-

A direct experience provides an ideal opportunity for vocabulary building. Speaking with a fireman and seeing a fire engine close up give these students the chance to learn and use new vocabulary in a meaningful context.

chase those they wanted to try and those they wanted to add to the soup they would make. Back in the classroom, they labeled and displayed the vegetables.

The next day Hally shared the book *Stone Soup* (Brown, 1947). After enjoying the story the children reenacted it, contributing the vegetables they had purchased to create a tasty version of their own. As their soup bubbled, Hally engaged the children in creating group stories using words from their vegetable map to describe their shopping and soup-making experiences. Then children worked together to illustrate pages for two big books, one called "Adventure at the Farmers' Market" and the other "Hard Rock Soup." The books they created, along with the copy of *Stone Soup,* were placed in the classroom library to be enjoyed again and again.

Third-grade teacher Joyce Souza was well aware that there were many new words in the texts her students studied and enjoyed. But when the texts could be worked into a theme or topic they were exploring, Joyce could build on her students' interest and background knowledge to help them gain meaning from more difficult material. She followed advice suggested by Patricia Herman (1988). After deciding on the important elements and sequence of thought in the text, she selected words in each text section that were critical to understanding and were likely to be met again by students. Next, she divided these key words into three groups. The smallest set represented the words she would directly teach because they were complicated or represented more abstract concepts. The second set was words that had unambiguous meanings and so could be learned from a dictionary or other resource, and the third set of words could probably be figured out from the text context.

As one of her literature groups prepared to read the novel *Sarah, Plain and Tall* (MacLachlan, 1985), Joyce found six new words, including three that she decided to teach before they read the chapter. To teach *prairie,* she began by writing on the board a phrase they knew—"only fields, and grass, and sky—as far as one could see"— and inviting students to add words or phrases that this phrase triggered. She wrote down their responses—farm, country, flat land, not a city or a town—and then added the new word, *prairie,* and discussed how it was related and how it might appear in the novel.

Joyce had her third graders begin their first research project on mammals with a mapping activity in order to help them gain familiarity with specific vocabulary related to the topic (for an example of a map see Figure 5.3). The mapping activity helped them pool their knowledge and correct their misconceptions. First, Joyce refreshed her own knowledge of natural history classifications, reviewing that mammals are ordered into carnivores, ruminants, rodents, and so on, and then into families (for example, canines are carnivores). She wrote the word *mammal* in the center of a large sheet of chart paper and asked students to name animals they thought were mammals and to explain why. Beginning with pets and farm animals, they named familiar mammals. Joyce wrote the names on the chart and grouped them roughly by family so that students could see resemblances among the groups. The groupings triggered their recall of other mammals.

Though Joyce did not expect all students to learn the more formal terms, she did introduce some of them. For example, on the second day of their discussion, she wrote the word *carnivore* and told the students that animals such as dogs, cats, tigers, and wolves are alike because of what they eat. She asked the children to consider how these mammals' diets are alike and led them to conclude that they are all "meat eaters." Through the same process, they identified the groupings of carnivores, herbivores, and omnivores. Joyce helped her students determine some of the features that define and distinguish the mammal families. She knew this information would be invaluable as they worked on their research. So she wrote key features and the family names, for example "front teeth for tearing" and "canine," supplying the critical information students might need to distinguish mammal families they knew less well. In this way the children developed a deeper understanding of mammals in general and an expanded vocabulary for describing them. Now they were ready to choose the mammal they wanted to study in more detail and begin their research.

Listening Activities

Young children enjoy hearing new words and talking about them, so when interesting words appear in stories they enjoy, and when the illustrations, story line, and style of the writer make the words sparkle with vivid meaning, children are likely to learn and remember a few of them. All the teachers read stories and informational books aloud to their students to introduce them to new words and expand their knowledge of words.

Hally and Joan usually followed a similar approach with their kindergarten and first-grade students. If they chose a book with interesting and rich vocabulary, such as *Jennie's Hat* (Keats, 1966), they usually introduced its genre, author, setting, or characters and then began reading. When they sensed that a word or phrase was not known, they stopped and discussed what it meant. Hally, for example, asked about the sentence "It's such a plain hat!" and had the children look at the picture clues to help them. Her questions helped students understand the story, made them more interested in new words, and gave them clues about how to use the story information to arrive at a possible meaning.

In the discussion that followed the story reading, Hally made a point to use some of the new words. When she said she really liked the way the birds said "thank you" to Jennie, Sebastian said, "Yeah. They made her hat beautiful." "Right. And fancy", said Hally. "And lovely," and "wonderful," and "lots of stuff on top," other children offered. "Good words," said Hally. "Let's see how many we can think of to describe Jennie's hat."

Hally and Joan treated some books differently because new words are remembered even better if the stories are reread. Cynthia Leung (1992), in her own work and in a review of others' work, offers evidence that repeatedly reading storybooks aloud, followed by giving children opportunities to retell the stories, promotes vocabulary growth. This step may be particularly important for kindergarten and first-grade children and children who are unaccustomed to hearing stories at home. They may need to hear stories three or more times before the new words are remembered.

Hally, for example, found that it was not easy for a few of her students to follow some of the stories she read aloud and that they sometimes became restless. During rereadings, however, as these students became more familiar with the stories, their attentiveness often increased. Nevertheless, Hally was careful in choosing books to reread. The books had to be favorites, with strong illustrations and story line. She noticed that when she reread these books, many of her students would choose to look at them on their own, comment about the characters' problems, and participate in discussions of the ideas. So rereading books became a Friday activity, with books that had been read only once before, and with books that had been repeatedly requested on previous Fridays. With everyone wanting to talk about the story or "read along," it was a noisy, happy way to end the school week. It also provided an impetus for her students to borrow the books for home reading.

Another way that Hally and Joan fostered vocabulary growth was to have students pantomime actions for stories they had read aloud. After reading an old favorite, *The Turnip* (Morgan, 1990), Joan had her first graders take turns pantomiming the action of trying to pull the turnip out of the ground. Then they talked about the characters' problem and ineffectiveness, how irritated or weak they felt, and then how surprised or thrilled they were when adding one more helper made them successful. Joan was able to infuse their discussion with new, relevant words.

When the teachers chose to read a book that fit a concept their students were studying, they were likely to plan an introductory activity before reading to give the students direct experiences with the concept. This approach was particularly important when the concept was unfamiliar and the students did not have a well-developed schema on which to build. Joan Lyons' first-grade students were about to study shadows. Early in their investigation, Joan used a lamp to demonstrate how light creates shadows against objects. Later, as she began to read *Shadow Magic* (Simon, 1985), she asked, "What do you need to make a shadow?" Now the students could talk about how shadows are made. After reading the book Joan had students help her construct a concept map describing how shadows can be made. Several familiar words and a few new ones appeared on the map. It served as the framework for a report that the class later developed about shadows in and around their school.

Jessie Michaels (Chapter 3) enjoyed watching her fifth-grade students' surprised reactions when they began to listen more carefully to texts that they knew, particularly the familiar commercials they heard on television. It was an excellent way of encouraging them to view language more objectively, rather than simply ignoring it or accepting it. In one project, she had them write down the words and phrases TV advertisers used to describe breakfast cereals. Their list included:

taste them again for the first time
a whole new kind of flake

toasted to perfection
a touch of brown sugar
natural whole wheat
multigrain
stays deliciously crisp in milk
the taste you can see
swirls of fun

They met in small groups to analyze the intent of the messages and how the words conveyed additional meanings, and then constructed and presented their own TV commercials.

Listening and discussing language take place in all grades with directed lessons and through incidental activities led by the teacher and sometimes the students themselves. Joan's first graders add words to a variety of charts, challenging their classmates to identify the meanings. For example, a list of color words is displayed, beginning with *red* and ending with Jeanie's recent contribution of *cerise.* Jessie's fifth graders maintain a bulletin board with the current slang rewritten into "proper" English. The students have a great time with the board, and Jessie is pleased with the way their recreations stretch their language usage. Often, the more expressive phrases become as much fun to say as the slang. The goal remains intact: students learn to listen to and use language to communicate in new and more complex ways.

KEY CONCEPT 2 STUDENTS SHOULD LEARN TO USE STRUCTURAL ANALYSIS TO EXPAND THEIR READING VOCABULARY.

STRUCTURAL ANALYSIS

We all know that as children become fluent readers, they encounter many new words. In the early grades, most new words are already in students' oral vocabulary but are new for them to read. In the later grades, many of the new words have familiar roots but look new because they have been combined with other words or with suffixes or prefixes. In first grade Joan Lyons directs some of her efforts to helping students connect their oral vocabulary to the written words they read. For example, she reminded them that a familiar word, such as *book* could refer to more than one, *books,* or could be snuggled against another word to form the compound word *bookshelf.* She wanted them to use words they already knew to figure out words that were new to them. By the fifth grade, Jessie Michaels was helping her students analyze written words into morphemes, or the meaning-bearing parts of words. For example, they learned that the word *insights* can be divided into three smaller units: *in-*, *-sight-*, and *-s*. They learned that each of these units is a morpheme. The *sight* part of the word is the root, or base word. The *in-* part is a prefix, which changes the meaning of the root, and the *-s* part is an inflection, which changes the word to a plural but does not otherwise affect its root meaning. Jessie's instruction with words they already knew helped the students recognize familiar roots in other multisyllable words, be more confident about word analysis, and have a better understanding about how meanings of words might be kept or changed when morphemes are added or deleted.

The importance of these word analysis tasks was explained by William Nagy and colleagues (1992), who found that an average fifth grader is likely to read around a million words of text in a year. About 10,000 of the words will be seen only once, often for the first time. Over half of the 10,000 words are derivatives of familiar words (*indebtedness, unromantic, metalware*) or inflections of more frequent words (*merges, merited*). About 1500 are proper names, and about 1000 are genuinely new words. As our teachers realized, this means that students who understand how to identify and analyze words will be able to read and understand over half of the new words that they see. To make use of such a powerful tool, Nagy and colleagues recommended that teachers provide explicit instruction, rely on examples to explain word structures, help students recognize the power of word analysis and its limitations, and apply structural analysis in text contexts.

Provide Explicit Instruction

Jessie's students came across many seemingly new words, so they often needed to carry out word analysis. In the process they discovered old words clothed in new endings or beginnings. To keep the tasks from becoming trivial, Jessie modeled the process of analyzing new words in context, using texts her students were reading. For example, when a group of Jessie's students were reading *Dragonwings* (Yep, 1975), she analyzed the word *mournful,* following the suggestions of Nagy and colleagues (1992, p. 8).

> Here's a word I haven't seen before. The first thing I'll do is see whether I recognize any familiar parts—a prefix, stem, or suffix—or perhaps it's a compound word. Okay, I see that I can divide this word into a stem I know, "mourn," and a suffix, "ful." I know you "mourn" when you feel sad. "Ful" means being full of . . . so this word must mean being filled with sadness. Now, I'll see if that meaning makes any sense in this sentence.

As a result of this modeling, students became more confident about doing the activity themselves.

Rely on Examples to Teach Structural Analysis

The teachers of younger children were able to introduce this guiding principle with the easiest morphemes so that students could begin to develop a sense of how root words are expanded to form other words. After reading *The Turnip* to her class, Joan Lyons presented a lesson based on suggestions by Sandra Condry (1979). She wrote the sentences "The old man lives on a farm. He is a _____." She asked her first graders to complete the sentence, and they discussed how the added word—*farmer*—is different in spelling and meaning. They considered other story-related words in a similar way: *work, worker; help, helper.* She also asked the children to consider how the "taking apart" strategy that they use when trying to identify words is like the "putting together" strategy they use to make longer words.

When Jessie wanted to teach her fifth graders that meanings of words could be discovered within word families, she began with examples of words they already knew well. She introduced the concept of word families with the word *drive* because she knew they would think of words in the same family that had prefixes or suffixes, such as *driving, driver, drives, drove, driven, driverless.* The word *drive* also provided an entry into compound words, with *overdrive, drive-in, driveway.* Making a list of word families was usually enough to spark a discussion of other words that were related meaningfully, as well as words that appeared to be related but were not, such as *drivel.* Jessie frequently helped her students apply this concept during their literature discussions. For example, one group reading the novel *Dragonwings* used the strategy to explore words such as *migrate, immigrant, immigrating,* and *immigration,* then *emigrate* and *emigrant.*

Building up or connecting word families was one step; understanding how to analyze longer words into their roots so as to recognize a familiar family was another. Taking words from the novel *Dragonwings,* Jessie wrote: *loneliness, separations, unperturbed, inhabitants.* She used these words to model ways of analyzing their roots to help determine their meanings within the context of the text. *Separations* and *loneliness* were useful examples because the roots were well-known words, and the analysis led the students into identifying familiar word families. *Inhabitants* and *unperturbed* provided another pattern because their roots are more difficult to determine or relate to the meaning of the targeted word. Jessie encouraged students to look carefully at the text context as well as root words to gain meaning.

On the board, this fourth-grade teacher displays cards with new vocabulary from the novels her students are reading. Students' interest in learning new words carries over from guided discussion lessons to their voluntary reading.

Recognize the Power and Diversity of Word Structure

Some root words and affixes are very productive, that is, they are used in large numbers of other words; others are not. The teachers were careful to use common affixes. They drew on work by White, Sowell, and Yanagihara (1989), who identified the following more common forms.

Inflected Suffixes

-s, -es
-ed
-ing

Common Suffixes

-ly
-er, -or
-ion, -tion
-ible, -able
-al, -ial
-y

-ness
-ity, -ty
-ment
-ic
-ous, -eous, -ious

Common Prefixes

un-
re-
in-, im-, ir-, il- (meaning "not")
dis-
en-, em-
non-
in-, im- (meaning "in" or "into")

over- (meaning too much)
mis-
sub-
pre-
inter-
fore-
de-

White and colleagues point out three complications to be aware of when teaching prefixes: inconsistent meanings (*un-*, *re-*, *in-*, and *dis-* contain at least two distinct meanings), false analysis (attempting to separate words that are not prefixed words such as *uncle, reason, invent*), and an overly literal interpretation (such as interpreting *indelicate* to mean "not fragile").

Joyce recognized that her students were frequently confused by prefixes. She used the ideas presented by White and colleagues to help her students develop strategies for using prefixes to gain meaning for unfamiliar words. Her lessons on prefixes made the following four points:

1. A prefix is a group of letters that go in front of a word. Joyce chose prefixed words from her students' reading as examples and then asked the students to locate others.

2. A prefix changes the meaning of a word. Joyce focused on the negative meanings of the prefixes: *un-*, *dis-*, *in-*, *im-*, *ir-*, and *non-*. When her students were reading *Sarah, Plain and Tall*, she wrote the sentence: Caleb was *unable* to remember his mama. Joyce helped the children note that when *un-* is peeled from *unable.* the word remaining is *able*. Students knew the meaning for *able*, so she asked, "What does *unable* mean? Does that make sense with what we know of the story? Remember, when you try to figure out words with a prefix, you should always check to see that the meaning makes sense." She used the same approach with the sentence: Papa was *disinterested* in singing.

3. When a prefix is removed, a word must be left. Joyce used the prefixes and approach introduced in Lesson 2 to point out that *able* and *interest* can stand alone as complete words.

4. Present alternative meanings of the prefixes that were introduced in Lessons 2 and 3. Joyce took advantage of Chantelle's discovery during her independent reading of *Sarah, Plain and Tall*. Chantelle had noted the sentence, "Papa reached into his pocket and *unfolded* a letter written on white paper." Joyce helped the students see that in this case *un-* means "the reversal of an action" rather that *not*.

Make the Limitations Clear

Text context is necessary to keep students from misidentifying words that seem to have familiar root words but cannot be explained in that way—that is, nonexamples such as *cargo, early, muster, current, curfew*. The teachers do not want students to assume unthinkingly that they could always find and rely on words that seem to be within the bigger words. So, when their texts contain words of this nature, the teachers add these nonexample words to their lists, expecting students to distinguish them and, when they checked against the text context, to explain how they knew from context or word analysis that these words did not contain recognizable roots.

Apply Structural Analysis in Context

Students need to apply structural analysis to whole texts to learn how to orchestrate word analysis, text context, and their own background knowledge. Affixed words and compounds can have quite different meanings depending on the context; students must learn to coordinate their analyses with their own sense of context. Jessie taught her fifth graders a two-part strategy for figuring out new words in context (from Herman & Weaver, 1988). She told her students to remember that there are two ways to come up with "best guesses" about unknown words:

1. Look into words. Identify familiar word features, roots, and affixes and remember past experiences with the familiar parts of the words.
2. Look around the words. Notice the flow of events and mood in that part of the text. Use nearby sentences and phrases, either behind or ahead, for other meaning clues.

To help her students remember the strategies, Jessie drew the diagram shown in Figure 5.2. Then she modeled the strategy using the word *wooers,* which students had noted in their reading. As the children looked *in* the word they recognized *-er* and said that it "means someone who does something, like *farmer* and *teacher*." They also noted that the word has an *s,* which makes it plural. They uncovered the base word *woo* but no one had heard of the word before. Next Jessie asked the students to review the events in the text *around* the word and then read the paragraph in which the word occurred. Through context and their understanding of suffixes, the students were able to bring meaning to *wooers.* Jessie often encouraged students to use the strategy, reminding them of the diagram as

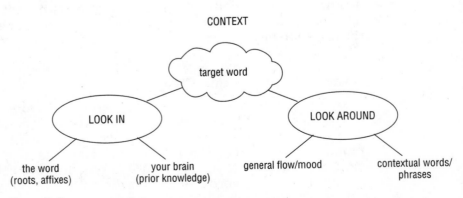

FIGURE 5.2
Visual Prompts for Context Strategy Instruction
Source: Herman & Weaver, 1988. Reprinted by permission.

they encountered unfamiliar words within their literature discussion groups.

Structural analysis is an important tool for students to learn. They should develop a number of strategies for using it, become aware of its limitations, and recognize possibilities for using it in concert with other strategies, such as checking the plausibility of meanings based on the text context. In the process of applying structural analysis to new words, students will learn when it is an appropriate tool and when it is not.

KEY CONCEPT **3** STUDENTS SHOULD LEARN TO COMBINE WORD- AND TEXT-READING STRATEGIES TO INCREASE THEIR GENERAL VOCABULARY KNOWLEDGE.

INSTRUCTION TO BUILD VOCABULARY

We know that vocabulary knowledge is fundamental to reading comprehension because words grant an ever-expanding conceptual base for understanding texts. Conversely, a dearth of vocabulary impedes word identification as well as comprehension. Although most vocabulary cannot be taught directly, if teachers focus on reading strategies that integrate new words with familiar background experiences, their students can use the strategies to increase their vocabulary knowledge. A second way is to learn words within a concept-of-definition framework. Another way is to learn new words within a conceptual frame. Regardless of which approach is used, students should be encouraged to accumulate as much information as possible from the context in which new words are located.

Integrating New Words Within a Knowledge Framework

When our teachers introduce new words or new concepts, they routinely help students form effective connections between new information and their background knowledge. They do this because forming good connections to old information makes the new information more understandable and easier to remember.

One approach, drawn from Dan Kirby and Carol Kuykendall (1985) and presented by William Nagy (1988), is to set up a hierarchy, using a "Thinking Tree." Joan Lyons used this idea as her first graders learned about transportation systems and their problems and how some of the problems can be solved. She began by listing the superordinate term *transportation* and asking, "What kinds of transportation are there?" The students' responses were written in a row with lines up to the superordinate term. Once the children had recalled the major methods of transportation, Joan asked them to consider the problems associated with each. Students had suggested cars, buses, airplanes, ships, and bicycles, and they now came up with problems regarding cost, danger, time, and air and noise pollution. The last step was to suggest solutions for some of the problems. Joan listed her students' ideas beneath the corresponding problems. For example, beneath cars, children had suggested that danger was a major problem and that possible solutions included wearing seatbelts, having airbags, not drinking when driving, and following speed limits.

Joyce Souza helps her third-grade students connect new words to concepts with semantic mapping. For example, during their study of birds, she chose to map the concept of flight because it effectively distinguishes birds from other vertebrates. By helping the students attend more carefully to the concept of flight she expected them to notice and learn new words associated with the concept. The first step was to put the word *flight* on the board, and ask students to think of words to describe how birds fly and words to talk about birds as they are flying. Then she asked the children to group the words into categories about bird flight. Their categories became: words describing movement, words describing what birds use to fly, and words describing noises associated with flight. Now the class had a way to compare birds in terms of patterns of flight. The map that Joyce and her students constructed appears in Figure 5.3.

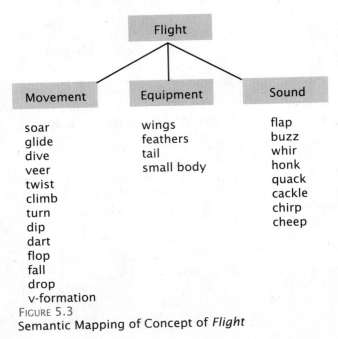

Flight

Movement	Equipment	Sound
soar	wings	flap
glide	feathers	buzz
dive	tail	whir
veer	small body	honk
twist		quack
climb		cackle
turn		chirp
dip		cheep
dart		
flop		
fall		
drop		
v-formation		

FIGURE 5.3
Semantic Mapping of Concept of *Flight*

The "movement" category served to introduce another lesson, one in which Joyce asked the students to think about differences among related words. Now the goal was to choose and think of words that best described the movement of the bird that they had chosen and that distinguished their bird from other birds. Joyce showed videotapes of birds to help the children visualize varying patterns of flight. So, for example, they learned that a robin's flight could be described in terms of diving, turning, darting, and twisting but that an eagle was more likely to soar.

Sounds that birds make was the subject of another activity. Joyce listed the words they had thought of and asked them to add other sounds that birds make, such as whistle, sing, tweet, cry, scream, and hoot. Again, they tried to fit the descriptors to the birds they had chosen and to compare their bird with others using the characteristic of sound.

To provide students with a general strategy for deriving the meanings of unfamiliar words in context, Jenkins, Matlock, and Slocum (1989) recommended that students use the following five-step approach:

1. Substitute a word or expression for the unknown word.
2. Check the context for clues that support your idea.
3. Ask if the substitution fits all context clues.
4. If it doesn't fit at all, try a new idea.
5. If it fits somewhat, revise your idea to fit the context.

To teach this strategy, Jessie Michaels first modeled the approach by showing students an unfamiliar word from their books, reading it aloud in the paragraph context, and showing them ways to substitute, check, and recheck to arrive at a plausible meaning of the word. She did this with the word *orbit,* which occurred several times in texts about space travel. Then she asked students to read another paragraph where the same word appeared and go through the steps themselves and, if necessary, revise their idea about the meaning of the word. Later, when they worked in groups, she had them explain to each other the strategies they used to make good guesses about the new words they found.

In the long run, of course, Jessie and the other teachers wanted students to realize that no one vocabulary strategy will be sufficient, and that they are in charge of identifying and tracking down a better understanding of words that are important to the text they are reading. To this end, Jessie gave special attention to vocabulary within their cooperative literature discussion groups. Drawing on a study of the reading of a novel in fourth grade by Fisher, Blachowicz, and Smith (1991), Jessie had students in each literature group take the roles of discussion director, vocabulary researcher, literary luminary, and secretary-checker. The four roles rotated each day. The vocabulary researcher was to select about five or six interesting words to teach to other group members from the chapter they were reading that day. After learning more about the words, the researcher led a vocabulary discussion, asking others in the group to locate the chosen words in the chapter. Next they tried to derive meanings from context or from their background knowledge, and then they confirmed their estimates or guesses or gave more accurate or more complete meanings.

Jessie found that allowing students to choose their own words for learning worked well. They identified unfamiliar words that were interesting to them, they shared knowledge about the words, and they applied reasonably effective strategies for locating, figuring out, and learning new meanings for important words in their texts. In so doing, they showed increasing independence in solving the problems around new words as they read.

Concept-of-Definition Framework

RATIONALE. Since one of our goals is to help students become independent in learning new words while reading, it may be important that they have a good *concept of definition,* as suggested by Robert Schwartz and Taffy Raphael (1985). These investigators pointed out that when skilled readers encounter a word they do not understand, they have the ability to work out a definition by using context and combining new information with existing background knowledge. Helping students develop this ability could contribute to their becoming much better readers.

How can teachers help children develop a concept of definition? According to Schwartz and Raphael, first, children often need help determining the type of information useful in defining words. Second, they need to know how the information should be organized.

The approach proposed by Schwartz and Raphael centers on the use of simple word maps, adapted from those described by P. David Pearson and Dale Johnson (1978). To construct an adequate word map, students need to bring together three pieces of information:

1. The class of which the concept is a part: What is it?
2. The properties that distinguish the concept from others in the same class: What is it like?
3. Examples of the concept: What are some examples?

The structure of a word map is shown in Figure 5.4; Figure 5.5 presents a completed word map for the concept of *sandwich.*

In the procedure developed by Schwartz and Raphael, students teach themselves new word meanings by understanding these three categories of information. Students can learn the strategy in a sequence of four lessons, as described below (adapted from Schwartz & Raphael, 1985). The procedure was tested with fourth and fifth

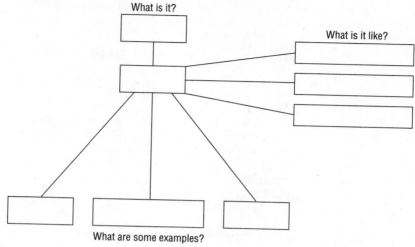

FIGURE 5.4
Structure of a Word Map

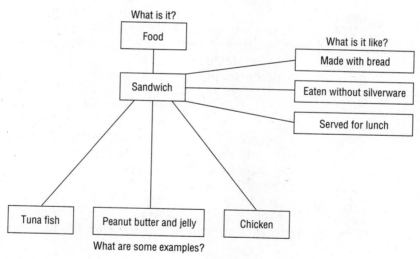

FIGURE 5.5
Completed Word Map for *Sandwich*

graders and can easily be used with students in any of the upper elementary grades.

FIRST DAY: PREPARATION. Before teaching the lesson, the teacher chooses three or more concepts the children already know. She uses these as examples in a categorization task showing the three components of a definition. For each concept, then, she has students prepare a list of information including the concept class, at least three properties, (what it is like) and at least three examples. Sample lists of information about two concepts, *soup* and *clown,* are shown below.

Soup	*Clown*
chicken noodle	wears a lot of makeup
served with sandwiches	Bozo
tastes good	a person
is a liquid	works in a circus
cream of mushroom	does funny things
eat it with a spoon	wears bright-colored clothes
vegetable noodle	likes children
made from milk sometimes	rodeo clown
served in a bowl	Oopsy
	has a large fake red nose

CONDUCTING THE LESSON. Begin by giving students explicit information about the purpose of the procedure and what they will be doing. Discuss with them how knowing the meanings of words helps with understanding the material being read. Explain to them that the procedure they will be learning will enable them to judge whether they know the meaning of a particular word.

Introduce the students to the structure of a word map (see Figure 5.4). Draw this structure on the chalkboard, putting the labels *What Is It?* above, *Examples* below, and *What Is It Like?* to one side. This gives you a place to list the information for class, examples, and properties. Explain to the students that this is a kind of picture that shows three things we generally know when we have a really good understanding of a word. Tell them that they will be learning what these three things are by completing word maps for a number of words they already know.

Have the students work from the concept lists that they prepared earlier. Ask them to place the information for each concept into the three categories in the word map. Here, for example, is an exchange between a teacher and students that occurred when the students were trying to categorize the information for the word *computer:*

T: To answer the question, "What is it?" you need a very general word. This is a word that would answer the question "What is it?" for many different words. Look on your list under the word *computer.* Can you find a very general word that answers the question, "What is it?" It could answer the question for *lawnmower,* or *dishwasher,* or *pencil sharpener,* as well as *computer.*

S: Machine.

T: That certainly is very general, and it does answer the question, "What is it?" Now we'll talk about the question "What is it like?" The answer to this question gives details about the word being studied. For example, the details for *computer* are descriptions of what computers are like. These descriptions tell things about computers and how they are different from other machines like lawnmowers, pencil sharpeners, or dishwashers. Can you find any?

S: Has a keyboard.

S: Can play games on it.

S: Has a screen to read from.

T: Yes, those are properties of computer; they answer the question, "What is it like?" To answer the last question, "What are some examples?" check the list again. Do you see any examples of computers?

S: Apple IIc.

S: IBM PC.

S: It isn't on the list, but there is the TRS-80 computer.

T: Excellent. You used information from the list, and also from your own experiences. (Schwartz & Raphael, 1985, pp. 201–202)

After working through a number of examples with the students, have them try to map and write definitions for some words on their own. They can begin by using words from the lists the class created earlier (e.g., soup, clown, computer). Working in groups of twos or threes, have them map a word of their choice using background knowledge to complete the map. Then have them write a definition for the word they just mapped. Here is an example of a definition students might have written after mapping the word *clown*:

A clown is a person who entertains you. He wears a lot of makeup and does funny things. He usually works in a circus. Some examples are Bozo and Oopsy and a rodeo clown.

SECOND DAY: PREPARATION. Look for a number of passages where information about the target word is presented in the surrounding context. Try to locate passages that give complete contexts, that is, provide three properties and three examples. Content-area materials can be a good source of passages, although you may have to modify them to make them more complete. An example of a complete context for the word *crops* is shown below:

Have you ever been to a farm? Have you ever seen a farmer work with his crops? Crops come from seeds planted by the farmer early in the spring. The farmer takes care of his seeds all spring and summer long. Early in the fall, crops are harvested and taken to market. At the market they are sold to people like you and me. Farmers can plant different kinds of crops. Some plant potatoes. Some plant onions. Some plant corn and tomatoes. Fresh crops sure taste good!

CONDUCTING THE LESSON. Let the students know that the purpose of the lesson is to teach them to locate in passages the information needed for a definition. Work through several sample passages with the students. Tell them what the target word is and ask them to mark the information to be put in the word map. Have them transfer the information to the map, then generate either oral or written definitions.

Once the students understand the approach, emphasize that it is not necessary to have exactly three properties or three examples. Let them know that some words have less than three properties or three examples and that more ideas important to an understanding of the word can often be included.

THIRD DAY: PREPARATION. This time look for a number of passages where the context is less complete. These "partial context" passages will not give all the information students need to complete a map and arrive at a definition for the target word. Here is an example of a passage providing only partial context (for *environment*):

> You hear a lot these days about our environment, but what exactly is it? We hear a lot of talk about a clean environment. Many parts of our environment need cleaning. The better our environment, the happier we can be.

CONDUCTING THE LESSON. Begin by letting the students know that passages will not always provide all the information they need to define a word adequately. Have them work through a passage as in the second lesson and identify the additional information needed. At this point the students may realize on their own that the missing information may be found in dictionaries and encyclopedias or in other books. If not, lead them to this conclusion. Encourage the students to use other references to complete their maps and definitions for the target words. Also, if they are not applying their own background knowledge, remind them to do so.

FOURTH DAY: PREPARATION. Again select a number of passages with only partial context. For each target word, make up an incomplete definition, one that lacks one of the three kinds of information or presents fewer than three properties or examples. Here is a sample for *astronaut:*

> The space shuttle is in space again, this time with five astronauts on board. What an exciting job to have! I'll bet people like John Glenn and Sally Ride really enjoy their work.
>
> *Definition:* Astronauts enjoy their work. Examples of astronauts are Sally Ride and John Glenn.

> _____ This is a complete definition.
> _____ This is not a complete definition.
> Things to add are: _____
>
> _____

CONDUCTING THE LESSON. Tell the students that the purpose of this lesson is to have them try to write down word definitions, incorporating all three kinds of information but without necessarily mapping it first. Ask them to think about the parts of the map and to try to put the information together in their minds.

Present the partial-context passages and incomplete definitions and ask the students to see if the definitions are complete. Tell them that they should write in the missing information for definitions they find to be incomplete. Discuss with the students the kinds of thinking they are using to decide what is missing from the definitions and where they might find the information needed.

Learning Within a Conceptual Frame

Some texts that students read and that teachers read to them contain new words that are not known but can be understood if placed within a conceptually meaningful framework. For example, Hally Simmons liked to use Hubbard's *C Is for Curious, An ABC of Feelings* (1990) with her kindergartners as they learned about feelings and emotions. The book's pictures presented a clear way of describing the concept through the actions of the pictured characters and Hally was then able to link them to the less familiar words of emotion. The *C* word, *curious,* for example, shows a character ready to look into a closed box. Hally asked the children how they felt when they saw something that was closed or wrapped up. From their responses, she was able to present the word *curious.*

Joan Lyons, reading the introductory chapter of *Winnie the Pooh* (Milne, 1957) came, on page 18, to,

"I think the bees *suspect* something!"

"What sort of thing?"

"I don't know. But something tells me that they're *suspicious!*"

Since understanding this word was essential to appreciating the story of Pooh's dilemma when hanging from a balloon above a bee hive, Joan stopped reading and asked how the students felt when something didn't seem quite right and they wondered what was going on. From their examples she introduced the word *suspicious* and had the children consider how the bees felt when they saw Pooh near their hive.

Joyce Souza extended students' knowledge of words and their concepts about mammals by helping them generate examples and nonexamples of mammals within a family. The students learned that "rodents" were the family that ate by gnawing on things and so they had large front teeth. They were able to apply this information to decide that rabbits, mice, rats, and squirrels belonged in this family and reject the possibility of pigs, horses, cats, or dogs being rodents. A small group of students played games with the idea later by creating a book of "oddities." They drew "pig rodents" with large front teeth and "horse canines" with their prey. Their examples of strange mammals reinforced their understanding of the concepts being studied and delighted their classmates as well.

Some new words are easily learned by imagining an action, an activity, or an interesting person and associating it with a new word. For example, students might imagine a sumo wrestler *flexing* his muscles, a young mother *embracing* a baby, a baker or pizza maker *kneading* dough. They might imagine the behavior of different, particular people as they *wail, proclaim,* or *make a retort.* They could imagine what action might accompany a *feud, conspiracy,* or *compromise.* Sometimes students place the word in its text context, imagining the word connected with a story character, but sometimes they let the image be free of the story. What makes this approach work is the vividness of the imagined activity and the personal distinctiveness of each word. Joyce and Joan did this activity after reading a story aloud, and found that it became a favorite game of their students. The children shared the images they created and helped one another construct more fully elaborated images, all of which facilitated identification and understanding of the word.

Jessie Michaels relied on a comprehensive approach to help her fifth graders understand new words in a text. Her first step was to lead a group discussion to elicit information about the topic. In a discussion about space travel, she noted that her students used words such as *rockets, space station,* and *satellites,* but made no connections to gravity and weightlessness, orbiting the earth, or relationships between earth and other planets in the solar system. As students read the text silently, Jessie asked them to list in their journals the words of which they were uncertain. Then she asked the children to arrange themselves into small groups to summarize the text ideas, discuss their problem words, and decide which ones interfered with their understanding. Certain problem words—*gravity, orbit, weightlessness,* and *solar system*—began to appear on their lists and could not be ignored. Their next step, for those problem words, was to reread and read ahead to see if they could use context to discover meanings. For the few words still remaining on their problem lists, they were to use other resources—not merely dictionaries, but encyclopedias, other books, and computer banks—to obtain more information about the new words. Finally, students from all groups compiled one combined list of problem words necessary for understanding the text along with explanations, interpretations, pictures, and outside source suggestions.

These lessons provided means for helping students learn to connect new and old information. They looked for relationships among words and discovered new ways of categorizing information. This strategy for forming connections among concepts helps students learn and remember new and more complicated information.

KEY CONCEPT 4   STUDENTS SHOULD BE MOTIVATED TO ATTEND TO NEW VOCABULARY DURING WIDE READING AT HOME AND AT SCHOOL.

MOTIVATING VOCABULARY DEVELOPMENT

Students learn to read some words through teachers' instruction, but there are many more words that students need to learn on their own. Estimates made by William Nagy and Richard Anderson (1984) suggest that students view as many as 90,000 distinct words during their 12 years of school. Although there is no way this many words can be directly taught by teachers, students do learn to read and understand most words. How is this possible? Nagy, Herman, and Anderson (1985) have argued that most words are learned not from instruction but in incidental ways, from encountering the words in school texts, from reading books, magazines, and newspapers at home and school, from viewing television, and from talking with others. The significance of this statement is that teachers must foster wide-scale reading and encourage students' attention to vocabulary, both in school and at home.

To nurture vocabulary development during wide reading our teachers maintained the following principles: they varied their support of independent reading to fit the reading situations, they fostered wide reading, and they encouraged students to be attentive to words during their independent reading.

Varied Support

Although there is no question that students should read widely, and read high-quality literature, some texts are more likely to promote learning from context. For example, it is easier to learn words from narratives than from expository passages, in part because words in narratives are better integrated into the text as a whole, and in part because concepts in expository texts are less familiar. Therefore teachers need to provide more contextual support when students are reading expository passages. Nagy, Anderson, and Herman (1986) explained further that "learning from expositions is especially dependent on relationships among concepts being made clear, and it may take repeated exposure, not just to the words, but to the system of ideas in a new domain, to produce a significant level of incidental learning" (p. 40).

To keep from overwhelming students with new terms and complex concepts in expository passages, Susan, Joyce, and Jessie relied on a four-category classification of words to guide them about when to let students learn on their own and when to provide explicit instruction (Graves, 1984).

1. *Type 1 Words:* These are words that students cannot read but are in their oral vocabulary.

   As students in Jessie's fifth grade read *Dragonwings* (Yep, 1975) they discovered words such as *nuisance* and *guardians* that some of them found difficult to read. Once they heard the words spoken, however, they recognized the words and understood their meanings.

2. *Type 2 Words:* These words are already in the students' reading vocabulary but with one or more other meanings.

   In *Dragonwings* students encountered words of this type, for example *demon* and *glider.* Though they had some background for these words, they gained new meanings through their reading and discussion of the novel.

3. *Type 3 Words:* These are words that are in neither the students' oral vocabulary nor their reading vocabulary. Although they do not have an available concept, a meaningful concept can be easily built.

   Other words the students discovered, such as *dowries* and *turret,* were completely unfamiliar to many of them. Jessie found she could connect *dowry* to property one owns before marriage, and a turret was easily visualized and shown in pictures of old houses.

4. *Type 4 Words:* These are the most difficult words to learn. The words are in neither the students' oral vocabulary nor their reading vocabulary. Moreover, they do not have an available concept, and a concept cannot be easily built.

   The students reading *Dragonwings* puzzled over terms such as *constellations* and *aerodynamics.* Jessie recognized that these are complex concepts and cannot be explained quickly. If word understandings are key to the story or would pique some students' interest (such as *aerodynamics*) Jessie encourages the students to research the concept. Reporting their findings to classmates increases everyone's understanding.

The classification system suggests that with type 1 and type 2 words teachers may allow students to learn the words incidentally, from reading. With type 3 words teachers need to provide some instructional support, and with type 4 words they need to provide extensive support, moving students from familiar to new concepts and then to new words.

Wide Reading

We know how important extensive reading is to language and vocabulary development. The main way to assure that students engage in wide reading is to make books accessible. All our teachers maintain classroom libraries, often set up in corners of classrooms with comfortable chairs or cushions, shelves of books, and a display of new and current-topic books. Hally was fortunate to have been able to capitalize on a special budget for book purchases to establish a substantial library for her kindergartners. The other teachers built their collections by frequenting garage sales, attending library sales and book fairs, and requesting contributions from students who had outgrown their books. All the teachers augmented their collections with books that they borrowed from the school and public libraries and with their accumulation of children's magazines. In addition, they arranged to obtain current subscriptions of magazines that fit their students' reading interests with the help of parent donations. Finally, they set up book clubs, so there were monthly opportunities for students to purchase books and to exchange books with one another.

With books attractively displayed and readily accessible in their classrooms, students could locate books that interested them, have books to read in their spare minutes, and borrow books for home reading. Although teachers found that setting up a library was time consuming at the beginning of the year, student helpers soon took over the tasks of cataloging, sorting, and checking books in and out. With a large assortment of books available to read in the classroom and to borrow for home use, reading soon became a common routine. (See Chapter 8 for additional information on making books accessible to students.)

Teachers will want to organize their schedules so that students have extended periods for reading. Time is planned for students to read from novels and informational books that follow the interests of literature groups or that fit into a whole-class unit of study. In addition, most teachers schedule a regular time each day for all members of the classroom community to read books of their own choosing. Teachers also encourage their students to spend time reading outside class.

Motivating students to *want* to engage in wide reading is also critical. Students should believe that reading is enjoyable, valuable to them, and not too difficult. Our teachers found a number of ways to make books interesting and worth students' time and attention. They introduced and promoted individual books by favorite authors or on topics in which students showed an interest. Hally and Joan read books to their kindergarten and first-grade students every day, and when they saw that a topic or author was especially appreciated, they found other books on the topic or by that author. They introduced these books by reading aloud opening lines or showing and talking about some of the pictures. They placed the books in a prominent place for students to read or borrow for home use. In third grade and even in fifth grade, Susan, Joyce, and Jessie read chapters or segments of books aloud to entice students to choose that book, or another book by the same author, to enjoy on their own. They also fostered peer recommendations of good books that students might not have considered reading, student reports about their favorite books, and incentive systems to encourage students to read more and to enjoy reading. (See Chapter 8 for more information on voluntary reading.)

Attention to Words During Independent Reading

Many teachers, particularly those of older children, heighten students' awareness of new and interesting language encountered during their independent reading by asking them to list some of those words (see Figure 7.5). Later, students share these words with their classmates, explaining why they found the words interesting, how they discovered their meanings, or why the words were important to the text in which they were discovered.

Teachers and students often maintain class charts with ever-growing lists of related words. Students continually add words that they encounter in their reading. One chart in Jessie Michaels' fifth-grade class contains words that describe ways of seeing. This chart began when students encountered the word *glimpse* in a novel they were reading. This was a new word for them and as they came to an understanding of its meaning, they began to generate similar words. A lively discussion ensued in which they explored the nuances of meaning for words such as *peek, glance, snoop, peep, sight, spy, stare.* The day Kelly was acting as vocabulary researcher, her literature group discussed the meaning for *scrutinize* found in their novel. They were excited to realize that they had a new contribution for this chart and were eager to share this with their classmates.

The Word Wizard procedure (Beck & McKeown, 1983) provides another means for encouraging students' sensitivity to new words and motivating their interest in vocabulary through independent reading. Students first identify interesting vocabulary in books they read and discuss during readers' workshop. They can then earn points for using or recognizing these words in other settings either in or out of school. Teachers allot a brief amount of time during readers' workshop for students to share words they saw, heard, or used, and to review their meanings. Students' points can be recorded on a class wall chart (see Figure 5.6). After every five points, students move into another category of "word expert."

Students need to read widely. They begin in kindergarten with books that are read to them, books they look at, memorize, and use to tell stories. They continue in the early and middle grades with a variety of books, both fiction and nonfiction. With a program that encourages wide reading and attention and interest in words, students can make extensive advances in their vocabulary development through independent reading.

SUMMARY

We opened this chapter by explaining that vocabulary learning is closely intertwined with reading, writing, listening, and speaking experiences and with abilities to recognize printed words. Words are not easily taught, and their meanings are not easily determined out of context. Moreover, because the number of words students need to learn is so large, they must learn most of their vocabulary in incidental ways, especially from wide reading. Teachers can support students' growth in vocabulary development by providing a diverse set of oral language activities, teaching students to analyze multisyllable words into their roots and affixes, and presenting ideas such as word families. In addition, teachers need to lead students to understand how to use a multiple set of strategies for learning, remembering, and interpreting word meanings. Finally, teachers need to encourage students to engage in wide reading on their own, both at school and at home. In these ways, students will accumulate a large reading vocabulary that will supply them with essential conceptual tools for understanding and learning from their texts.

◀ ACTIVITIES

Reflecting on Your Own Literacy

Labov (1973) pointed out that words can be "slippery customers, and many scholars have been distressed by their tendency to shift their meanings and slide out from under any simple definition" (p. 341). Find a few words that are good examples of Labov's observations. Be prepared to share and discuss your examples.

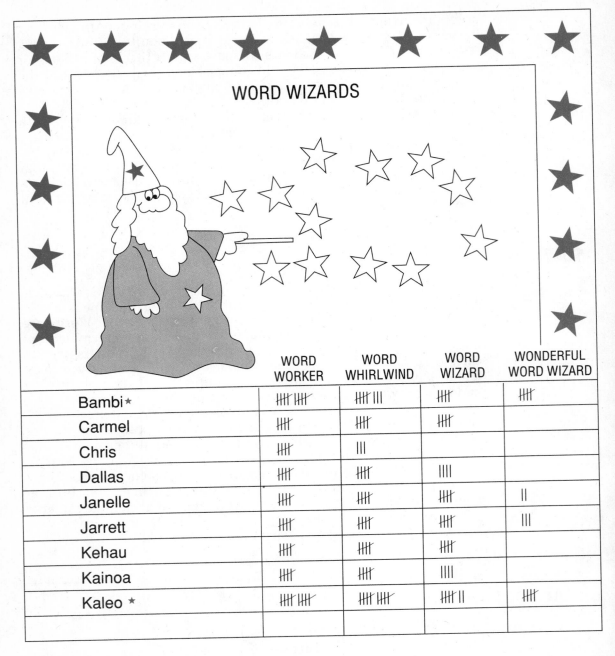

WORD WIZARDS

	WORD WORKER	WORD WHIRLWIND	WORD WIZARD	WONDERFUL WORD WIZARD
Bambi ⋆	‖‖‖ ‖‖‖	‖‖‖ ‖‖	‖‖‖	‖‖‖
Carmel	‖‖‖	‖‖‖	‖‖‖	
Chris	‖‖‖	‖‖‖		
Dallas	‖‖‖	‖‖‖	‖‖‖	
Janelle	‖‖‖	‖‖‖	‖‖‖	‖
Jarrett	‖‖‖	‖‖‖	‖‖‖	‖
Kehau	‖‖‖	‖‖‖	‖‖‖	
Kainoa	‖‖‖	‖‖‖	‖‖‖	
Kaleo ⋆	‖‖‖ ‖‖‖	‖‖‖ ‖‖‖	‖‖‖ ‖	‖‖‖

FIGURE 5.6
A Word Wizard Chart
Source: J. Carroll, ed. (1992), Literacy Curriculum Guide, Early Education Division, Kamehameha Schools/Bernice Pauahi Bishop Estate, p. 141.

Applying What You Have Learned to the Classroom

Choose a novel appropriate for students in grades 4 to 6. Read the first chapter. Then go back through the chapter and identify vocabulary (words or phrases) that might fall into the following categories (some words or phrases may fit in more than one category):

1. those which are important to an understanding of the novel,
2. those which can be learned as part of the teaching of new concepts,
3. those whose meaning can be grasped (at least in part) from context, and
4. those which might be hard for students to read but which are probably in their oral vocabulary.

Prepare a plan for vocabulary instruction based on selected words and phrases. Explain why you chose to teach these particular words and phrases. Provide a justification for your instructional approach.

BIBLIOGRAPHY

References

Beck, I. L., & McKeown, M. G. (1983). Learning words well—A program to enhance vocabulary and comprehension. *The Reading Teacher, 36*(7), 622–625.

Bissex, G. (1980). *GNYS AT WRK: A child learns to write and read.* Cambridge, MA: Harvard University Press.

Condry, S. (1979). A developmental study of processes of word derivation in elementary school children and their relation to reading. Unpublished doctoral dissertation. Ithaca, NY: Cornell University.

Davis, G. (1944). Fundamental factors of comprehension in reading. *Psychometrika, 9,* 186–197.

Feitelson, D., Kita, B., & Goldstein, Z. (1986). *Effects of reading series-stories to first graders on their comprehension and use of language.* Haifa, Israel: University of Haifa, School of Education.

Fisher, P., Blachowicz, C., & Smith, J. (1991). Vocabulary learning in literature discussion groups. In J. Zutell & S. McCormick (Eds.), *Learner factors/teacher factors: Issues in literacy research and instruction.* Fortieth Yearbook of the National Reading Conference. Chicago, Il: National Reading Conference.

Freebody, P., & Anderson, R. (1983). Effects on text comprehension of differing proportions and locations of difficult vocabulary. *Journal of Reading Behavior, 15,* 19–40.

Gallas, K. (1991). Arts as epistemology: Enabling children to know what they know. *Harvard Educational Review, 61,* 40–50.

Graves, M. (1984). Selecting vocabulary to teach in the intermediate and secondary grades. In J. Flood (Ed.), *Promoting reading comprehension*. Newark, DE: International Reading Association.

Herman, P. (1988). Vocabulary knowledge. In C. Carroll (Ed.), *Literacy resource notebook*. Honolulu, HI: Kamehameha Schools.

Herman, P., & Weaver, R. (1988). *Contextual strategies for learning word meanings: Middle grade students look in and look around*. Paper presented at the National Reading Conference, Tucson, AZ.

Jenkins, J. R., Matlock, B., & Slocum, T. (1989). Two approaches to vocabulary instruction: The teaching of individual word meanings and practice in deriving word meaning from context. *Reading Research Quarterly, 24,* 215–235.

Kirby, D., & Kuykendall, D. (1985). *Thinking through language, Book one.* Urbana, IL: National Council of Teachers of English.

Labov, W. (1973). *The boundaries of words and their meanings.* In C. J. Bailey & R. Shuy (Eds.), *New ways of analyzing variation in English.* Washington, D.C.: Georgetown University Press.

Leung, C. (1992). Effects of word-related variables on vocabulary growth through repeated read-aloud events. In C. Kinzer & D. Leu (Eds.), *Literacy research, theory, and practice: Views from many perspectives.* Forty-first Yearbook of the National Reading Conference. Chicago: National Reading Conference.

Mezynski, K. (1983). Issues concerning the acquisition of knowledge: Effects of vocabulary training on reading comprehension. *Review of Educational Research, 53,* 253–279.

Nagy, W. (1988). *Teaching vocabulary to improve reading comprehension.* Urbana, IL: National Council of Teachers of English.

Nagy, W. E., & Anderson, R. C. (1984). How many words are there in printed school English? *Reading Research Quarterly, 19,* 304–330.

Nagy, W., Anderson, R. C., & Herman, P. (1986). *The influence of word and text properties on learning from context.* (Tech. Rep. No. 369), Urbana: University of Illinois, Center for the Study of Reading.

Nagy, W., Herman, P., & Anderson, R. C. (1985). Learning words from context. *Reading Research Quarterly, 20,* 233–253.

Nagy, W., Osborn, J., Winsor, P., and O'Flahavan, J. (1992). *Guidelines for instruction in structural analysis.* (Tech. Rep. No. 554) Urbana-Champaign: University of Illinois, Center for the Study of Reading.

Pearson, P. D., & Johnson, D. D. (1978). *Teaching reading vocabulary.* New York: Holt, Rinehart & Winston.

Schwartz, R. M., & Raphael, T. E. (1985). Concept of definition: A key to improving students' vocabulary. *The Reading Teacher, 39*(2), 198–205.

White, T., Sowell, J., & Yanagihara, A. (1989). Teaching elementary students to use word-part clues. *The Reading Teacher, 43,* 302–308.

Suggested Classroom Resources

Brett, J. (1987). *Goldilocks and the three bears.* Spring Valley, NY: Dodd, Mead.

Brown, M. (1947). *Stone soup.* New York: Macmillan.

Cowley, J. (1986). *Yuk soup.* San Diego, CA: The Wright Group.

Hubbard, W. (1990). *C is for curious, an ABC of feelings.* San Francisco: Chronicle Books.

Keats, E. J. (1966). *Jennie's hat.* New York: Harper & Row.

MacLachlan, P. (1985). *Sarah, plain and tall.* New York: Harper & Row.

Milne, A. A. (1957). *The world of Pooh.* New York: Dutton.

Morgan, P. (1990). *The turnip.* New York: Philomel Books.

Simon, S. (1985). *Shadow magic.* Fairfield, NJ: Lothrop, Lee & Shepard Books.

Yep, L. (1975). *Dragonwings.* New York: Harper & Row.

Further Readings

Blachowicz, C. L. Z., & Lee, J. J. (1991). Vocabulary development in the whole literacy classroom. *Reading Teacher, 45*(3), 188–195.

Cooper, J. D. (1993). Vocabulary development in the literacy program. Chapter in Cooper, J. D., *Literacy: Helping children construct meaning* (2nd ed.). Boston: Houghton Mifflin.

Mason, J., Peterman, C. & Kerr, B. (1989). Reading to kindergarten children. In D. Strickland & L. Morrow (Eds.), *Emerging literacy: Young children learn to read and write.* Newark, DE: International Reading Association Publications.

6 CLASSROOM ORGANIZATION AND MANAGEMENT

The [third-grade teacher] provided a great deal of information to the students about the standards in the classroom and how, when, and why they applied. This information was "structured" in the sense that the teacher made explicit connections between events, their antecedents and consequences, and the expected student role, and she consistently followed through on her predictions, building credibility for her statements. This was especially evident during the first 3 weeks of school. For example, she said on the second morning of school, "Every morning when you come in, there will be math on the board for you to do," and then she followed through with this pattern throughout the year. Also on the second morning, she explained that the morning schedule would typically include movement between classes for reading, but that for 2 weeks they would be doing something different, thus communicating to students about an exception to a regular pattern rather than changing patterns after 2 weeks without warning. In several instances during the first few weeks, she noted students' progress and good behavior and linked their success to their own actions, making clear the links between cause and effect. Corrections or reminders were accompanied by explanations such as, "If you drop paste on the floor, please wipe it off well because someone could slip on it and get hurt."

As the year progressed, the classroom ran fairly smoothly, with students adept at moving from one event to another quickly. The work accountability system was clearly in evidence, and its consistent use was another example of structuring of information for the students, in that consequences were predictable because the teacher enforced the system. For example, in one observation, students had a designated place to turn in certain assignments, and an aide immediately checked another assignment when completed. Before dismissal for lunch, the teacher collected all work and then called out the names of students who were finished and could leave for lunch. Throughout the year, the teacher provided a great deal of information about time to the students, such as pointing out how many minutes were left in the period to finish up work, or saying to a student who appeared to be off-task that his reading group would begin in 5 minutes. These time references focused students' attention on the passing of time, thus providing information that went beyond a correction of off-task behavior.

Although opportunities for self-regulation on school tasks were not very evident early in the year, the fall observations did reveal that procedures for water, bathroom, and pencil sharpening were in place and running smoothly without teacher permission. The teacher did provide some choices in early fall assignments (e.g., names for a graph, symbols for class map) and commented on student self-regulation when it occurred (e.g., "Jennie, I like the way you use your time," to a girl who had chosen to keep working on an assignment when others took a bathroom break. On another occasion, when a girl finished a reading assignment and resumed work on an earlier math paper, the teacher noticed and said, "Good, you're getting that math done. That's a good idea too.") Sometimes, the teacher would cue students' behavior without explicitly telling them what to do, which might have been a way of easing students into more thinking for themselves (e.g., she held up a science book, saying, "If you see what I am holding up, you will know what to get ready for next.").

By mid-year and the spring observations, there was more direct evidence that students were making task-related decisions and functioning independently. For example, students spontaneously began their assigned classroom jobs. When doing morning math, students regularly chose where they wanted to sit and work. For some other assignments, students could make choices about where to work and were allowed to get into the hall when they wanted to work with partners. Apparently, no management problems resulted from this. Students also had the option of joining a more advanced math group for instruction when they finished their regular assignments. During afternoons, students sometimes had a period for finishing work, and they independently monitored what they needed to do and in what order.

Many of the teacher's messages to students, especially corrections, relayed the message that they had choices and could control themselves. For example, she said to a boy who had been inattentive in reading group, "Go to your seat and put your head down. When you really want to listen, you can come back." In several ways, the teacher conveyed expectations and opportunities for students to make informed choices about how they would meet task demands in her classroom. This occurred within an environment where relationships were warm, humor was frequent, and students were not at risk for failure on tasks (because the teacher provided them with adequate information about the tasks and the accountability system). (Anderson, Stevens, Prawat, Nickerson, 1988, pp. 290–291)

◀ OVERVIEW

Teachers need well-crafted systems for organizing and managing their classrooms. Newer ways of teaching students to read and write and to evaluate their progress give them more opportunities to make decisions and more chances to work on their own and with classmates. Teachers now entrust greater responsibilities to students and ask their help in maintaining the classroom structure that they create together; a sound management system is critical to making this work. Furthermore, well-run classrooms are more important than ever because of the many students who require social support from adults and a secure, predictable classroom environment.

When students understand that their teachers want to establish a stable and supportive place for them to learn and that they will be able to play a useful role in building this structure, they are more likely to feel that they belong. Their classrooms become safe, friendly places where they can explore new ideas and acquire new skills. As Carole Ames (1992a, p. 253) noted, "In the classroom, a sense of 'I belong here' is very important. It is more than a feeling of acceptance by one's peers; it is a belief that one is an important and active participant in all aspects of the learning process."

However, because teachers and students usually construct classroom rules, procedures, and schedules during the first few weeks of the school year, little of the role students play in creating this structure is apparent to an outsider. It may not be clear to a beginning teacher how the structure was created or agreed upon.

In this chapter we describe the processes for setting up and maintaining an effective classroom organization and management system that promotes a positive social milieu for learning. The four key concepts for this chapter blend social and organizational characteristics of instruction with motivational and volitional dimensions of learning.

KEY CONCEPT 1: A prosocial environment serves as an effective structure for literacy learning.

KEY CONCEPT 2: Classroom management principles provide an indispensable framework for reading instruction.

KEY CONCEPT 3: Reading and writing instruction should be organized and scheduled in ways that are coordinated with instructional goals.

KEY CONCEPT 4: Reading and writing goals are better achieved when students are motivated and have the drive to learn.

◀ **PERSPECTIVE**

A Constructivist Approach

Throughout this book we have presented new trends for teaching reading and writing. We have shown how whole language and a process approach to writing are part of a movement toward constructivism, a concept that was presented in Chapter 1. An important feature is that students are actively involved in their own learning. For example, Hally Simmons allows kindergartners to begin the day by selecting books to look at or read. Later in the day, they choose from several classroom centers for their explorations of literacy. In the other grades, students consider topics to write about and books to read. Giving students real choices makes them more involved in their own learning. When reading and writing tasks draw on personal goals, students learn how to plan and use strategies to read and write. Students can understand how to take responsibility for their own learning from kindergarten on.

Constructivism refers to a way of learning that is situated in the here and now and depends on authentic rather than contrived tasks. However, authentic learning activities and tasks are often more complicated, and so our teachers model the procedures and present ideas graphically before recasting them as more abstract concepts. For example, Joan Lyons often reads part of a story to her first graders as a way of modeling the process of reading. She encourages them to join her in the reading, and then lets them continue on their own when the language is familiar or the story line becomes obvious. She often has students assist one another as they reread a familiar story, and then reread parts that they especially enjoyed. After several opportunities to read familiar materials, they will become confident about reading new stories on their own.

In a constructivist setting school tasks, in addition to being authentic, are shaped by productive teacher-student communications and peer interactions. Teachers and students ask and answer real questions and solve real problems. For example, Hally helps her kindergarten students communicate with her and with classmates using classroom mailboxes. They write to one another and to her. She writes notes to them and responds to their notes. Susan Meyer's third graders know that if they are facing a problem reading a story or writing about it, they can write a note for the message board to request help. Jessie Michaels arranges for her fifth graders to take turns assuming different roles in their reading workshop groups as they coach and learn from one another. In these ways, students learn to communicate with one another, solve problems together, and work in collaboration.

Students become actively involved in the management process when teachers include their ideas in the inner workings of the classroom—its management and structure. For example, Hally's kindergartners help label shelves and boxes and then refer to the labels as they put away books and writing materials. They realize that classmates will find them more easily. Susan's third graders accept the responsibility for designing and setting up a classroom literacy bulletin board and in the process learn a great deal about group planning, sharing tasks, and carrying out projects that are useful to everyone. Joyce Souza's third graders participate in decisions about their classroom routines. They are also notified about the schedule, as well as any changes in it, and their involvement helps them to plan their work and take charge of starting and completing it. These approaches help students assume a shared sense of ownership and responsibility for the classroom.

Students are better able to evaluate their progress realistically if teachers are sensitive to differences in rates of learning and success, show them self-appraisal techniques, and work with those who are unduly sensitive to risk or anxiety about failure. Joan's first graders decide when they are ready to present their favorite story excerpts or their written pieces to classmates. Susan attends to her third grade students' concerns and social problems and then finds a story that is relevant. Story discussions often focus on the characters' similar problem and possible solutions; then they talk about ways of supporting one another and managing their own problems, of caring for themselves and others, as suggested by Nell Noddings (1992).

School achievements are treated as confidential and students are not encouraged to compete with one another. Susan recognizes her students' achievement privately so that they will not be disheartened by others' successes. She also bases achievement on a wide selection of competencies and on students' progress and growth rather than on a few accomplishments. She recognizes differences in students' resource and time management skills and accepts a flexible framework for completing assignments. As a result, her students more readily accept responsibility for their own learning and better understand their own strengths and weaknesses.

An emphasis on personal goals helps students develop an interest in learning. To that end, Susan involves her students' families in the classroom literacy program, which is described in Chapter 8. Jessie motivates students by incorporating their preference to work with one another into the academic plans and goals. Her students are usually organized into small groups based on interest and recognized for differing achievements and competencies. They are also encouraged to practice different roles in their peer-guided discussions (such as with reciprocal teaching, which is described in Chapter 9).

A constructivist outlook is a way of learning and teaching that can enhance students' interest in learning, involve them in the process, and engage them in the necessary steps of helping themselves and supporting one another throughout the school day.

KEY CONCEPT   1   A PROSOCIAL ENVIRONMENT SERVES AS AN EFFECTIVE STRUCTURE FOR LITERACY LEARNING.

A CARING ENVIRONMENT

A prosocial classroom environment is one in which students are offered opportunities to establish and work as a classroom community (Benninga et al., 1991). They learn about helping themselves and one another and about how to work together. They are likely to have a sense of concern and respect for each other, understand how to collaborate to achieve academic and social goals, and be more interested in the literacy learning process for themselves and others.

Teachers who establish a prosocial classroom community are supplanting an earlier favored management system that relied on formal assessment and academic ranking, external motivations, competition among students, and individual achievement. Although teachers in many American classrooms still rely on a competitive atmosphere and tangible rewards for achievement, many others prefer a cooperative environment and a structure that fosters internally motivated goals. A prosocial environment helps more students to make academic gains, and enables teachers to establish a more positive and encouraging classroom atmosphere for literacy learning.

When students develop a sense of commitment to classroom norms and values, a prosocial environment is possible. Teachers foster this sense of commitment by establishing clearly defined procedures that embrace students' opinions and preferences about routines, roles, schedules, and implementations of lessons. For example, Hally, the kindergarten teacher, begins the year by giving students free-choice times. She then solicits their preferences about short, whole-class activities and offers familiar activities that they can work with independently. Later, as described in Chapter 2, she introduces the library center and, once students understand the procedures for using centers already available, adds new ones. In third grade, Joyce discusses with students how long their sustained silent reading period should be, as described in Chapter 8. Jessie has her fifth-grade students solve their own classroom problems in group meetings. When management and organization problems arise, Jessie holds a class meeting. Students present problems from their perspective and, with advice from classmates and the teacher, figure out possible resolutions and mutually agreeable solutions.

A prosocial environment is enhanced when teachers organize their teaching so that students share tasks and work cooperatively. One way that teachers establish a sense of cooperation is to have students discuss what books, authors, and topics they want to read and learn about and what writing skills they want to acquire. At the beginning of the school year, after students describe what aspects of literacy they can do well, what they want to learn, and how they want to learn, teachers can arrange interest groups to research shared topics, read particular stories or novels, or pursue the writings of particular authors.

The teachers encourage collaborative learning in the readers' and writers' workshops. When working independently, students may ask one another for help on an assignment, read to one another, and share their writings. When working in small groups on joint research projects (see Chapter 4), they may collaborate with a partner on projects, help one another, and complete assignments together. However, the teachers don't assume that students will work together effectively at first. Joan's first-grade students must learn to respect and appreciate one another's efforts and skills. Joan first has them set up clearly defined problems and anticipate how to work out a solution. She prompts them to notice partner sharing by asking them to describe what they have learned from their partner. When they review one another's work, she reminds them to state at least one positive quality of a classmate's writing before making a criticism or suggestion. These steps—defining, planning, evaluating success, and reviewing gains—help them pay more attention to the sharing process and to its benefits.

Kindergarten students also learn about working and playing together. Hally asks students to share and to accept any children who want to join them in their work and play activities, a suggestion Vivian Paley made in her 1992 book, *You Can't Say You Can't Play.* She established the policy after long discussions with the students. At first it was not easy for them to accept the idea that anyone could join their game or work with them, but they eventually realized that it was the fairest way for everyone. Jessie's fifth-grade students learn about helping and caring for others not only by reading to Hally's kindergartners in the buddy program, which is described in Chapter 8, but also by following community events. She has students bring in newspaper stories about current community events and school issues. They also acquire firsthand experiences of management of the environment by working on school maintenance and community beautification projects. Jessie then has students describe their efforts and reactions by writing reports for their school newspaper.

The teachers cultivate social understanding not only through projects but also through literature. There are many stories in which the themes reveal social and emotional problems and portray cultural perspectives and differences. The teachers choose books that exemplify cultural diversity, prosocial values, or social problems and difficulties. Hally uses picture storybooks to widen children's knowledge of rural life and to acquaint them with ways that children in other countries live. Joan and Joyce read books that fit students' problems, such as a playground bully, worrisome strangers, or problems at home, such as divorce, sickness, death, or a parent losing a job. Valuable discussions often follow the reading aloud.

In this environment, teachers try to avoid using public and competitive recognitions, such as displaying teacher-selected "best" written pieces. Instead, students might keep track of their progress with portfolios, as described in Chapter 7. When they can see and appreciate their own gains, they are more likely to want to continue making progress. Establishing individual, intrinsic reasons for learning also improves students' self-esteem. As a result, and without an atmosphere of competition, teachers are more able to weave academic classroom goals with social values and to institute a general sense in the classroom of mutual support and caring.

Overall, with a stable prosocial environment, teachers can blend lessons and literacy activities with procedures that foster student support and cooperation. When students are given a voice in setting up the rules of their classroom, they share its responsibilities and learn how to establish and maintain a community within which productive learning takes place. When the goal is for everyone to progress rather than for a few to excel, the classroom becomes a friendlier place.

KEY CONCEPT 2   CLASSROOM MANAGEMENT PRINCIPLES PROVIDE AN INDISPENSABLE FRAMEWORK FOR READING INSTRUCTION.

PRINCIPLES OF CLASSROOM MANAGEMENT

Well-managed classrooms are places where students become fully involved and use their time wisely, whether working alone, with peers, or with the teacher. Students are also able to assume responsibility for their own learning goals even when the teacher is not working directly with them. Kindergartners, for example, can be engaged in several projects, with some working on a mural together, helping one another choose and depict objects that fit their theme, while others are working with blocks, drawing, or looking at books. First graders can share favorite books with one another and confidently ask for help from classmates rather than from the teacher. Older students can discuss stories without the teacher, join in group-developed writing assignments, and negotiate shared tasks on projects emanating from reading or writing assignments.

How do teachers attain well-organized classrooms? How do they acquire cooperating, academically involved students, and with little evidence of direct instruction or disciplinary intervention? The answer is, not easily, although a skilled teacher establishes the basic framework within the first few weeks of school. To help beginning teachers create a well-organized classroom, we present eight general characteristics (Smith & Misra, 1992).

1. Rules. Teachers can establish rules at the beginning of the year with the active participation of students. For example, Joan introduced the idea of constructing useful classroom rules to her first graders by discussing safety rules that they already knew about. After considering rules for riding in the bus and crossing the street, she had them suggest possible problems if there were no safety rules. Then they considered what rules they needed for their classroom, both for the sake of safety and respect for others, and for establishing efficient routines.

One set of rules they needed was about how to get started when they arrived in the morning, which is described in Chapter 8. Joan made sure her students had a small number of rules, no more than seven. They thought of putting coats away, checking in library books, and signing up for a sharing activity. She helped them frame rules that were realistic, clearly stated, and positive, describing what students should do, not what they should not do. Joan put the rules in a prominent place and explained how to interpret a rule using examples and nonexamples. During the first few weeks of school, she reminded the students of the rules and praised them for following them. She helped them revise rules that didn't seem to work or that were no longer needed. She also monitored their compliance with the rules and set up consequences for the few students who did not want to follow them.

When rules are fair, students know what they are supposed to do, and when they have participated in the construction of the rules, most will cooperate and will even help errant students remember and follow the rules. Good rules that students accept allow the classroom to operate more smoothly and the teacher to pay closer attention to lessons and students' needs.

2. Classroom routines. Classroom routines should be determined gradually, beginning in the first week of the school year. The goal is a stable daily pattern that everyone can count on. Hally began kindergarten classroom routines in ways that eased students gradually into more complexity. The idea came from an Australian reading-writing classroom that was described by Andrea Butler and Jan Turbill (1984).

In week one, after establishing library and home centers, Hally set aside the first hour for a writers' workshop, and activity time. She let students select books to look at and then called them together for a morning message activity. After that, they could choose an activity or center such as the library, message, blocks, home, or art. In week two, Hally worked on routines for the writers' workshop, inserted right after the morning message. She also made contacts with parents and the fifth-grade teacher to secure parent aides and student buddies who would listen to and help students read. In week three she set up the listening and computer centers, and began meeting with individual students to identify their early literacy skills and help them begin at the right level. In the next few weeks she streamlined the routines, and with newly-added math and science centers, she provided an "investigation time" when students could observe, count, calculate, estimate, and carry out experiments. She also began meeting with small groups for reading. In the afternoon she read to students a book that coordinated with a literacy topic or an investigation project, and the rest of the day involved applying literacy activities to arts, crafts, music, and other creative activities.

Joan began her first-grade program in a similar manner. In week one, she showed students how to use their library and writing centers. She set aside the first two hours for writers' and readers' workshops. Students read or reread familiar books of their own choosing and learned the arrangements for borrowing books to take home. They also began to write every day on topics of their own choosing. At the end of the first week, Joan reviewed the written pieces and set up ongoing records to keep track of students' spelling, sentence structures, writing form, and complexity of story structure. In week two, Joan streamlined the routines for monitoring independent reading. She arranged to meet with students in small groups to discuss literature and noted their reading strategies, skills, and attitude toward book reading. She also contacted parents to obtain helpers. In week three she set up a listening center, and added math and science centers. She began meeting with individual students about their language, reading, and writing progress. In week four she consolidated routines and sorted out problems. In the next few weeks her math and science time was extended as an investigation time, and she added arts and crafts activities coordinated with book topics and writing and science projects.

3. Materials. Teachers check before the school year starts to make sure that they have all of the reading and writing materials they expect to use in the fall. They stock the classroom library with books that fit students' age and likely interests, the time of the year, and topics that they plan for the first month. They also decide on procedures for distributing, using, returning, and storing books and other materials. Then, when students arrive and they discuss what and how they want to learn, materials can be added or replaced and lessons adjusted. Attending to these details at the beginning of the year assures a steady, clearly presented startup.

4. Scheduling. Teachers will have smoother-running classrooms if everyone can anticipate what will happen during the school day and from week to week. A predictable schedule helps students plan and work within organized time frames. The teachers in this book constructed schedules by blocking most of the morning for readers' and writers' workshops. Blocking provides flexibility, allows students to complete work at different rates, and makes it possible to engage students in unscheduled events that flow from class discussions. Sometimes teachers alternate activities that students particu-

The organization of this classroom features a bookline, with children's published books prominently displayed.

larly like with those that they enjoy less, and they arrange for breaks after particularly difficult lessons. By October, for example, Hally's schedule for kindergartners' writers' workshop and activity time alternates easy and more difficult activities. She begins with free-choice reading and continues with the morning message and writers' workshop. Then, after a recess break, she meets with students in small groups while other students engage in center activities. The morning ends with a read-aloud story.

Susan's morning schedule for third graders, described in detail in Chapter 1, incorporates many of the same features. Free reading is followed by an hour each of writers' and readers' workshops. As students work on their own writing, Susan confers with individuals. Then she meets with one group at a time to discuss their novels while others are reading and writing about their books. Jessie's fifth-grade schedule is presented in Chapter 3. There, students begin with a readers' workshop, and Jessie works with two of the three groups each day while the third group meets in peer-led discussions. Then comes the writers' workshop, four times a week.

The teachers post their schedules in prominent places in their classrooms and send copies home to parents. They try to avoid revisions in the schedule, but when they need to make a change, they announce it at the beginning of the day or week and post the revised schedule. When lessons take less time than planned, the teachers always have other interesting endeavors ready.

5. Seating. There are very different ways to seat students in a classroom. Many kindergarten teachers post students' names on their tables, but fixed spaces are not necessary when students keep their belongings in lockers or cubby holes and tables are set up with activities for students to choose from. When they gather for a whole-class song or discussion activity, some teachers have fixed places in a circle; others let students determine where to sit. Similarly, when they meet to hear the teacher read aloud or take part in student presentations, they sit together on the rug facing the leader's chair, either in preassigned places or in places they have selected. The teacher makes seating decisions based on the nature of the activity as well as on students' ability to attend, regardless of group size or the students' distance from the teacher or one another.

In our first- and third-grade rooms, students have their own desks grouped into fours by the teachers to form small group tables. Joan and Joyce decided student placements beforehand so that more and less able students would be available to assist one another on writing projects. In the fifth grade, students rearrange their own desks frequently because Jessie organizes many lessons around interest-based projects. Students often group and regroup themselves depending on the activity, and often use a table at the back of the room for planning activities such as skits, writing projects, story debates, or reports.

All of the teachers have a desk for themselves, located near the back of the room. While the students are in class, the teachers spend little or no time at their desks, preferring to circulate around the room to assist or observe students when not conducting lessons. Only after school, when preparing for the next day or writing in their journals, do the teachers sit at their desks.

6. Rate of success. Teachers want their students to have challenging assignments but not be discouraged or frustrated by unsuccessful efforts. Even first graders quickly realize which classmates are becoming proficient readers, and by third grade some will stop trying if they believe they are too far behind. This means that teachers need to determine how to encourage all students and show them how they are making progress in reading and writing. Teachers need to be aware that students vary in their tolerance for risk and frustration, in their willingness to postpone goals, and in their level of anxiety when they work on hard problems. They also need to notice students' varying knowledge about how to judge their own achievement, recover from mistakes, and seek out and secure help from others.

Appropriate rates of success are easier to establish with readers' and writers' workshops. Jessie embedded an effective system into her workshops, as detailed in Chapter 7. At the beginning of the year she had students review their folders, consider what they did well as readers and writers, and decide on new goals. After sharing their thoughts with one another, students wrote out their new goals and placed them in their literature response logs and writing folders. Each week they reviewed and updated these goals.

The workshop framework allows teachers time to work with individuals; they review folders and students' plans and goals and judge their progress. They can permit more flexible, individually geared assignments. Learning teams can be set up, with each selecting its own collective project; this way, students assume personal responsibility for setting and achieving goals and are more likely to be motivated to achieve. This framework permits variation in lesson length so that teachers can capitalize on unexpected teachable moments to help students understand new ideas better or make closer connections to new ideas. Thus, teachers can help students set up projects and achieve goals that more closely match their interests and talents.

7. Lesson implementation. Teachers develop lessons in advance at three planning levels. Plans that encompass year-long goals and satisfy the school district's guidelines include selection of basic books or anthologies, setups for classroom libraries and other centers, projected literacy themes and goals, and notes about the classroom structure and general strategies and approaches. Quarterly and monthly plans are directed to integrating and linking literacy projects with other curriculum subjects, reviewing goals accomplished and determining new goals, reviewing students' portfolios with them and their parents, and discussing accomplishments and goals with students. For example, as presented in Chapter 7, Joyce has third graders choose one written response to literature and one piece of personal writing for their portfolio. Weekly and daily plans maintain continuity and connections among goals, tasks, and projects. Jessie, for example, has fifth graders review their literature response logs and writing folders each week to evaluate their progress and update their goals. Setting up these short- and long-term plans that include students' ongoing goals promotes greater flexibility and minimum disruption of the regular schedule.

8. Lesson process. Teachers work with students individually, in small groups, and with the whole class within readers' and writers' workshops. The principles and procedures are not scripted but determined by what is taking place at the moment.

The teachers provide students with numerous opportunities to discuss, comment on, and ask about stories and informational texts they have read. Using a number of different ways to guide students' thinking—such as the experience-text-relationship framework (Chapter 3), concept-text-application approach (Chapter 4), and directed reading-thinking approach (Chapter 4)—makes lessons more engaging. The teachers also direct students to analyze their texts by mapping the underlying concepts (Chapter 5) and build vocabulary from structural analysis of words (Chapter 5). Lively discussions also arise based on arguments about story intent or meaning, and full participation ensues when students present summaries and personal reactions to the texts.

The teachers share responsibility with students for learning by offering work choices, listing several things to do but letting students choose what to do first, letting them set their own priorities, and letting them choose a partner to work with. They help students determine and work toward specific short-term and long-term goals and arrange for them to check their own work and evaluate their own progress. They also make sure that the lesson environment is well connected to students' other work across science, math, and social studies, and is explicitly linked to concepts already learned, such as similarities among genres, characters, settings, or authors' writing styles.

In all of these ways, then, teachers create well-organized classrooms where the structure is clear to students, procedures are fair to everyone, and lessons are related to students' needs and goals.

KEY CONCEPT 3   READING AND WRITING INSTRUCTION SHOULD BE ORGANIZED AND SCHEDULED IN WAYS THAT ARE COORDINATED WITH INSTRUCTIONAL GOALS.

ORGANIZING TO SUPPORT GOALS

For years teachers in the United States have taught reading to students in small groups, usually three groups, representing high, middle and low reading abilities. However, as Richard Allington pointed out from his observations of classrooms (1983), "low groups" frequently progress slowly and do little actual book reading. Students in lower-achieving groups may have lower self-esteem, particularly if it is public knowledge that they are not achieving as well as other students. They may feel stigmatized or trapped as poor readers, especially if they perceive that they do mindless skill and drill work while other students read interesting stories and do high-level thinking activities. So, for a number of reasons, low-achieving students can be more difficult to teach, and putting all of them together into one work group compounds instructional problems.

Fortunately, a framework built on readers' and writers' workshops permits teachers to set up more flexible arrangements and

Introduction to day's workshop activities (first five minutes)

Teacher explains to the whole class any new activities and reminds children about ongoing activities and projects. Children ask questions about the work.

Small group lessons (one hour and forty minutes)

Teacher signals that children should begin work. Teacher meets for twenty minutes with each of the reading groups. Teacher gives lessons with an ETR or other systematic method of comprehension instruction and also teaches particular word identification or vocabulary skills.

Wrap-up (last five to ten minutes of the workshop period)

Completed assignments are handed in. Teacher discusses with the whole class their progress at learning centers. Teacher also asks for reactions to the work and for suggestions for future work. Occasionally, or as scheduled in place of the wrap-up, students present projects and written pieces to the class.

FIGURE 6.1
Sample Daily Schedule for Small-Group Instruction

gives all students opportunities to work with one another and to share literacy learning activities. Much of the reading instruction will still occur in small groups, but the groups are based on student's interest in topics rather than ability. Furthermore, a workshop framework easily accommodates individual meetings and student-led sessions (for example, Jessie's peer-guided groups described in Chapters 3 and 8).

When instruction takes place in small groups, it might follow a schedule such as that shown in Figure 6.1. During each small-group lesson, some of the other students would be preparing for their meeting with the teacher, perhaps by reading the text or writing about how the text connects with their own experiences and feelings. Students who had already met in a teacher-led group could be rereading the text with a classmate, considering reactions to the text or to the small group discussion, writing in their literature response logs, reading another text.

A workshop framework also makes whole-class instruction feasible. Teachers can read stories or chapters from books to the whole class and lead a discussion. Everyone is likely to be attentive if the activity is interesting. Before a story is read, teachers might engage students in a discussion of the author, setting, or topic, or have students predict the story focus on the basis of the book's cover and title. After reading a story, teachers could have students retell or summarize the plot or relate events to their own experiences.

Grouping to Foster Cooperation and Shared Responsibility

Small groups can be the most effective setting for teaching and interacting with students. However, the main criticism of small groups is that when they are based on ability, low-achieving students may be stigmatized. By following the four solutions below, teachers may gain the benefits of small groups while avoiding this drawback.

1. FOSTERING A MULTIDIMENSIONAL CONCEPT OF ABILITY. Teachers should evaluate students on more than one dimension by determining their different skills, competencies, and strengths, a concept that is further explained in Chapter 7. When teachers foster a multiple concept of ability rather than a single concept, students begin to look for, notice, and appreciate each other's strengths (Marshall & Weinstein, 1984). As a result, no one will feel incompetent at everything, and everyone can be praised for particular talents and accomplishments.

To foster a multiple concept of ability, teachers should look beyond students' reading fluency. Look for other valid reading talents such as an ability to act out the part of a story character, construct good analogies to explain an idea, make interesting predictions about stories, give useful examples that help other students understand new words or story concepts, or critically evaluate text information. Consider also students' talents at oral and written expression, group leadership, task perseverance, and attention to details and accuracy. Then, help students use their special abilities as part of the readers' and writers' workshop lessons and projects. These actions will help students differentiate aspects of their own reading, encourage them to improve their skills, and may help them see that hard work will increase their literacy competencies.

2. IMPROVING THE CLASSROOM STATUS OF LOW-ACHIEVING STUDENTS. Separating students by ability, as discussed earlier, can depress lower-achieving students' achievement, since their self-esteem and status in the classroom are jeopardized (Hallinan, 1984). Since ability grouping has a number of advantages, however, teachers who want to continue using ability grouping should work to enhance the status and self-esteem of lower-achieving students.

Greta Morine-Dershimer (1983) found that an effective tactic to enhance students' classroom status is to increase their participation in classroom discussions. Because students who are called on become more visible to their classmates and recognized as children-who-know, they achieve a higher status, and become students whom others turn to and learn from. She observed that teachers could help students improve their status by calling on them to describe their lesson-related experiences and problem-solving ideas, not merely to describe remembered text information. Teachers were then able to call on high-, middle-, and low-achieving students about equally, and all could contribute effectively to the discussion.

3. HETEROGENEOUS GROUPING. An alternative to setting up groups of students who have similar tested reading competencies, or homogeneous groups, is to set up groups whose members represent a wide ability range, or heterogeneous groups. This enables students to work with a larger number of their classmates, and it permits teachers to set up more flexible instructional groupings. It may improve the status and self-esteem of low-achieving students, though teachers usually have to help them become full participants.

Noreen Webb and Linda Cullian (1983) observed teachers who mixed students of high, middle, and low ability into groups of three and four. This arrangement successfully fostered students' achievement and their social interactions if teachers assigned tasks to be completed by the groups and the groups learned to work together. To achieve cooperation, helpfulness, and coordination of effort, teachers circulated among the groups as they worked, coaching as necessary.

In another study, Noreen Webb set up groups composed of high and middle achievers and other groups of middle and low achievers (Webb & Kenderski, 1984). She found that the groups were able to work more effectively if students explained things to one another; to do that, teachers needed to show students how to explain their ideas and answers to one another. The research on heterogeneous grouping shows, then, that the arrangement can be effective, and that teachers will usually need to monitor and promote cooperation among group members to achieve academic and motivational benefits.

4. COOPERATIVE LEARNING AND FLEXIBLE GROUPING. Another alternative to homogeneous groupings is for teachers to form cooperative learning groups of four or five students. These mixed-ability learning teams are monitored and rewarded for individual as well as group accomplishments. Stevens, Madden, Slavin, and Farnish (1987) worked on ways to manage this approach for reading and writing lessons. Basically, they recommend a cycle of four activities:

1. Teacher instruction to the group.
2. Team practice in which students work in teams to master the material, using materials assigned by the teacher or determined in coordination with the team. Depending on the specificity of the material, students could work on items and check answers with one another, reach and discuss common answers, read and discuss story information, and assess one another to make certain that everyone on the team will succeed on individual assignments.
3. Individual assessment by the teacher on students' knowledge of the information or skill in accomplishing the task.
4. Team recognition, with students' scores on individual assessments summed to form team scores that are used to earn certificates or other honors.

Stevens and his colleagues describe one application of this cycle in which students work on a story and followup activities in pairs. After reading a text silently, they read to each other and help each other with difficult words and obscure ideas until they can read fluently and with understanding. They receive questions about the story, grammar, and new words and work together to answer these questions and write their personal response to the story. They might also practice new and difficult words with their partner, summarize or paraphrase the main points of the story, and pretest each other on spelling words.

Additionally, once a week teachers provide whole-class instruction on a reading comprehension skill, after which partners join with another pair to work on followup assignments. Twice a week teachers provide whole-class lessons on specific writing and language mechanics, and three times a week students are involved in writing activities in which they plan, draft, review, revise, and edit their pieces, again with the support and advice of team members and conferences with the teacher. They also share their writings in whole-class meetings.

This is an elaborate cooperative learning plan that was successfully carried out by third- and fourth-grade teachers. In both grades teachers assigned two hours per day to the reading and language arts lessons, so a number of aspects of this approach could be applied to the reading and writing workshop periods that we advocate here.

KEY CONCEPT **4**   READING AND WRITING GOALS ARE BETTER ACHIEVED WHEN STUDENTS ARE MOTIVATED AND HAVE THE DRIVE TO LEARN.

MOTIVATING STUDENTS

Teachers obviously want all of their students to be motivated to learn and voluntarily to assume responsibility for their own learning. Most high-achieving students are already self-motivated and self-directed. Presenting them with good learning activities and interesting reading materials is usually sufficient. But lower-achieving students often need something more. Modifying instruction in several ways can inspire these students to want to learn and be more willing to try.

Modifying the Classroom Environment

Unlike high achievers, low-achieving students typically have decreasing motivation to learn over the years they attend elementary school, according to Ames (1990, 1992b). Fortunately, she found

TARGET Area	Strategies
Task	Design tasks for novelty, variety, individual challenge, and active involvement. Help students set realistic, short-term goals. Help students develop organizational skills for task completion.
Authority	Involve students in decision-making and leadership roles. Help students develop self-management and self-monitoring skills.
Recognition	Recognize individual progress and improvement. Assure equal opportunities for rewards.
Grouping	Use flexible and heterogeneous grouping arrangements. Involve students in group learning.
Evaluation	Give opportunities to improve. Use criteria of individual progress, improvement, and mastery. Involve students in self-evaluation. Make evaluation private and meaningful.
Time	Adjust time or task requirements. Use flexible scheduling. Help students organize and manage their work.

FIGURE 6.2
Instructional Strategies Within TARGET Areas
Source: After Epstein, 1988, 1989; from Ames annual meeting of the American Educational Research Association, Boston, April 1990.

that teachers can regain students' motivation to learn in school. Her approach is to train teachers to shift classroom practices so that students learn to identify, work on, and master their own academic goals. This orientation involves modifying six dimensions of the classroom learning environment, dimensions that Joyce Epstein (1988, 1989) initially identified using the acronym TARGET (see Figure 6.2).

Tasks in readers' and writers' workshops should be interesting, challenging, and varied, but not overwhelming. For example, the experience phase of ETR (Chapter 3) makes book reading personally interesting, and the succeeding story discussion can vary to fit the type of story and story focus. Having students keep portfolios in which they collect and review their work weekly or monthly helps to assure that they will establish clearly defined reasons for doing tasks. Well-defined, short-term goals are necessary for low achievers in particular, because they need to manage more of the work on their own and then see themselves making progress. Short-term goals also should be alternated with long-term goals when students are reading long stories or novels and engaged in lengthy projects.

To make sure that students are motivated to begin a new assignment, such as a new story, teachers might read an opening segment or, as Jessie did in Chapter 3, pique students' curiosity with a brief introduction. Then, they can observe students as they begin the work, since that is often the hardest time for students, and help them review plans and goals or consider alternative projects.

The *authority* dimension focuses on increasing student responsibility. This can occur if everyone participates in classroom processes, from establishing rules to setting up task goals and selecting and accomplishing assignments. One result is that a number of leadership roles can be turned over to students. Teachers need to monitor the sharing of roles, however, by making sure that girls as well as boys and low as well as high achievers have opportunities to be successful leaders. Sometimes this means coaching students about how to be a leader, helping them select appropriate leadership activities, or helping them achieve expertise in an area in which they want to be a leader. There are usually many opportunities during the workshops for students to advise one another, choose from among books to read and topics to write about, discuss goals and ways to achieve them with the teacher and classmates, and set up guidelines for completing projects and tasks. Opportunities such as these enable students to assume responsibilities and lend them a sense of personal control over what they are learning as well as a sense of ownership over their accomplishments.

Recognition involves noticing students' efforts and improvements, not merely their accomplishments, which increases the likelihood that all students will be noticed. Recognitions and rewards should be confidential so they can't be used for social comparison. A pat on the shoulder, a brief note at the bottom of a student's paper, and a detailed response to portfolio work are simple but meaningful rewards. Recognition should be used for specific but laudable attainments so that students know clearly why they are being recognized and will connect it with hard work and effort. These steps help students to attend to their efforts to learn and the process of achievement, not merely to the outcome, and so promotes greater self-motivation.

Grouping arrangements can be varied so that students have opportunities to work with different classmates in small groups, based on common interests for some tasks, on common, group-identified objectives for others, and on reading ability at other times. These flexible assignments and alternate groupings encourage cooperation and enable students to coach one another as well as to assume more control over their learning.

Evaluation can be an ongoing part of classroom events with the use of writing portfolios and literature response logs. For example, as described in Chapter 7, Joyce has third graders write about what they have learned and what their new goals are each month. Then they talk with a partner about what they have learned and what they ought next to accomplish, perhaps then modifying their new goals or plans. Jessie has fifth graders create a "showcase portfolio" each quarter, a shared teacher-student evaluation of progress for parents to view, comment on, and write in. The portfolio contains a reading response log piece, a writing piece, comments by students and the teacher, and students' cumulative voluntary reading list.

Before having students take their end-of-year, nationally normed, group achievement tests, teachers can explain to students how to take the tests (Chapter 7) so that they understand how and why these tests are unlike their regular reading and writing activities. If teachers also give end-of-unit or ongoing progress tests, they can offer test retake opportunities so that students can work toward improvement.

Teachers may want to evaluate students informally. They can listen to students read and discuss materials they have read and written about, review students' written responses to their reading and their written pieces, and look over students' self-evaluations. Viewing many different facets of students' competencies gives teachers more valid and fairer evaluations of their progress. They can help students see that earlier attempts to read or write need not be reminders of failure but signs of progress and can help them understand what and how they are learning. Students are then more likely to compare their performance with their own past efforts and not against others in the class.

The *time* dimension pertains to matters such as workload, instructional pace, and allotment of time for completion of assignments and projects. The teachers adapt these factors to differences in individual students' ability and rates of working by allowing students opportunities to plan their schedules and time commitments. Then students will be better able to complete their work despite these individual differences.

With TARGET, students will feel more motivated to learn because the teachers consider every dimension of the learning process. Moreover, all students can become an integral part of their classroom group and feel that they are constructive participants. Positive perceptions about their progress as learners and about their role in determining school tasks and goals will influence how they approach learning and use their time. These perceptions will also have a positive influence on their judgments about their ability, their willingness to apply strategies, and their feelings of satisfaction. Tasks will become personally relevant and meaningful and offer personal challenges. Students will have a better sense of control over process or product, and they will be encouraged to create intrinsic purposes for learning. They will be more likely to believe that they can accomplish a task if they make a reasonable effort. Overall, then, students will be more fully and actively engaged in their work and managing their learning.

Volition

A belief that they can learn, an interest in learning, and a willingness to put forth effort to learn, however, may not be sufficient to sustain all students. They also have to understand *how* to work effectively and successfully. Classroom TARGET dimensions lead to an interest in learning and a willingness to try, but, as Lyn Corno (1993) explained, students must also understand how to apply themselves to their school work. "Volition is taken to mean 'strength of will....' Adjectives include, for example, conscientious, disciplined, self-directed, resourceful, and striving. All imply an ability to buckle down to tasks that goes beyond goal-directedness or persistence in the face of difficulty. To do something 'of one's own volition' is to do it by one's own resources and sustained efforts, independent of external source or pressure" (p. 14).

Volition can be applied to classroom activities in terms of cognition and self-management (see Thomas, Strage, and Curley, 1988). These activities are summarized in Figure 6.3 and described next.

COGNITIVE ACTIVITIES. The cognitive activities of selecting, comprehending, remembering, integrating, and monitoring are components in the process of learning. Students need to incorporate them so they can take charge of their learning. We suggest ways to convey each of these concepts to students.

Selection activities can be rephrased for students as "My Plans." Student plans can be made through responses to four questions:

1. Where will I find materials that fit my goals?
2. What information do I need?
3. How will I record the information?
4. How will I use the information?

For example, in Chapter 4, Joyce has third graders initiate research on birds. She prepares them by making available a large set of books, pointing out particularly good books, reviewing with students what they already know about their topic, and having them consider and write out what they want to learn. After students share the information with a partner, she reminds them to refer back to what they wanted to learn as they choose materials, decide what to record and how, and make sure that the information fits their purpose. This is a hard step for some students, so she observes them carefully, has them work with partners, and coaches in-

Cognitive activities:	
Selection *(activities that facilitate focusing selectively on material)*	Seeking out criterion information Differentiating important from unimportant information Recording important information Organizing and highlighting information
Comprehension *(activities that enhance understanding of the material)*	Previewing the material Noting hard-to-understand points Using context cues Consulting resources and references
Memory enhancement *(activities that enhance the memorability of the material)*	Reviewing the material Using mnemonic strategies Using self-testing methods Making memory aids (charts, flashcards) Matching study strategies to memory demands of the test
Integration *(activities that promote integration and the construction of relations)*	Putting material in one's own words Construct ideas/answers that go beyond the information given Using relational aids (diagrams, time lines) Relating information across sources Relating course content to prior knowledge
Cognitive monitoring *(activities that serve to monitor learning and evaluate progress)*	Knowing what you haven't yet mastered Keeping track of personal strengths and weaknesses in processing skill
Self-management activities:	
Time management *(activities that provide the opportunity to learn)*	Establishing sufficient time to complete activities Keeping track of time Scheduling time Meeting time commitments Distributing time over tasks
Effort management *(activities that serve to promote and maintain the disposition to learn)*	Establishing a productive study environment Setting learning and achievement goals Initiating effort Securing the necessary materials Maintaining attention and avoiding distractions Providing incentives to learn
Volitional monitoring *(activities that serve to monitor and evaluate the productivity of one's study habits)*	Keeping track of the adequacy of time and effort management activities Monitoring attention Assessing strengths and weaknesses in study habits

FIGURE 6.3
Classes of Self-Directed Learning Activities
Source: Thomas, Strage, & Curley, 1988. Reprinted by permission of The University of Chicago Press.

dividuals as needed by asking them to review with her their goals and plans.

Comprehension activities can be termed "Actions." A number of possible actions could be employed by students as they read and record information, so Joyce lists some actions on the board to remind them to use book and text cues as they study the materials and to write relevant information in their notes. She recommends that they look for the name of their bird in the table of contents, the index, and chapter headings. They quick read to find information about the bird by scanning, reading headings, and reading first and last sentences. They record important and interesting information using their own words. To help students carry out these tasks on their own, Joyce models her comprehension and recording activities and then has students present some of their approaches.

Memory enhancement and integration can be termed "Remembering" and "Connecting." Remembering involves reviewing material, using memory aids or mnemonic strategies, and self-testing what has been learned. This was not relevant to the bird research project. However, Joyce does want students to connect and integrate new with known material. Their K-W-L summary sheet helps; they can see simultaneously what they knew, what they wanted to learn, and what they had learned. This summary sheet also makes it easier for them to restate the important ideas in their own words, go beyond the text information in their discussions and written reports, and discuss how they related the new information to material they already knew.

To monitor their cognitions, teachers remind students to "Check and Evaluate." To do this, Joyce sets up conferences with students, reviewing their drafts and reminding them about how to check that the material they were gathering fits their plans and goals and that the project is still feasible. Students know that their plans and goals are guidelines that can be adjusted if they find more interesting or more relevant information.

SELF-MANAGEMENT ACTIVITIES. Self-management has been described in a number of ways in this chapter; to present it from the perspective of the student, it can be termed "Managing My Work." There are three aspects: management of time dimensions, management of effort, and monitoring progress.

Students need to become responsible for managing their time wisely. Joyce helps them set up long-term, realistic timelines and targets for work completion. She also supports daily progress and short-term goals by discussing plans at the beginning of the workshop period and success in meeting the goals at the end of the session.

Effort management means discussing with students productive ways of setting up their projects. Joyce helps them choose appropriate materials. She makes sure that their questions keep them focused on their goal rather than divert or distract them from it. She also encourages them to maintain their efforts even with a difficult assignment or a lengthy project.

Monitoring progress involves discussing how to view and appreciate progress. Joyce points out improvements in note taking and in writing and editing the reports. She also demonstrates ways for students to appraise their success in achieving their goal and has them check that their report answered their questions. She conveys much of this information in conferences with students. Then, as students became familiar with her suggestions and advice, she hears them questioning, coaching, and advising one another in similar ways.

Teachers can support students' efforts to accomplish their learning goals and offer concrete suggestions and strategies for carrying out their plans and goals successfully. When teachers combine motivational dimensions of learning with techniques to accomplish tasks, students become more interested in learning, make an effort, and sustain it to its completion.

SUMMARY

Social, motivational, and volitional dimensions of teaching reading and writing broaden and complicate instructional models, and these changes mark a major modification in conceptions of effective classroom instruction. Nonetheless, they add dimensions of learning that experienced teachers have long known. How teachers interact with students, how they inspire them to become interested in literacy, and how they persuade them to take on challenging projects for their own good are and have always been essential aspects of effective teaching.

The first key concept describes how a prosocial environment establishes a cooperative rather than competitive environment and gives students partnership roles in setting up workshop projects and in developing team responsibilities for learning.

The second key concept suggests behind-the-scene dimensions for managing a classroom. Teachers can set up rules, routines, materials, and schedules, in collaboration with students. They can also adjust seating arrangements, success rates, and lesson processes based on input from students. With the advice and active involvement of students, classroom management becomes a joint responsibility.

The third key concept presents issues about grouping students for instruction. Different grouping patterns achieve different goals, but readers' and writers' workshops allow a more integrated approach. Also, groupings are flexible and lead students toward noticing differing talents among their classmates and working in cooperative structures.

Finally, the fourth key concept describes how motivation and volition play crucial roles. When students play a more substantial role in organizing their reading and writing goals, and when they are coached about how to direct their own learning and work in collaboration with classmates, they are more likely to be motivated to learn, to assume responsibility for their own learning, and to continue making an effort to learn even when it is difficult for them.

◀ **ACTIVITES**

Reflecting on Your Own Literacy

Think back to when you were in elementary school. Choose one year when you were in the primary grades (kindergarten through third grade) and one year when you were in the intermediate grades (fourth through sixth grade). For each of these years, describe how your teacher organized the classroom. What say did students have in the way the classroom was run? Did literacy instruction occur mainly through whole-class, small-group, or individual instruction? Was the emphasis on competition or cooperation? How did the teacher recognize student achievement? Then, on the basis of what you have learned in this chapter, describe what you would wish to keep the same, and what you would wish to change, about each of these classrooms.

Applying What You Have Learned to the Classroom

Observe in a classroom for the morning or, if possible, a full day. Listen and watch for prosocial behavior by students toward one another and modeled by the teacher. Look for private and unobtrusive recognitions of achievement, community governance (student-assisted classroom management), student input about work plans and activities, collaborative learning and support, encouragement, and students helping one another. Be as objective as possible. Describe the observed prosocial behavior and write down exactly what is said and done. Then offer your interpretation or reaction to the events. Finally, review your observations and comments. When do students make prosocial contacts with one another? How does the teacher foster prosocial interactions? How might they be increased?

BIBLIOGRAPHY

References

Allington, R. (1983). The reading instruction provided readers of differing ability. *Elementary School Journal, 83,* 548–559.

Ames, C. (1990). Achievement goals and classroom structure: Developing a learning orientation in students. Paper presented at the annual meeting of the American Educational Research Association, Boston.

Ames, C. (1992a). Classrooms: Goals, structures, and student motivation. *Journal of Educational Psychology, 84,* 261–271.

Ames, C. (1992b). Achievement goals and the classroom motivational climate. In J. Meece & D. Schunk (Eds.), *Students' perceptions in the classroom.* Hillsdale, NJ: Erlbaum, pp. 327–348.

Anderson, L., Evertson, C., & Brophy, J. (1982). *Principles of small-group instruction in elementary reading.* (Occsasional Paper #58). East Lansing, MI: Institute for Research on Teaching, Michigan State University.

Anderson, L., Stevens, D., Prawat, R., & Nickerson, J. (1988). Classroom task environments and students' task-related beliefs. *The Elementary School Journal, 88,* 281–296.

Benninga, J. S., Tracz, S. M., Sparks, R. K., Jr., Solomon, D., Battistich, V., Delucchi, K. L., Sandoval, R., & Stanley, B. (1991). Effects of two contrasting school tasks and incentive structures on children's social development. *The Elementary School Journal, 92,* 149–168.

Brophy, J. (1984). The teacher as thinker: Implementing instruction. In G. Duffy, L. Roehler, & J. Mason (Eds.), *Comprehension instructions: Perspectives and suggestions.* New York: Longman.

Butler, A., & Turbill, J. (1984). *Toward a reading-writing classroom.* Rosebery, Australia: Bridge Printery Pty Ltd.

Corno, L. (1993). The best-laid plans: Modern conceptions of volition and educational research. *Educational Researcher,* March, 14–22.

Epstein, J. (1988). Effective schools or effective students: Dealing with diversity. In R. Haskins & D. Macrae (Eds.), *Policies for America's public schools: Teacher equity indicators.* Norwood, NJ: Ablex.

Epstein, J. (1989). Family structures and student motivation: A developmental perspective. In C. Ames & R. Ames (Eds.), *Research on motivation in education,* vol. 3. New York: Academic Press, pp. 259–295.

Hallinan, M. (1984). Summary and conclusions. In P. Peterson, L. Wilkinson, & M. Hallinan (Eds.), *The social context of instruction: Group organization and group processes.* New York: Academic Press.

Marshall, H., & Weinstein, R. (1984). Classroom factors affecting students' self-evaluations: An interactional model. *Review of Educational Research, 54,* 301–326.

Marx, R., & Walsh, J. (1988). Learning from academic tasks. *The Elementary School Journal, 88,* 207–220.

Morine-Dershimer, G. (1983). Instructional strategy and the "creation" of classroom status. *American Educational Research Journal, 20,* 645–662.

Noddings, N. (1992). *The challenge to care in schools.* New York: Teachers College, Columbia University.

Paley, V. (1992). *You can't say you can't play.* Cambridge, MA: Harvard University Press.

Smith, M., & Misra, A. (1992). A comprehensive management system for students in regular classrooms. *The Elementary School Journal, 92,* 353–371.

Stevens, R., Madden, N., Slavin, R., & Farnish, A. (1987). Cooperative integrated reading and composition: Two field experiments. *Reading Research Quarterly, 22,* 433–454.

Thomas, J., Strage, A., & Curley, R. (1988). Improving students' self-directed learning: Issues and guidelines. *The Elementary School Journal, 88,* 313–326.

Webb, N., & Cullian, L. (1983). Group interaction and achievement in small groups: Stability over time. *American Educational Research Journal, 20,* 411–423.

Webb, N., & Kenderski, C. (1984). Student interaction and learning in small-group and whole-class settings. In P. Peterson, L. Wilkinson, & M. Hallinan (Eds.), *The social context of instruction: Group organization and group processes.* New York: Academic Press.

Further Reading

Doyle, W. (1986). Classroom organization and management. In M. Wittrock (Ed.), *Handbook of research on teaching* (3rd ed.). New York: Macmillan, pp. 392–431.

Routman, R. (1991). *Invitations: Changing as Teachers and Learners K–12.* Portsmouth, NH: Heinemann.

Solomon, D., Watson, M., Schaps, E., Battistich, V., & Solomon, J. (1990). Cooperative learning as part of a comprehensive program designed to promote prosocial development. In S. Sharan (Ed.), *Cooperative learning: Theory and research.* New York: Praeger, pp. 231–260.

Webb, N. (1982). Student interaction and learning in small groups. *Review of Educational Research, 52,* 421–445.

7 ASSESSING PROGRESS AND EVALUATING INSTRUCTION

An administrator responded to questions concerning the results of the school's child-centered, active approach to learning.

"The bottom line is, we don't have graffiti on our walls. The bottom line is that we have an increasing number of students who are graduating out of our high schools with higher and higher skills. The bottom line is that our businesses are telling us that we're doing better, or not doing better. The bottom line is that parents are telling us we're satisfied, or not satisfied. The bottom line is that we're still getting the best people in our classes as teachers."

"In other words, the bottom line, as far as you're concerned is not just a simple score on a test."

"A simple score on a test, in a multicultural, multiracial society, is the kiss of death to opportunity for all people."

"Why?"

"Because it negates the past of people! Would you give a test tomorrow morning in this school, or in an elementary school, when you know that in that classroom you're going to have children who two days ago were in Managua, in the middle of a civil war? Would you give a test—the same test—to a child who is sitting next to this youngster, who has grown up in an upper-middle-class neighborhood, who has only known English, and whose parents are university professors? Would you give the same test to a child who also comes from a middle-class background, but who hasn't had breakfast, and whose parents just had a fight and are about to split? The same test? The same morning? And would you say that this is an objective way of finding out what kids know? That it's reasonable? That it's the bottom line? Even business doesn't do that! Even business doesn't treat their employees that way. Why do we treat kids that way?" (Brown 1991, p. 226–227)

◀ OVERVIEW

First we will look at three classrooms to consider some of the ways first-grade teacher Joan Lyons, third-grade teacher Joyce Souza, and fifth-grade teacher Jessie Michaels assess and evaluate their students' literacy learning. Then, in the key concepts, we distinguish three assessment goals and offer a way to integrate them. The three assessment goals are drawn from work by Linda Vavrus and Robert Calfee (1988). One goal is for assessment results to guide teachers' planning and to help them improve their instruction in the classroom. A second is to help monitor students' growth and progress, and a third is to provide appropriate information about individual students who may need special instruction or services.

The first key concept describes initial assessment goals. The goals include measures of students' literacy development and background knowledge, which teachers can use to plan their instruction. The second key concept presents ongoing assessment goals. We suggest ways to monitor and record students' literacy growth over time. The third key concept explains focused assessment, or ways to understand how to teach students who present significant problems or challenges. Finally, in the fourth key concept we present an integrated plan that you can use to weave the three goals into your instruction.

KEY CONCEPT 1: Teachers should assess students at the beginning of the school year to gain information about their background knowledge and literacy development.

KEY CONCEPT 2: Teachers should use portfolios to monitor and record student progress throughout the school year.

KEY CONCEPT 3: Teachers may use focused assessment of individual students to gain special insights into their strengths and needs.

KEY CONCEPT 4: Teachers should integrate assessment with classroom instruction, recognizing the inseparability of instruction and assessment.

◀ PERSPECTIVE

Assessment in Three Classrooms

First Graders Prepare For Standardized Testing

It is May, and three first graders are involved with folders containing samples of their work in reading and writing from throughout the school year.

Shelly: Look, Karla and Dan. See how I used to write. I only made capitals. Now I write lower-case letters too. And look. I never used to put periods.

Karla: Look at the books I read in September. Baby books! This week I read *Henry and Mudge* [Rylant, 1987]. It's a chapter book, you know.

Shelly: Here's what I wrote about *Amelia Bedelia* [Parish, 1963]. It's my favorite book because she is so silly. She gets things all mixed up. I read some other books about her too.

Dan: Here's my reading tape. In September I read, "Here . . . is . . . some . . . bread. Here . . . is . . . some . . . mmmmeat." This time I taped *Mice at Bat* [Oechsli, 1986]. I read it fast. It is easy for me now.

These first-grade children have been actively involved in evaluating their learning throughout the school year. Joan Lyons has encouraged them to save their written responses to literature, lists of book titles they have read, audiotapes of their oral reading, and stories they have written. Two plastic crates sit on a bookshelf and contain folders for each child. The children have easy access to their folders and have been adding things and noting their progress throughout the year. Joan Lyons has helped the children articulate personal learning goals and decide how they might meet them. The children often speak of their growth as readers and writers; they are proud of their accomplishments.

As Joan Lyons watches and listens to these young readers and writers she is confident in her knowledge of their strengths and needs. In addition to the products the children saved, Joan has regularly used sticky labels to record evidence of her students' literacy development. The children add the labels to a special form in their folders. Joan has regularly recorded the children's behaviors as they read aloud to help her understand their use of text cues such as context and letter sounds. And she has maintained records to help her monitor student growth and to guide her instruction (see Figure 7.6 for an example of a teacher-developed checklist).

Yet, now it is May and Joan Lyons has been feeling a tinge of discomfort. Standardized tests will be administered to her first graders soon. How will the children respond to them? How will they perform? Joan discovered an article by a first-grade teacher (Reardon, 1990) that suggested ways to prepare children instructed in a literature-based approach for standardized testing, and decided to adapt that teacher's ideas.

After this morning's read-aloud from *Puss in Boots* (Brown, 1952), Joan Lyons asked what kind of book or genre the children thought it was. They identified it as a fairy tale and talked briefly about other books and genres they had recently read.

Teacher: Today we will find out about another kind of reading—reading-test reading.

Joan Lyons gave the children a practice page from a standardized test. She asked them to read the page and write anything that they noticed. Then they gathered together to share their discoveries.

Kenji: It's short. Not like stories in books.

Karla: It's not really a story. It's only part of a story.

Verner: There aren't any pictures.

Shelly: There are questions, then A, B, C.
Sam: What do they mean, A, B, C?

After further sharing, Joan Lyons used the children's ideas to form a list of the features of reading-test reading (adapted from Reardon, 1990, p. 34):

You can tell reading-test reading by the way it looks.

It has no pictures.

It has questions and you can choose only one answer.

The stories on the page don't all go together.

The stories aren't whole stories.

You shouldn't think what the stories mean to you. Just answer the questions.

It's tricky like a puzzle or code.

During the next few days, Joan plans to have the children work with a portion of the practice test booklet for about 20 minutes of each readers' workshop. She will encourage them to work with partners just as they normally do when they read and share books with one another. Each day they will come together to compare their insights and discoveries about this "new" kind of reading.

Third Graders Use Portfolios

Joyce Souza remembers when she thought of assessment as the annual standardized test and the end-of-unit measures in the basal reading series. Only recently has she come to place more value on her own judgment and insights as an evaluator of student learning.

The day before school began two years ago, Joyce opened the packet of cumulative files passed on from last year's second grade teachers in order to learn about her new students. She had planned to form tentative reading groups based on the children's results from the standardized test given the previous spring.

As Joyce looked through the files, she noted that one second grade teacher had also included end-of-the-year work samples for each of her students. That teacher had attached her own written comments to each child's work and the students had written personal letters that began, "Dear Third-Grade Teacher." In their letters the children told what they thought they had learned about reading and writing in second grade and what they hoped to learn as third graders. Joyce learned that Brandi's favorite author was Mercer Mayer and that Brandi plans to read "hard books" in third grade. She noted that most of Frederick's written responses included cleverly drawn illustrations. Frederick was looking forward to reading "interesting nature books." Joyce reflected on how much more she knew about these children's literacy development from their work samples and the accompanying comments than she learned from the test scores of the other students.

Last year Joyce decided to join other teachers in her school to explore portfolio assessment. She was not sure of the exact techniques or procedures involved, but she was committed to trying. She believed that with the support of her colleagues, they would all learn together. And they did.

Now that Joyce is using portfolios for a second year, she feels much more confident. During the two years she has explored a variety of assessment procedures, learned from mistakes, and has continued to make refinements. She believes her efforts have been rewarded by an increased knowledge of each student's literacy development and her greater awareness of them as people.

 Today is the last school day of February and, as in previous months, the students will use the language arts period to review their portfolios. Each month the children choose a written response to literature and a piece of personal writing for their portfolios. Joyce asks that they write down their reasons for choosing the piece, what they learned, and their new goals, and staple them to their selected pieces.

The literature responses that the children chose this month show the usual variety. Chantelle has selected a comparison between Rebecca's search for the ovenbird in *One Day in the Woods* (George, 1988) to a time when she and her family heard a woodpecker and tried to locate it. Chantelle said she chose that piece because she and her family "had a *very* fun time that day." She learned that "the author probably likes to explore the woods like my family does." Her future goal is "to read more nature books." Matt selected his retelling of *Saving the Peregrine Falcon* (Arnold, 1985), which includes his interpretation of the author's message. He said he chose it "because I wrote a lot of details," he learned "why people want to save the falcon," and his future goal is to "learn more about endangered birds."

This month Joyce asked all the students to include their research reports in their portfolios. A few students have chosen additional pieces as well. She asks them to evaluate their reports by noting how much they have learned.

> *Teacher:* Look back at your K-W-L sheets [see Figure 4.4]. How can you tell you have learned new information about your birds?
>
> *Jermaine:* There's lots of information in my *L* columns and just a little in the *K* column.
>
> *Ryan:* I checked off five of my questions in the *W* column because I found the answers.

Joyce also focuses the students on their growth in the research process.

Teacher: Think about writing your first report on mammals. Was doing the research easier this time? Think about the kinds of books you used and how you wrote and organized your information.

Matt: Alphabetical order! In the encyclopedias you gotta look at the second letter . . . and the third letter. . . . (The children laugh as they remember their struggles and insights during mini-lessons on locating information about their topics.)

Randi: My notes are shorter. I don't write whole sentences any more. I read a section, close my book, and just write the important information I remember.

Teacher: Good ideas! How about the informational books we shared together?

Boyd: They gave us ideas for how to write our reports.

Next Joyce Souza asked the children to spend some time rereading their K-W-L questions and notes, their drafts, and their final reports.

Teacher: Then I'd like you to write an evaluation. (She writes on board.)

1. The most important things I learned by doing this project are _____ .

2. How I feel about this project _____ .

3. My goals for my next research project are _____ .

Teacher: After you have written your evaluation, you should talk it over with a partner. Your partner may have some ideas that you will want to add. I will meet with Jamal, Karl, Chantelle, and Dede to discuss their projects.

Joyce has been pleased to note the growing sophistication in her students' evaluative comments. In September they measured their growth in terms of "knowing all the words" and "reading thick books." Through regular discussion and practice they have become more aware of how they are learning and what is helpful to them as learners. Her evaluations of Jamal, Karl, and Dede indicate that they will benefit from some additional support. Because Chantelle and Dede worked together on their project, Joyce included Chantelle in the group. Joyce thinks Chantelle will provide a good model for the other three students as they discuss their evaluations together.

After the children have written their evaluations, Joyce will fill in the checklists that she and her colleagues developed to highlight student goals and achievement (see Figures 7.3 and 7.6 for examples of teacher-developed checklists). Joyce finds these checklists helpful in providing her with information about her students' strengths and needs. They also suggest instruction she should provide for individuals, small groups, and whole-class mini-lessons.

Fifth Graders Reflect on Their Own Literacy

Jessie Michaels began the school year by asking her students to consider the questions "What is reading?" and "What is writing?" As the students responded she recorded their ideas on chart paper. When Jessie reviewed the responses she noted the range of their knowledge about the functions and uses of literacy.

To Darrah reading meant "being able to understand a story"; Tonya had offered, "When you look at words to figure out a story," and Travis had said, "Knowing the ideas, the action, what's happening!" In defining writing the students' responses included "communication," "using words," "explaining something," and to sensitive Mariko, "explaining your feelings."

Jessie has planned for her students to be involved in monitoring their own literacy learning throughout the school year. This initial discussion began the process.

Next Jessie asked her students to consider what they do well as readers and writers. She suggested that they look through their literature response logs and their writing folders and write down their ideas. Later, she asked each student to share an accomplishment with the group.

Guillermo shared, "I am learning how to understand the book and its meaning." Robyn said, "I can concentrate when I read and not get distracted." Edouard noted, "I remember to put the correct punctuation at the end of a sentence."

Then Jessie felt that the students were ready to begin forming their own goals for learning. She explained that they would be setting goals, working toward them, reviewing their goals, and formulating new ones throughout the school year. She suggested that they return to their logs and folders to think about what they might want to work on next. What could they do to become better readers and writers?

After that, the students shared their discoveries in another group discussion. This discussion helped them clarify their goals, react to one another's ideas, and consider whether their proposals were realistic. As students committed to personal goals, they wrote them on forms that they dated and stapled in their reading logs and writing folders.

Every week Jessie takes a few minutes for the students to review their goals, to look for evidence that they are working toward them, and to share with a partner what they have done. Then Jessie asks a few students to share with the whole class. This activity serves to remind the students of their goals and reflect on their accomplishments.

On this day in late October, Jessie is introducing the idea of *showcase portfolios* to her students.

Teacher: So far this year we have been thinking about our growth as readers and writers. What have we done?

Several children contribute to a review of their ongoing involvement in setting and working toward goals.

Teacher: Today I want to share a special way that we will be able to show to one another, as well as to your parents, that you are, indeed, growing as readers and writers. This year each of you will create a folder of your special work. We will call it a showcase portfolio. Every quarter you will place at least one piece from your reading response log, and one finished piece of writing along with your notes and drafts, into this portfolio. Your voluntary reading lists will go there too. Five of my students from last year let me borrow their portfolios so that I could share them with you. You'll notice that all five are different in the cover design and how they are organized. These students also chose to include additional information that they thought was unique or special about them as readers and writers. But each portfolio is the same in that it has the students' goal sheets, a table of contents, at least four reading and writing samples, book lists, comments about the work written by that student, other students, me, and often the student's parents. Questions?

Darrah: How do we know what to put in?

Teacher: Let's talk about that. Ideas?

Through their discussion the students concluded that the reading and writing pieces they select should be pieces they are especially proud of and will probably show that they are meeting their personal goals. They thought their selections should reflect their learning from text and reveal their personal interests. They also decided that the reading and writing they do as special projects or outside school could be important additions to their showcase portfolios.

Robyn: My mom always says, "How are you doing in school?" Sometimes I don't know what to tell her. I should show her my portfolio.

KEY CONCEPT 1 TEACHERS SHOULD ASSESS STUDENTS AT THE BEGINNING OF THE SCHOOL YEAR TO GAIN INFORMATION ABOUT THEIR BACKGROUND KNOWLEDGE AND LITERACY DEVELOPMENT.

AN EXPANDED VIEW OF ABILITY

Traditionally, assessment of students has drawn upon only two aspects of ability: verbal or linguistic abilities, and logical or mathematical abilities. Although these two aspects predict how well students are likely to do in school, they are not adequate measures of their success after school.

But what about other abilities? When teachers are aware of their students' other abilities, they can better help them develop their full learning potential. For example, do students have musical, athletic, or analytic skills? Do they make friends easily, do they show leadership characteristics, and are they able to communicate their personal needs to others?

You might assess students at the beginning of every school year by gathering information about several dimensions of ability. You might construct a questionnaire for students and their parents to complete. You can talk with students and parents in order to learn about students' interests, their outside school activities, and their other strengths.

Some teachers begin the school year by sending letters like this one shared by Lucy Calkins (1990, p. 15):

> Dear Parents,
>
> I'm writing to ask you to help me become a partner with you in your child's education. I will only have your child for a short time in this trip through life—just one fleeting school year—and I want to make a contribution that lasts a lifetime.
>
> I know my teaching must begin with making your child feel at home in my classroom, and with helping all the children come together into a learning community made up of particular, unique individuals, each with his or her own learning style and interests and history and hopes. Would you help me teach well by taking a quiet moment to write me about your child? What is your youngster like? What are the things you, as a parent, know that would be important for me to know? What are the child's interests? I want to know how your child thinks and plays and how you see your child as a learner and a person.
>
> Respectfully yours,

You may also want to learn of the extent to which students' home and community environment supports schooling. Is English spoken at home? Have parents established a routine, such as reading to children in the early years and allowing them to read at bedtime or at another regular time? Do students read outside school and if so, what and how often? Given the importance of voluntary reading (a topic discussed in Chapter 8), you will want to know its extent as soon as possible. You might inquire about the availability of literacy materials, including library books, in the home and community and also about parents' understanding of the important role they need to play in monitoring their children's homework, encouraging out-of-school reading, and supervising television viewing.

As you noted at the beginning of this chapter, students' portfolios are sometimes shared as students move from grade to grade. The artifacts contained in the portfolios will provide insights into each student's special strengths and interests.

A FRAMEWORK FOR ASSESSMENT

The six aspects of literacy introduced in Chapter 1 (see Figure 1.2) provide a broad curriculum framework. Teachers who use such a curriculum framework to guide their instruction will find it logical to use the same framework as a guide for their assessment.

In earlier chapters you noted how teachers considered assessment a part of their ongoing instruction. This chapter further describes how student achievement can be monitored within a curriculum that recognizes the importance of both the affective and cognitive dimensions of literacy.

EXAMPLES OF BEGINNING-OF-THE-YEAR ASSESSMENT

Informal Assessment

FUNCTIONS OF LITERACY. How do your students use literacy in their daily lives? There are a number of questions that you could ask informally or give as a short written questionnaire. Here are some suggested topics.

Book sharing with friends

Use of school and community libraries

Opportunity to select and purchase books

Membership in book clubs

Subscription to children's magazines

Size of home library of books they can read

Amount of reading at home and whether it is a regular activity

Favorite book, author, or reading topic

Diary keeping

Use of writing for certain purposes

Amount, purpose, and type of out-of-school reading

Interest in particular topics or literature

Educational television viewing

In addition, question students about the time they spend with activities such as sports, music, art, TV viewing, and playing with friends. You can use the students' responses to compare the amount of time they engage in literacy activities with the time spent in other endeavors.

Hally Simmons has adapted an informal assessment developed by Maria Weiss and Ranae Hagen (1988) to show kindergarten children's awareness of the functions of print as defined by reading materials commonly found in a literate environment, and the children's view of the reasons for reading in our society. She shows each student reading materials one at a time as part of a group of three items, asking the child to identify the one item she names. (In their study, Weiss and Hagen used a storybook, menu, newspaper, telephone book, magazine, shopping list, letter, TV schedule, calendar, and set of directions.) If the child correctly identifies the item, Hally asks *why* people read that particular material. In the final portion of the interview she asks the child to pretend that he has met someone who knows nothing about reading. How would the child explain to that person why people read? As the child responds, Hally records his ideas.

By looking at students' responses to informal assessments such as these, teachers gain insight into their experiences with a variety of printed materials and learn how they view their uses to convey meaning. Teachers can also learn of the children's overall view of reading. Is it a meaningful and useful activity in which they want to engage?

BACKGROUND KNOWLEDGE OF TOPICS. Before establishing the major themes and topics for the school year, it is wise to determine how much information students already know. What background knowledge do they have? What topics does the whole class know next to nothing about? On which topics do students vary a great deal in their knowledge? Answers to all of these questions will help you plan your instruction.

Joyce Souza chose a word-association assessment suggested by Betty Holmes and Nancy Roser (1987) to use with her third graders. Because the larger theme of their year-long science and social studies curriculum is interdependence and conservation, she began their study by saying, "Tell me everything you can think of that relates to the word *conservation*." The students began by making individual lists in their learning logs and then brought these lists to the whole group. Joyce wrote CONSERVATION on a sheet of chart paper and then recorded the students' responses. As subtopics developed, Joyce asked the students to organize their sharing around the related ideas (see Figure 7.1).

Joyce finds this to be a relatively effective and efficient way to evaluate students' background knowledge. The knowledge she gains helps her determine her own instructional goals and assist her students in planning their individual goals.

METACOGNITION. Students ought to be asked how they learn and what strategies they use to read, write, study, remember information, and complete assignments. If you want to know about your class in general, your questions could be carried out through group

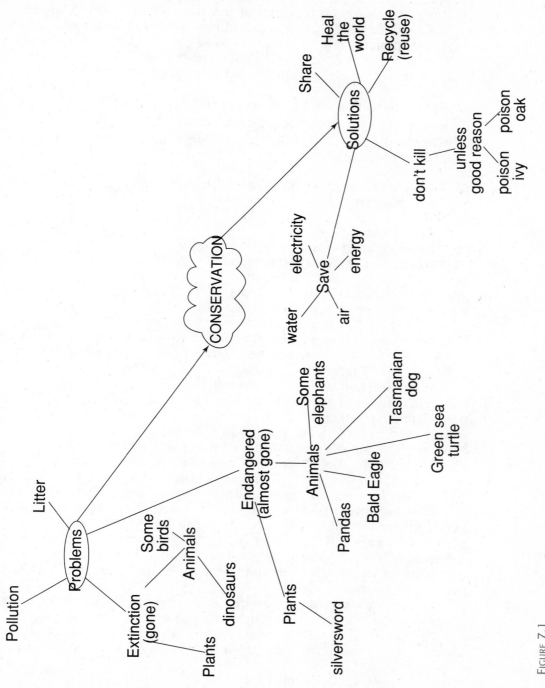

Figure 7.1
Word Association Assessment for *Conservation*

discussion. If you want to know about particular students' strategies, then individual interviews or written questionnaire responses will be needed. Here are some possible ways to ask questions about metacognition.

Scott Paris and colleagues (1992) asked third graders questions to learn of their understandings about literacy:

Do you think you are a good reader and writer?

What makes someone a really good reader?

When you think of yourself as a reader, what would you like to do differently or better?

Stupey and Knight (1988) asked three questions of three- to ten-year-old children:

1. What is reading?
2. What is reading for?
3. What do people do when they read?

Responses were evaluated in terms of four levels of ability: a single idea, relating one idea to another, relating one set of ideas to another set, and describing abstract relationships. They found that older children gave higher-level answers. You could use these questions, along with similar ones for writing, to help you understand your students' literacy awareness.

In unpublished work, Jana Mason and colleagues held a discussion with students at the end of kindergarten, first grade, and second grade. They asked them to talk about what next year's students would need to do to learn to read or to become better readers. After a five-minute discussion, students were given paper on which to draw or write the three ideas that they thought were the most important for next year's class. Those who drew or used invented spellings were asked to tell what they had drawn or written so that their ideas could be recorded. Even in kindergarten, most children could describe important ideas. This approach can be done at the beginning of first and subsequent grades; ask, "What do you think your class needs to learn this year to be good readers?" Variations in response will provide helpful information about students' awareness of the process of learning to read.

Jeanne Paratore and Roselmina Indrisano (1987) suggest a process interview that is intended to show how children view the reading process. Their interview questions, which include the following, can be asked in a written form for older students:

How do you choose something to read?

How do you get ready to read?

When you come to a word you can't read, what do you do?

If the text you are reading does not make sense, what do you do?

When you have a question you can't answer, what do you do?

What do you do to help remember what you've read?

How do you check your reading?

If a young child asked you how to read, what would you tell him/her to do?

Informal assessment measures like these will provide you with invaluable information about your students' literacy development and interests. The information will guide you in making instructional decisions for the class as a whole and for individual students.

Formal Assessment

Formal assessment information reporting on general concepts such as word attack, vocabulary, and comprehension will likely be available to you as you begin the school year. However, this information is usually reported as scores in these general areas, so teachers do not find it particularly useful.

You are probably familiar with these assessment instruments. Standardized testing took off in the mid 1940s and continues at nearly every level of schooling today. Standardized tests, with multiple-choice responses, are administered to large groups of students and, to reduce costs, are machine scored.

Norm-referenced, standardized tests are intended to show whether students have learned what others in the same grade typically have learned. That is, they assess students' performance in relation to the performance of a large, representative group of students. The scores represent overall achievement rather than a particular ability. In some schools the tests are given every year; in others they are used for sorting purposes, typically in the first, fourth, and seventh grades. Scores are likely to be in every child's cumulative folder to mark progress through school.

Typically, norm-referenced reading tests contain subtests of decoding, comprehension, and vocabulary to measure a student's relative success. You can examine and compare the reading achievement of your students with students the test makers have determined are typical. You can use the tests at the beginning of the school year to learn which students are below the norms for that grade and are likely to need a more concentrated reading program, and which are above and will benefit from an accelerated program. You cannot use them for diagnosis of individual students.

All items on a norm-referenced test are scored as either right or wrong. The total number that a student gets right is called a raw score. Interpretations are made from the raw score to compare students in terms of percentile ranks, stanines, and grade equivalents.

A *percentile rank* describes the likely rank of a student's score in terms of the percent of the total. A rank of 1 percent is given to students who score the lowest, 50 percent to students in the middle. A *stanine* is a number from one through nine; one represents the poorest performance, five is average, and nine is the best. Stanines are useful because they show each child's score in terms of deviations from the normed average, or the population mean. You can interpret a stanine of four, five, or six (or a percentile from 23 to 76) as representing a fairly typical score, a stanine of three (or a percentile from 11 to 22) as borderline, and a stanine of two (or a percentile from 4 to 10) as a low score. A stanine of seven (or a percentile of 77 to 88) represents an above-average score and eight (or a percentile from 89 to 95) is a high score. A score in stanine one (or a percentile from 0 to 3) is exceptionally low, while a score in stanine nine (or a percentile from 96 to 99) is exceptionally high.

A *grade-equivalent score* compares the performance of a child to the average performance of groups of children in the different grades. The number expresses level of reading achievement in grades and tenths of grades. For example, a score of 3.9 is supposed to mean the score that would be earned by the average third grader at the end of the school year.

We do not recommend relying on grade-equivalent scores because they do not have adequate statistical properties for making either comparisons among children or decisions about instruction. Particularly high and low scores cannot be reliably translated into reading materials. For example, a third grader who obtains a grade-equivalent score of 6.5 on a reading test is not necessarily reading at the sixth-grade level. Likewise, a third grader who tests at grade 1.5 may not need a first-grade book.

It is very important that you use standardized test information cautiously, since student motivation, interest, and anxiety levels can affect scores. Consider test scores to be just one indicator among many. The informal means of assessment that we discussed earlier can provide authentic information that is more valid to you as a teacher than that gained from inauthentic formal assessments, which simply provide ranking information. Assessment information is considered authentic if it is derived from actual literacy learning situations in the classroom. It is considered inauthentic if it is derived from a contrived testing situation unrelated to ongoing learning in the classroom. The formal tests do not divulge process information such as how a child is thinking, or particular content information, such as whether a child knows all letters of the alphabet. In the next key concepts, you will learn of some other effective ways to evaluate students' literacy development. By using multiple measures for evaluation you are able to form a more complete picture of your students and your instruction.

TEACHERS SHOULD USE PORTFOLIOS TO MONITOR AND RECORD STUDENT PROGRESS THROUGHOUT THE SCHOOL YEAR.

ONGOING MEASURES OF STUDENT PROGRESS

You have seen the value of using authentic materials such as children's literature for reading instruction and you recognize the importance of encouraging students to respond to their reading in authentic ways such as through literature discussions. Literacy instruction should be meaningful, ongoing, and occur in authentic contexts. So, too, should assessment. Portfolio assessment provides an authentic means for evaluating students' ongoing literacy growth and development.

> Authentic assessment is not a single method. It includes performance tests, such as conversations in a foreign language; observations, open-ended questions where students tackle a problem but there's no single right answer; exhibitions in which students choose their own ways to demonstrate what they have learned; interviews, giving students a chance to reflect on their achievement; and portfolios, collections of student work. The list is limited only by the criterion of authenticity, is this what we want students to know and be able to do? (Mitchell, 1989, p.5)

While portfolios are not the only form of authentic assessment, we believe that their structure and the values they represent provide a meaningful context for ongoing evaluation.

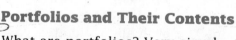

Portfolios and Their Contents

What are portfolios? Very simply, they are folders in which you and your students place a range of examples to represent their accomplishments over time; these examples can be used to plan and evaluate your teaching and students' progress. Several characteristics are important to a well-developed portfolio assessment system:

1. Assessment captures and capitalizes on the best each student has to offer, rather than criticizing or finding errors.
2. Assessment is an ongoing part of instruction. Teachers don't have to take time away from instruction, nor students from learning, for assessment to take place.

3. Assessment informs instruction. The process of learning is as important to record as the outcome of learning (the product).
4. Assessment is multidimensional, including cognitive, affective, and social processes.
5. Assessment provides for active, collaborative reflection by both teacher and student.
6. Assessment is authentic. Children are assessed while they are actually involved in literacy learning (Lamme & Hysmith, 1991, p. 629).

You will recognize that these characteristics underlie the portfolio systems described in all the classrooms at the beginning of this chapter, although use of portfolios in each classroom was unique. While the systems in those three classrooms present evidence of students' ongoing literacy development, and involve students as well as teachers in evaluation, they also represent the distinctive character, experiences, and members of each classroom. Diversity is expected and encouraged within a student portfolio system (Tierney, 1991, p. 42).

The students and teachers in the classrooms we described included a variety of items in their portfolios. The examples we shared are only a few of an almost limitless range of possibilities. When making selections it is helpful to think within categories; this will ensure a variety of indicators to build a complete picture of students' development (Valencia, 1990, p. 339). Our categorization of portfolio items includes observational notes, work samples, and record-keeping forms.

OBSERVATIONS. Shavelson and Stern suggest that informal observations of students engaging in authentic literacy events give teachers an opportunity to bring together their knowledge about how children become literate and their teacher intuition about why children perform in certain ways. This kind of reflection can form the basis of instructional decisions far more accurately than test scores (cited in Harp, 1991, p. 38). Teachers who conscientiously and systematically observe students come to view observational information as central to their evaluation strategies.

When teachers first begin observing and recording anecdotal notes, they are often concerned with the focus for their observations. Most important, teachers should be focusing on the positive—what students *can* do. The evaluation pictures you create of your students should be based on their present abilities, not their deficits. You should also be selective in the notes you record. Teachers working with Lamme and Hysmith (1991) evolved two guidelines for determining what and how much to record for each student:

1. Record information on process that is not readily available elsewhere, such as in artifacts or checklists.

Teachers made notes of strategies they saw children using. How do students go about selecting a book to read? What do they do when what they are reading does not make sense? How do they gain spellings for new words they want to write? Teachers also noted students' interest in activities, their concentration, and their interactions with one another.

2. Observe each child, but be selective so that observation notes that are taken are actually useful in informing instruction and assessing progress.

Teachers often find it difficult to maintain systematic observations within the context of a busy classroom. To make recording a habit, many teachers begin with a recording schedule. First they examine their daily plans to determine a time when their students are independently engaged in literacy activities. Then they make a schedule for observing particular children or particular interactions. After they feel more secure with the process, they select and record noteworthy events as they occur. You will recall that Joyce Souza took time as her students settled into writers' workshop to observe and selectively take notes.

It is also important that your observations be ongoing. The evaluation of children's literacy development must be based on many observations in a variety of situations. Limited observational data will be no more helpful that the limited information provided by a standardized test.

Teachers have devised a variety of means for recording their observations. Joyce Souza prefers a simple clipboard and class list. She begins a new sheet at the start of each week. Some teachers organize spiral notebooks into topic sections; others have a page for each child. Some teachers, like Joan Lyons, use sticky labels which are later filed in the students' portfolios or in a box containing cards for every student. Hally Simmons carries computer labels on a clipboard. She records information about individual children on separate labels along with the date. The labels are then transferred to forms kept in the students' portfolios. Usually the children are given responsibility for attaching the labels to their portfolio pages (see Figure 7.2). This is a convenient method for organizing ongoing observational information.

Checklists are another system that many teachers prefer. Often teachers within a school will formulate a list of behaviors based on their instructional goals and knowledge of their students. They use these checklists periodically to monitor students' progress toward the goals. Figure 7.3 shows a checklist for recording students' ownership of reading.

WORK SAMPLES. Examples of students' work provide living proof of their literacy development. When we examine students' writing we can see that they are including more information, they are becoming more thoughtful, and their pieces are better organized. Samples based on their reading show that they are reading longer

Name _____

Reading	Writing

FIGURE 7:2
One Technique for Recording Student Observations: Using Blank Form and
Computer Labels

TEACHER'S NAME _____

STUDENT'S NAME

1. ENJOYS READING												
2. CONFIDENCE, PRIDE												
3. CONTRIBUTES TO LIT-ERACY DISCUSSIONS												
4. SHARES BKS W/OTHERS												
5. DEVELOPING PREFERENCES												
6. READS FOR OWN PURPOSE												
7. READS OUTSIDE OF SCHOOL												
8. RECOMMENDS BOOKS												
9. LEARNS FROM READING												
10. OBTAINS BOOKS NON-CLASSROOM												
11. SETS GOALS FOR READING												
12. EVALUATES LEARNING												

FIGURE 7.3
Recording Student Observations with a Checklist
Source: Carroll, 1992.

and more challenging books, that their responses are more thoughtful, and that they are making personal connections to what they are reading.

Who and what should determine the focus for the work samples collected in portfolios? We think that this should be a collaboration between children and their teachers. We also believe that goals should help guide what is placed into portfolios—the goals of students as well as those of the teacher.

In our classroom examples earlier in this chapter you saw that all three teachers give students opportunities to set their own learning goals (see Figure 7.4). Their students are also encouraged to examine their classwork for evidence that they are growing toward their goals. First-grader Karla wanted to write her own story about the characters in *Harry and the Lady Next Door* (Zion, 1960) and chose to place that story in her portfolio. Fifth-grader Sharita included her research report on Kwanzaa. The work products that students select for their portfolios should reflect the goals they have for themselves as learners.

Teachers' goals also determine the selection process. Sheila Valencia (1990, p. 339) points out that decisions about what to assess must grow out of curricular and instructional priorities. Goals of instruction must be broad rather than overly specific. The teachers you have read about throughout this text are guided by goals such as summarizing the plot of a story, understanding the author's message, relating the author's message to one's own life, gaining meaning from informational text, using word-identification skills to construct meaning, and exhibiting an interest and desire to read. You will recall that Joyce Souza and Jessie Michaels regularly asked their students to choose a response to literature for their portfolios. The responses document their students' growth toward these larger goals. When instructional goals are not clear to both students and teachers, portfolios become merely files of meaningless materials.

Time must be allotted for adding and removing portfolio samples. Some teachers, like Joyce Souza, schedule time each week for adding specified items. They also encourage students to contribute to their portfolios in more spontaneous ways. Valencia distinguishes between required evidence and supporting evidence. Required evidence enables teachers to look systematically across students as well as within each student. Required samples, for example the literature responses of Joyce Souza's and Jessie Michaels' students, and the daily reading logs from all our classrooms, match teachers' instructional goals and are included in every student's portfolio.

Supporting evidence is selected independently by students or collaboratively by teacher and students. It may result from a spontaneous activity, such as a literature group's decision to write a letter to a favorite author, or it may be individually determined, such as Sharita's research on Kwanzaa. "Supporting evidence is critical to

NAME _____

READING GOALS

Write about the goals you have for yourself as a reader.
Date _____

Write what you have done to accomplish your goals.
Date _____

_____

Write about the new goals you have for yourself as a reader.
Date _____

Write what you have done to accomplish these goals.
Date _____

FIGURE 7.4
Recording Student Goals

building a *complete* picture of a student's literary abilities because it adds the depth and variety typically missing in traditional assessments. It provides the opportunity for teachers and students to take advantage of the uniqueness of each classroom and each student by encouraging the inclusion of a variety of indicators of learning" (Valencia, 1990, pp. 339–340).

Teachers and students have devised many ways for organizing work samples within their portfolios. Students often decide as a group how to structure them. Students can take over responsibilities such as stamping the dates on their pieces, devising sections for readers' workshop and writers' workshop samples, and constructing a table of contents. Other teachers are comfortable allowing children to create their own personal arrangements. However the portfolio is organized, the important consideration is that the contents communicate to its most critical evaluators—teachers, students, and parents.

RECORD-KEEPING FORMS. A third category of portfolio information may be classified as record-keeping forms. These forms usually serve to summarize and synthesize information related to student learning. Such records may be kept by students, teachers, or by students and teachers working collaboratively.

Forms with questions to assess children's understanding of the functions and uses of literacy may be used at the beginning of the school year. Teachers of young children will need to interview them individually and record the students' responses. Older children can take more responsibility for responding to the questions in writing. Even young children are usually able to maintain their own book logs on which they record titles, authors, and their opinions of the books they have read. Older children may also log the pages read each day, the genres of their books, and interesting vocabulary that they encounter (see Figure 7.5). Students may list the titles of the writing pieces they have published. They may also keep a running list of skills and strategies that they use independently.

Some teachers ask students to add these kinds of records to their portfolios on a regular basis, perhaps quarterly. Others ask that they be added when forms are complete.

Some of the record-keeping forms that teachers maintain can be appropriately placed into student portfolios as well, such as running records (see Key Concept 3) and summary checklists. These summarizing records provide a structure for teachers to synthesize the information from students' work products, responses, and observations in order to make instructional decisions. Figure 7.6 shows a checklist that kindergarten through sixth-grade teachers use to organize and focus information about their students' reading development. You will note the broad goals they have defined for student learning and how portfolio data can be used to support evaluations.

READING LOG

NAME _____

DATE _____

DATE	TITLE & AUTHOR	RATING (1-5)	TYPE OF BOOK	INTERESTING WORDS

FIGURE 7.5
A Blank Reading Log

READERS' WORKSHOP STUDENT DATA CHECKLIST

TEACHER: GRADE: SCHOOL: DATE:

GRADE LEVEL BENCHMARKS   S=Satisfactory   D=Developing   **STUDENT NAMES**

EVALUATION COLUMNS
+ = Exceeds grade level benchmarks
✔ = Meets all grade level benchmarks
− = Doesn't meet grade level benchmarks

INSTRUCTIONAL READING LEVEL
[E, PP, 1^1, 1^2, 2^1, 2^2, 3^1, 3^2, 4, 5, or 6]

Hears or reads literature that represents a variety of cultural perspectives (K–6)

SMALL GROUP DISCUSSIONS

Participates in small group rdg. discuss. (K–6 teacher-led, 4–6 student-led)

Shares written respon. to lit. in sm. groups (K–6 teacher-led, 4–6 student-led)

Shows facility with lang. through quality respon. during small grp. discuss. (K–6)

Notes & discusses new or interesting language in small groups (2–6)

Uses multiple vocabulary strategies (3–6)

Responds in a variety of ways during small group discussions (4–6)

EVALUATION: (K–6) [+, ✔, −]

WRITTEN RESPONSE: Aesthetic

Writes personal responses to literature (K—listening, 1–6—reading)

Comprehends and writes about theme/author's message (2–6)

Applies/connects theme to own life/experiences (2–6)

Makes connections among different works of literature (3–6)

Applies, connects content text information to own life/experiences (4–6)

EVALUATION: Aesthetic response (K–6) [+, ✔, −]

WRITTEN RESPONSE: Efferent

Comprehends and writes about characters & events (K only—listening)

Comprehends & writes about characters, prob./goal, events, solut./outcome (1–2)

Reads nonfiction and shows understanding of content (2–6)

Writes summary that includes story elements (3–6)

Uses clear, meaningful lang. to express ideas in writ. respon. or summaries (3–6)

Reads different genres of fiction & shows understand. of genre characteristics (4–6)

Understands elements of author's craft (5–6)

EVALUATION: Efferent response (K–6) [+, ✔, −]

FIGURE 7.6
Reading/Listening Data Collection Checklist
Source: Carroll, 1992.

Most teachers schedule regular times during the school year to focus on record-keeping forms of this kind. They may choose to prepare them quarterly, or just prior to parent conferences or the preparation of report cards.

Student Evaluation of Portfolio Information

Portfolios are effective ways to engage students in the evaluation of their own learning. In our earlier examples you saw how even young students could set goals and reflect upon their growth. In order for students to be involved, portfolios must be easily accessible. They must become an integral part of classroom life so that items will be added, contents will be reflected upon, and new goals will be set on a regular basis.

Our classroom examples showed many ways of involving students with portfolios. Teachers of young children may routinely ask students to choose their best piece of work and tell why they chose it. The students' responses are written on index cards and attached to the chosen piece of work.

Some teachers have involved students by sharing scales of development in reading and writing. They use pieces of students' work to exemplify stages on the scale, usually actual work products from former students. A fifth-grade teacher may share and discuss, for example, memoirs judged to be below, at, and above her expectations for end-of-year fifth graders. Teachers find that when they create such awareness, students are helped to set goals for themselves. When teachers ask students to place themselves along the scale, they are often amazed by students' insights into their own development.

Jane Hansen (1992, p. 100) suggests asking students to reflect upon these three questions:

1. What have you learned recently in reading (writing)?
2. What would you like to learn next to become a better reader (writer)?
3. How do you intend to go about learning how to do that?

Robert Tierney (1991, p. 153) describes an elementary classroom in which students are asked at the end of each grading period to sort through their reading and writing projects to make their portfolio selections. They write notecards to clip to each piece, explaining why they chose it and its origin. After their portfolio selections are made, they develop a self-evaluation summary detailing what they see as their strengths and future goals.

Teacher Evaluation of Portfolio Information

Bill Harp (1991, p. 48) suggests that teachers adopt a "Yours, Ours, and Mine" approach as they evaluate and reflect on portfolio information alone and with their students. Such an approach permits students to take the lead in goal setting and yet it recognizes the teacher's responsibility in instructional planning.

This was the approach taken in a classroom described above by Tierney (1991). The students submitted their self-evaluation summaries and their portfolios to the teacher. The teacher met individually with all students while developing her own written narrative evaluation, then planned interventions to guide future contacts with individual students and with small groups.

Through portfolios and portfolio conferences teachers will gain valuable insights into their students' developing skills, interests, and attitudes. Portfolios provide teachers with a wealth of material upon which to base instructional decisions. Observations, student work samples, records, and students' own reflections contribute a range of information about each student's learning (see Figure 7.7). Portfolio assessment supports teachers in becoming true evaluators—evaluators who reflect on their own work and set new goals for their teaching and learning.

KEY CONCEPT 3   TEACHERS MAY USE FOCUSED ASSESSMENT OF INDIVIDUAL STUDENTS TO GAIN SPECIAL INSIGHTS INTO THEIR STRENGTHS AND NEEDS.

INDIVIDUAL ASSESSMENT

There is not sufficient time in the school day to make a detailed assessment of each student. However, there will be a few students in your class about whom you are puzzled. They are not responding to your instruction or do not seem to be making adequate progress. You will want further information.

You may gain additional insights into these students' learning with more frequent use of the observations and evaluations that we discussed in Key Concept 2. You may also find that specialized assessments can help you understand the learning of these children. When choosing more focused assessments for individual students, you must consider the authenticity of the measures. Because all your students are engaged in authentic literacy activities throughout the day, individual assessments should come from authentic, meaningful texts.

Contents of students' literacy portfolios

Joan Lyons Grade 1	Joyce Souza Grade 3	Jessie Michaels Grade 5
Functions of literacy assessment		
Beginning-of-year parent questionnaire	Beginning-of-year literacy questionnaire	Beginning-of-year literacy questionnaire
Assessment of letter names and sounds		
Writing samples	"Published" writing pieces and all accompanying drafts	"Published" writing pieces and all accompanying drafts
Running records		
Oral reading tapes		
Written/drawn responses to literature	Written responses to literature	Written responses to literature
		Samples of writing and reading in multiple genres
Voluntary reading logs	Voluntary reading logs	Voluntary reading logs
	Records of new vocabulary	Notes of vocabulary study
	Personal learning goals and reflections	Personal learning goals and reflections
		Written review of portfolio contents
Anecdotal notes	Anecdotal notes	Anecdotal notes
Checklists	Checklists	Checklists
Students' own selections	Student's own selections	Students' own selections

FIGURE 7.7
Contents of Students' Literacy Portfolios

Running Records

As discussed in Chapter 2, running records are an excellent means of assessing the word-reading strategies of beginning readers. They can also be used to provide information about older children who are still struggling to decode text.

Marie Clay (1985) suggests that teachers use running records to note the strategies students are using or not using while reading. As the student reads aloud, the teacher notes exactly what the child says and does. Then the teacher evaluates the student's responses, noting his dependence on meaning, structure, and visual cues. She looks at every error and asks herself, "What made him say that?" By noting the child's use of strategies, the teacher can establish meaningful goals for instruction.

When Karl began third grade in Joyce Souza's classroom, he was one of a small group of students whose facility with reading was significantly below average. Joyce decided to closely monitor Karl and the others with weekly running records so that she might provide them with consistent, ongoing instructional support. Figure 7.8 shows part of a running record that Joyce took early in the school year as Karl read from *Commander Toad and the Big Black Hole* (Yolen, 1983).

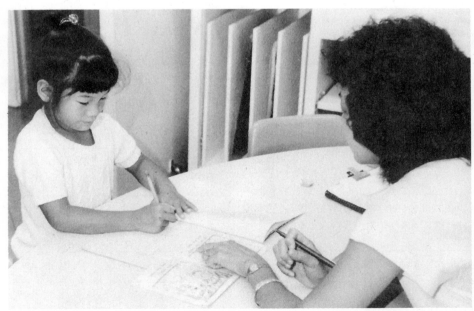

The teacher uses focused, authentic assessment to gain further insights into this student's learning. Individualized assessments help guide the teacher's instructional decisions about the needs of special students.

RUNNING RECORD SUMMARY

Name___Karl_____ Date_____ Recorder_____

Title___Commander Toad and the Big Black Hole_____ Reading Level_____

Running Words = _____   Error Rate = _____   % Accuracy = _____   Self-Correction
Errors   Ratio =

Easy_____ Instructional_____ Hard_____

ANALYSIS OF ERRORS (Cues used and cues neglected)

_____

_____

Page		E	SC	E Cues	SC Cues
34 ✓ ✓	Party / Peeper	1		MS(V)	
Search / scratches ✓ ✓ ✓		1		MS(V)	
What / With ✓	trick / stick	2		MS(V)	
✓ ✓ ✓ ✓ ✓				(M)SV	
✓ ✓					
✓ ✓ trick✓					
✓ ✓ trick / sticky ✓		1		MS(V)	
✓ ✓ tron / tongue		1		MS(V)	
✓ get✓ / giant		1		MS(V)	
✓ ✓	shrow / crew	1		MS(V)	
✓ ✓					

FIGURE 7.8
A Running Record Summary
Source: Clay, 1985.

When Joyce evaluated Karl's reading, she learned that he usually attended to the beginning letters of words but often failed to check for further visual cues. Also, Karl frequently ignored the meaning of the text. When he read something that did not make sense, he continued on without attempting to self-correct.

Joyce planned for Karl to have increased opportunities to read books that were easy for him, to build his fluency and confidence. She encouraged him to monitor his understanding by attending to meaning and sense making. Joyce included Karl, along with a few of her other students, in a series of mini-lessons focusing on ending and medial letters using words from the books they were reading. Joyce has also encouraged Karl in his writing throughout the day. She knows the benefits of writing for supporting students' development of word-reading strategies.

Informal Reading Inventories

The informal reading inventory (IRI) has long been a popular approach for measuring children's reading ability. IRIs provide information about the level of reading material the child can handle independently, the child's use of specific skills and strategies, and the nature of reading problems. They can help students better understand themselves as readers and serve to evaluate their progress (Johnson, Kress, & Pikulski, 1987, pp. 3–4). You can use IRIs to help evaluate children who join the class partway into the school year. Some teachers have used IRIs to guide their selection of reading materials for their classrooms. They are also a useful approach for understanding the reading performance of older students who have difficulty with more complex text.

Text used to construct an IRI is typically a sampling from the materials you are using for instruction at several levels of difficulty. You should begin the evaluation with materials the child can read easily, and continue with increasingly more difficult text. The IRI usually consists of several activities, including:

1. A discussion between you and the child. This discussion is designed to assess the student's prior knowledge about the topic of the selection.
2. The child's oral reading of the text. The teacher carefully records the child's oral reading performance.
3. An assessment of the child's comprehension of the passage. You may ask the child a series of questions about the selection or ask her to retell all she remembers.
4. The child's silent reading of text that is parallel in difficulty to that read orally.

5. An assessment of the child's comprehension through questions or retelling.
6. An evaluation of the child's ability to efficiently and rapidly locate information in the silently read selection.
7. An assessment of the child's listening comprehension if you find it important. You read the selection aloud and then use questioning or retelling procedures. (Johnson, Kress, & Pikulski, 1987, p. 8)

A text is thought to be at the right level for instruction if a child reads 90 to 94 percent of the words correctly and answers at least 75 percent of the questions. It is thought to be appropriate for independent reading if the child can read 95 percent or more of the words correctly with 90 percent accuracy. Word recognition of less than 90 percent *or* comprehension of 50 percent or less is thought to be at the frustration level, indicating that the passage is too difficult for the child.

It is important to remember that the purpose of IRIs is to guide your instructional planning. If you record the student's responses on tape, you can return to the assessment to gain further insights about the child's use of literacy, such as language development from the retellings or judging the pattern of strategies or cue systems used during oral reading.

Reading Comprehension

Karen Wood (1988) offers a way to organize important comprehension information on an individual profile card (Figure 7.9). Her approach is a structured observation with holistic scoring that is controlled by the teacher but is not intrusive. Wood makes a point of allowing the child to be evaluated after both oral and silent reading, with varying text genres and levels of text difficulty, different recall procedures, and varying degrees of collaboration. These allow the teacher to determine how a student works and learns best by systematically varying the more important reading comprehension variables.

If appropriate to the needs of your students, Wood's profile can be extended to include assessment of word-reading strategies taken from running records. Again, the instrument would involve structured observations and holistic scoring. Word-identification accuracy, reading fluency, and self-monitoring are added to the profile.

Word-identification accuracy can be evaluated at three levels of reading:

1. easy (95 to 100 percent of words accurately read or self-corrected);

Name Eric Matthews   Date September 3   Grade 3

	Reading type		Genre					Recall mode			Degree of guidance			Overall compr.	Comments
	Oral	Silent	Poetry	Plays	Realistic fiction	Fantasy	Nonfiction	Free recall	Probed recall	Infer, predict	Background knowl.	Preteaching vocab.	Assist during rdg.	(1 = none, 2 = some, 3 = most, 4 = all)	
Level 2₂ p. 41	✓				✓			✓	✓		—	—	—	3	A little choppy at first, then very fluent with accurate recall
Level 2₂ p. 76	✓			✓				✓	✓	✓	—	—	—	4	Very fluent reading and retelling
Level 2₂ p. 168		✓					✓	✓	✓	✓	—	—	—	4	Needs no assistance—has control over word recognition and comprehension
Level 3₁ p. 101	✓				✓	✓		✓	✓		—	—	—	2	Some fluency problems & sketchy recall (e.g., misread "trail" for "trial," "beautiful" for "body")
Level 3₁ p. 96	✓							✓	✓	✓	✓	✓		3	With help, recall is improved; can predict and infer (e.g., Why do you think . . .)
Level 3₁ p. 66		✓					✓	✓	✓		✓	✓	✓	4	Had difficulty recognizing "ambulance" – "emergency". Defined "Red Cross" & "swerved." This helped!
Level 3₁ p. 119		✓					✓	✓	✓	✓	✓	✓		4	Tried with and without guidance. Comprehension is improved with help.

Overall assessment: Eric's comprehension while reading silently seems better than while reading orally. Can retell in own words at level 3, but gives more detail when probed or prompted. With assistance, seems to benefit from instruction in this material.

Appropriate placement level 3₁

FIGURE 7.9
Individual Comprehension Profile
Source: Wood, 1988.

2. instructional (90 to 94 percent of words accurately read or self-corrected);
3. hard (less than 90 percent of words accurately read or self-corrected).

   Reading fluency can also be gauged with three levels:

1. expressive and smooth;
2. some expression and some hesitation or rereading that is choppy;
3. word-by-word reading, voice pointing or finger pointing.

Self-monitoring of word identification can be assessed with three levels:

1. rereads and self-corrects half or more of errors using picture, printed word, and text cues;
2. rereads or self-corrects occasionally or fewer than one in four errors and uses only one or two cue sources;
3. seldom rereads or self-corrects and uses only picture or printed word cues or appeals for help.

The revised profile card is shown in Figure 7.10.

KEY CONCEPT 4

TEACHERS SHOULD INTEGRATE ASSESSMENT WITH CLASSROOM INSTRUCTION, RECOGNIZING THE INSEPARABILITY OF INSTRUCTION AND ASSESSMENT.

INTEGRATING ASSESSMENT WITH INSTRUCTION

Throughout this chapter we have emphasized the importance of integrating assessment and instruction. In this key concept we present the teaching-learning cycle, a sequence of steps that allows you to use assessment information to improve your instruction. It synthesizes ideas from the instructional approaches we have discussed in earlier chapters with the suggestions made in this chapter for using ongoing assessment and evaluation.

The Teaching-Learning Cycle

STEP 1: ASSESSING STUDENTS' NEEDS BEFORE BEGINNING AN INSTRUCTIONAL UNIT. Effective teachers want to have some idea of what their students know and can do based on their own instructional goals as well as goals from their school's or district's curriculum. You can compare those goals with information about students' knowledge

Name _____   Date _____   Grade _____

Text Level	Genre					Word Identification			Recall Mode			Degree of Guidance				Comments
	Poetry	Plays	Realistic fiction	Fantasy	Nonfiction	Accuracy	Fluency	Self-monitor	Free recall	Probed recall	Infer/predict	Bkg. knowledge	Pret. Vocabulary	Assist read	Overall comp.	

Overall assessment:

FIGURE 7.10
Revised Individual Reading Profile

and interests that is in their portfolios. The purpose is to find out which goals or objectives individual students already seem to have met, and which might be helpful to focus on next.

You may also want to measure their background knowledge of specific units or topics to be studied. We presented some suggestions for doing this in the first key concept of this chapter, in the informal assessment section. When you have information about students' current knowledge and understandings, you will be better able to plan your instruction so that it will meet students' needs and heighten their learning.

Your skill as an observer is most helpful in establishing a system of useful, ongoing assessment within the classroom. Listen carefully to students' responses during the instruction of a reading lesson to determine their level of understanding. For further information about their capabilities, carefully examine their written responses. As you interact with students, note their problem-solving strategies and how successfully they are using them. In other words, every

Assessment is fully integrated with instruction in this classroom setting. By carefully observing students as they read and write, the teacher is able to monitor progress and make informed instructional decisions.

contact with the students, in person or through their written responses, can provide you with information about your instruction.

You will not want to omit this initial step. Obviously, an effective classroom program cannot be developed on the basis of sheer guesswork. This assessment step allows you to gather information about your students to make informed rather than haphazard instructional decisions.

To illustrate the connection between assessment and instruction, we will return to our third-grade classroom. Joyce Souza is particularly concerned with her students' long-term reading comprehension development. Many of her major goals are in this area. After the students had read and discussed a few nonfiction selections within literature groups, Joyce decided that most of the students seemed ready to organize important text information into written summaries. She checked this by making notes of students' oral responses during their early literature group discussions and by looking at their written responses to the books they had read.

STEP 2: SETTING IMMEDIATE GOALS FOR INSTRUCTION. The next step is to set immediate goals for instruction, or specific objectives for student learning. On the basis of your observations and the information in students' portfolios, you can evaluate what skills and strategies students use well, and what instructional opportunities they might benefit from next. Then you can plan instruction and opportunities that will help them move toward independence.

You should seek to meet your immediate goals through a combination of activities. Instruction may be through teacher-led activities (see Step 3 below), through activities pursued by small groups of students working with indirect teacher support, or through independent endeavors (these last two are part of Step 4).

In our example, Joyce's immediate goal was to help her students develop an understanding of how to summarize information from the nonfiction text with which they were engaged in their literature groups. She wanted them to understand that summarization is a useful concept for understanding and recalling information. She wanted them to learn the process of summarization within a meaningful context.

STEP 3: PROVIDING INSTRUCTION TO MEET GOALS. In Step 3 the teacher provides instruction on concepts that build upon children's strengths. She provides the scaffolding necessary for her students to acquire new skills and knowledge.

Joyce Souza introduced her students to summarization with a general discussion of what a summary is, why it might be important to construct one, and how she would help them. She led them to understand why summarization is an important instructional goal. As she met with each literature group, she selected a section from their book and asked the students to reread it to themselves. Then she modeled how she would summarize the paragraph. She invited the students to comment on her summary.

Next, students took responsibility for creating their own summaries. Sometimes they worked collaboratively, sometimes independently. They constructed oral summaries, and wrote summaries in their learning logs. Joyce continued to give them feedback about the process and encouraged them to help one another. They contrasted how many facts they recalled after reading with how many they recalled after reading and summarizing. Joyce and the students made notes to add to their portfolios concerning their responses to the lessons or their movement toward independence.

STEP 4: PROVIDING STUDENTS WITH OPPORTUNITIES FOR APPLICATION AND DISCOVERY. Having introduced the new process or information in Step 3, students should have opportunities to apply the concept or skill in a slightly different way. Opportunities for discovery will grow out of their involvement in learning activities that require them to use their skills and background knowledge to gain new understandings on their own.

Joyce Souza's third graders had many opportunities to apply their understanding of summarization and to discover ways it might further their learning as they engaged in independent research projects. The series books with which they began their studies provided a meaningful context for summarizing, and because the texts were easy most students were able to pursue their interests with independence. Joyce recognized that her instructional goal helped her students meet their personal goals of learning more about their research topics.

STEP 5: CHECKING ON STUDENT PROGRESS. Teachers should check often to see that their students are progressing in a satisfactory way toward meeting their instructional goals. Observations, work samples, and record-keeping forms will provide the information you need to evaluate student progress.

Joyce Souza noted her students' initial struggle with summarizing. With guided practice most of them became comfortable with the process, though a few students did not seem to be able to construct a summary without considerable help from others. These same students found it difficult to summarize information on their research topics, and a recently administered informal reading inventory also confirmed this difficulty.

STEP 6: PROVIDING ADDITIONAL INSTRUCTION. When students are not progressing satisfactorily, as shown by the evidence you collect in Step 5, you will want to provide further instruction. This means going back through Steps 3 and 4 within the same teaching-learning cycle.

Joyce Souza provided additional instruction for the students who continued to struggle with summarization. She met with this small group of children on several occasions to read and discuss other nonfiction selections in addition to their regular reading groups. Using easy articles from children's magazines such as *Ranger Rick* and *Zoo Books* Joyce modeled the process of summarizing, gradually releasing increased responsibility to the students so that they could try out the approach by working together. She asked the children to write independent summaries of selected sections of text which they later shared and discussed with one another.

In addition, she asked these children to include a summary of the central theme as they responded to the books they chose for voluntary reading. As the students in this group shared their responses, Joyce encouraged them to note how the concept of summarization could be applied to the wide variety of books they read.

Some of these students chose to add work samples and written comments about summarizing to their portfolios. Joyce added her own observational notes and checklist information to document the students' progress.

Going Ahead: Setting New Goals

When your evaluation shows that students have met the immediate learning goal, new instructional goals are determined. Joyce Souza targeted specific vocabulary development related to their study of mammals as her next goal. The students continued to use the concept of summarizing with different factual selections, thus allowing for some review as well as new learning.

SUMMARY

In this chapter we provided you with a perspective about the role of assessment in your classroom and its relationship to your instruction. In the first section we described how three teachers meaningfully link assessment and instruction in their classrooms. The first key concept provided ideas for assessment information that is helpful as you begin a new school year. This information will give you insights into your students' literacy development and interests. In the second key concept we suggested ways to set up portfolios that are used collaboratively by students and teachers to monitor and record progress during the school year. The third key concept discussed ways of gaining additional information about individual children. In the last key concept we explained how you might integrate assessment information into classroom instruction by following the teaching-learning cycle.

◀ ACTIVITIES

Reflecting On Your Own Literacy

Consider how you use reading and writing in your own life. Begin to create a portfolio that represents you as a reader and writer. Evaluate your portfolio and set goals for future growth. Then meet to share your portfolio and goals with someone else. Plan to meet again in a month to review your portfolios and assess your progress toward your goals.

Applying What You Have Learned to the Classroom

Talk with a classroom teacher to discover how he or she assesses students' abilities and development in reading and writing. How does the teacher use assessment information to plan and guide instruction? Consider your findings in relation to the key concepts in this chapter.

BIBLIOGRAPHY

References

Brown, R. G. (1991). *Schools of thought.* San Francisco, CA: Jossey-Bass.

Calkins, L. (1990). *Living between the lines.* Portsmouth, NH: Heinemann.

Carroll, J. (Ed.). (1992). *Literacy curriculum guide.* Honolulu, HI: Kamehameha Schools/Bernice Pauahi Bishop Estate, Early Education Division.

Clay, M. (1985). *The early detection of reading difficulties.* Portsmouth, NH: Heinemann.

Hansen, J. (1992). Students' evaluations bring reading and writing together. *The Reading Teacher, 46,* 100–105.

Harp, B. (Ed.). (1991). *Assessment and evaluation in whole language programs.* Norwood, MA: Christopher Gordon.

Holmes, B., & Roser, N. (1987). Five ways to assess readers' prior knowledge. *The Reading Teacher, 40,* 646–649.

Johnson, M. S., Kress, R. A., & Pikulski, J. J. (1987). *Informal reading inventories* (2nd ed.). Newark, DE: International Reading Association.

Lamme, L. L., & Hysmith, C. (1991). One school's adventure into portfolio assessment. *Language Arts, 68,* 629–640.

Maxim, D. (1990). Beginning researchers. In N. Atwell (Ed.),*Coming to know: Writing to learn in the intermediate grades.* Portsmouth, NH: Heinemann.

Mitchell, R. (1989). What is "authentic assessment"? *Portfolio, the Newsletter of Arts PROPEL, 1*(5), 5.

Paratore, J., & Indrisano, R. (1987). Intervention assessment of reading comprehension. *The Reading Teacher, 40,* 778–783.

Paris, S. G., et al. (1992). A framework for authentic literacy assessment. *The Reading Teacher, 46*(2), 88–98.

Pearson, P. D., & Valencia, S. (1987). Assessment, accountability, and professional prerogative. In J. Readance & R. Baldwin (Eds.), *Research in literacy: Merging perspectives.* Rochester, NY: National Reading Conference.

Reardon, S. J. (1990). Putting reading tests in their place. *The New Advocate,3*(1), 29–37.

Searly, D., & Stevenson, M. (1987). An alternative assessment program in language arts. *Language Arts, 64,* 278–284.

Stupey, D., & Knight, C. (1988). *Concepts about reading from a developmental perspective.* Presentation at the annual meeting of the National Reading Conference, Tucson, Arizona.

Tierney, R. J. (1991). *Portfolio assessment in the reading-writing classroom.* Norwood, MA: Christopher-Gordon.

Valencia, S. (1990). A portfolio approach to classroom reading assessment: The whys, whats, and hows. *The Reading Teacher, 44* 338–340.

Vavrus L., & Calfee, R. (1988). *A research strategy for assessing teachers of elementary literacy: The promise of performance portfolios.* Presentation at the annual meeting of the National Reading Conference, Tucson, Arizona.

Weiss, M. J., & Hagen, R. (1988). A key to literacy: Kindergartners' awareness of the functions of print. *The Reading Teacher, 41,* 574–578.

Wood, K. (1988). Techniques for assessing students' potential for learning. *The Reading Teacher, 41,* 440–447.

Suggested Classroom Resources

Arnold, C. (1985). *Saving the peregrine falcon.* Photographs by R. Hewett. Minneapolis, MN: Carolrhoda Books/Nature Watch Books.

Brown, M. (1952). *Puss in boots.* New York: Scribner's.

George, J. (1988). *One day in the woods.* Illustrated by G. Allen. New York: Thomas Y. Crowell.

Oechsli, K. (1986). *Mice at bat.* New York: Harper & Row.

Parish, P. (1986). *Amelia Bedelia.* New York: Harper & Row.

Rylant, C. (1987). *Henry and Mudge: The first book of their adventures.* Riverside, NJ: Bradbury Press.

Yolen, J. (1983). *Commander Toad and the big black hole.* New York: Coward-McCann.

Zion, G. (1960). *Harry and the lady next door.* New York: Harper & Row.

Further Readings

Cambourne, B., & Turbill, J. (1990). Assessment in whole language classrooms: Theory into practice. *The Elementary School Journal,* January, 337–349.

Davies, A., Cameron, C., Politano, C., & Gregory, K. (1992). *Together is better: Collaborative assessment, evaluation & reporting.* Winnipeg, Canada: Peguis Publishers.

Educational Leadership (1989, April). Redirecting assessment (special issue).

Eggleton, J. (1990). *Whole language evaluation: Reading, writing, and spelling.* Bothell, WA: The Wright Group.

Graves, D. H., & Sunstein, B. S. (Eds.). (1992). *Portfolio portraits.* Portsmouth, NH: Heinemann.

Kubiszyn, T., & Borich, G. (1990). *Educational testing and measurement: Classroom application and practice* (3rd ed.). Glenview, IL: Scott, Foresman.

Language Arts (1991, December). The whys, whats, and hows of literacy evaluation (special issue).

Traill, L. (1993). *Highlight my strengths: Assessment and evaluation of literacy learning.* Crystal Lake, IL: Rigby.

Videotapes

Making Meaning: Integrated Language Arts—Assessment (1992). Alexandria, VA: Association for Supervision and Curriculum Development.

Traill, L. (1993). *Learning Running Records.* Crystal Lake, IL: Rigby.

Traill, L. (1993). *Using Running Records.* Crystal Lake, IL: Rigby.

8 FOSTERING INDEPENDENCE AND A LOVE OF READING

Five adults speak of developing their love of reading:

[*Reader A:*] As the youngest daughter of a family of four girls, I can't remember when I didn't read. I had started to enjoy books by myself before I went to school. Never can I recall any direction from my family as to what I should read or whether the material was appropriate for my age or would enrich my experiences. I read what I wanted to or simply selected available books that were being enjoyed by members of my family. My home had a good library with many periodicals. It was natural to pick up books and magazines. The monthly arrival of *St. Nicholas Magazine* and *Youth's Companion* were days of anticipation, but equally so were the delivery dates of adult magazines. . . .

[*Reader B:*] My intermediate teacher brought boxes of books into the schoolroom. We children could browse them at our leisure and read to our heart's content. This was when I read *Black Beauty, Robinson Crusoe, Beautiful Joe* and *The Pony Boy Riders*. . . .

[*Reader C:*] Starting in the fourth grade, I always ordered books from Scholastic Book Services. This and the small shelf of books in the classroom served as my main source of reading material. . . .

[*Reader D:*] We had a good many books at home and I had a friend who had a good library. We exchanged books and enjoyed talking about our reading. . . .

[*Reader E:*] During the summer months the library had a reading program in which I participated. After reading a certain number of books, a summary of which was made for the librarian as each book was returned, the reader was awarded a certificate and a gold star. At the time, I considered my certificate to be a prized possession (Carlsen & Sherrill, 1988, pp. 62, 64, 65, 71, 110).

◀ OVERVIEW

We begin this chapter with another look into three of our classrooms to see how Joan Lyons, Susan Meyer, and Jessie Michaels help to extend their students' enjoyment of reading. In the first key concept we focus on steps teachers can take to promote students' independent application of reading and writing strategies. In the second key concept we look at voluntary reading and discuss methods teachers can use to promote children's choosing to read on their own. In the third key concept we consider how children can support one another's reading development within and across classrooms. The fourth key concept deals with the importance of schools and families working together to further children's literacy development.

KEY CONCEPT 1: Students should grow toward independence in literacy as teachers gradually release responsibility to them.

KEY CONCEPT 2: Students should have opportunities to read independently for their own enjoyment and information.

KEY CONCEPT 3: Students should have opportunities to support one another's literacy development as members of an extended community.

KEY CONCEPT 4: Students' proficiency and interest in literacy should be strengthened through connections between home and school.

◀ PERSPECTIVE

Fostering a Love of Reading in Three Classrooms: First Graders Enjoy Access to Books

Books seem to be everywhere in Joan Lyons' first-grade classroom. Child-made stories on huge pieces of butcher paper hang on wires from the ceiling. Others sit open, accordion style, on bookshelves. A large bulletin board colorfully displays the children's single page stories with drawings of their families. Joan's husband helped her construct narrow boxes, which stretch across the middle of the children's worktables. A variety of trade books are placed side by side in these boxes, covers visible, inviting children to read throughout the day.

The classroom library, "The Book Nook," is the focal point of the classroom. Children enter the area through an open doorway. The entrance is surrounded by students' own "advertisements" for their favorite books. One colorful poster proclaims "We love Clifford and Emily Elizabeth" and is signed by Karla, Verner, and Stan. Another lists "Books we can read by Joy Cowley." The children have written the titles and drawn accompanying illustrations. The Nook contains a great assortment of big books, predictable books (see Chapter 2), and trade books of a variety of genres and formats. There are child-authored books and students' writing about books. A beanbag chair, pillows, two small rocking chairs, and a variety of stuffed animals invite children to settle in. A tank of tropical fish is surrounded by related titles such as *Swimmy* (Lionni, 1983) and *How to Set Up an Aquarium.*

Though it is still early in the school year, classroom routines are well established. A list near the front of the room reminds the children:

1. Put your things away neatly.
2. Mark your attendance card.
3. Check in your library books.
4. Sign up to share.
5. Sharpen your pencils.
6. Choose a book and begin reading.

The children know they may enter the classroom up to 15 minutes before school officially begins, as long as their teacher is present. By the time the morning bell rings, most children have completed their responsibilities and are settled with a book.

At the sound of the bell, Joan Lyons encourages a few children to complete their tasks and picks up her own book. Each day begins with teacher and children enjoying books of their own choosing for 10 to 15 minutes. Teachers of older children call their period of voluntary reading "SSR" (sustained silent reading). Joan laughingly calls hers SNR (sustained noisy reading), though with the children she uses the term OTTER for "our time to enjoy reading." She has found that it is very difficult for her young students to read silently; many are helped by hearing themselves read aloud, and many enjoy reading and sharing with one another. So Joan has decided that, at least for the first half of the school year, she won't be bothered by the noise. As long as the children are involved and enjoying books, her goals for independent reading are being met.

Now, after ten minutes, Joan hits three quiet tones on the xylophone. Some of the children carefully place book markers into their books, some return books to the shelves and boxes, and a few carry their books as the group gathers together on the carpet.

As the group assembles, Joan engages the children in reading a few rhymes from charts in large print. She points to the words of "Over in the Meadow" and the children enthusiastically read along.

T: Any requests?

Orlando: "One, Two, Buckle My Shoe."

Again the children read together. After another request, Joan asks, "Does anyone have something they'd like to share about their reading this morning?"

Shelly: Me and Bridgett read three books by Joy Cowley.

T: Good for you! What are the titles?

Bridgett: Ice Cream, Noise—

Shelly: —and *Grandpa, Grandpa.*

T: Are they all on the list by our Book Nook?

Bridgett: Not *Noise.*

T: Did you enjoy it?

Shelly and Bridgett: Yeah! Everyone said, "Yukka-dukka, yukka-dukka, yah-yah-yah!"

T: It sounds like you girls will want to add the name of that book to our list. We'll all be interested to see what kind of picture you decide to draw to match with the title. Anyone else?

Orlando shares that Alex let him look at the book his grandparents sent for his birthday. Kenji says he read *Hop on Pop* for the third time. Sandi says that Dan helped her read the story that his reading group wrote yesterday.

T: Let's check our a.m. list and see who has signed up to read to us this morning.

Joan Lyons has a place on the chalkboard marked a.m. and p.m., each followed by the numbers 1, 2, 3. Children write their names after the numbers to indicate that they would like to read aloud to the class either in the morning or in the afternoon just after lunch. Sometimes they read an entire book, other times they select a favorite part from the book they took home and read with their families the day before.

T: I see Kenji's name is first on our list.

Kenji takes the chair in front of his classmates, holds up his book, and says, "The title of my book is *Eat* by Diane Paterson. It is a very funny book."

Kenji begins reading confidently to his appreciative audience.

Third Graders and Their Parents Share Literacy Activities

As Susan Meyer's third graders arrived at the classroom one January morning, Reggie announced to Susan and Ming that his mom said she would be able to finish typing and printing Ming's story at her office today. Reggie would bring it to school tomorrow. Kenyatta carried a bag with blank books, which she placed in the publishing area. Her family had sewn the books together so that the children could have another form in which to publish their stories.

This year Susan had decided to extend the involvement of her students' families in the classroom literacy program. She had been very pleased with the results. In other years Susan has had contact with parents at school open houses, parent conferences, and through newsletters, notes, and occasional phone conversations. She explained her program and encouraged family reading. Because most of the parents worked outside their homes, she did not expect them to have time to participate in the day-to-day activities of the classroom.

With her own two girls in school, Susan became more aware of the value and benefits of parent participation in the school's program. Despite their busy schedules, she and her husband have found positive ways to contribute to their daughters' school experiences. This year Susan decided to offer additional options to the parents of her students.

Susan planned to actively encourage parental involvement in November, during the first scheduled parent conferences. She had been using assessment portfolios for two years, and she often shared materials from the portfolios during her meetings with parents. This year, however, she decided to make the portfolios a central part of the conferences. She wanted to heighten parents' understanding of the relationship between her curriculum goals and the literacy activities in which the students engaged.

Before the conferences, she gave her students time to explore, organize, and talk with one another about their portfolios. She met with the children individually, asking them to tell why the pieces were included. She helped the children explain what they were proud of and why, what they needed to work on, and how they might do that.

Then, two days before the conferences were scheduled, the children took their portfolios home to review with their parents. Susan also sent a form encouraging parents to make positive statements about their child's accomplishments along with any concerns or questions they might have. The parents came to the conferences with their child's portfolio and with a much clearer understanding of the child's literacy development. Susan found that the 20-minute conferences with these parents were much more focused than her conferences in other years. She noted, too, that when she clearly communicated her philosophy through examples of students' learning, parents discovered ways to support their children's literacy development.

At the end of their discussions, Susan told parents that she would continue to keep them informed through newsletters and notes. She also invited the parents to participate more directly in the literacy experiences of the classroom. She had a list of suggestions, but hoped that parents would think of others suited to their own talents and circumstances. Susan was prepared to accept all offers.

Lindsey's father works a late shift and volunteered to organize a schedule for family members who could spend some time each week in the classroom. Now, with his team of four mothers, one grandmother, and one grandfather, Susan and her students can count on an extra adult almost every day for an hour during their workshop time. Susan provides ongoing guidance to this team so they know how to confer with children about their writing, help with publishing, and work with children like Bobby who can benefit from additional support in reading.

Some parents have taken on home projects. They take care of filling out book club orders, return and pick up community library books, type students' published stories, and contribute book-making materials.

Other family members find ways to visit the classroom at least once during the year. Susan has encouraged them to celebrate their child's birthday, or another special day of their choosing, by telling a story or sharing a book. Today is Esteban's birthday. His mother has arranged her lunch break so that she could come to the classroom right after the students' lunch period. Esteban introduced his mother and Ms. Martinez sat in the author's chair to read *The Cat's Meow* (Soto, 1987). The students were delighted with Pip, the Spanish-speaking cat, and were interested in exploring some of the vocabulary he spoke in the story. Ms. Martinez promised to leave the book in the classroom library so that the children could continue to enjoy it on their own.

Then Esteban and his mother shared another surprise with the class. Last evening they had written out the words to the song "Happy Birthday" in Spanish. They helped the children learn the words, then they joined together to sing "Cumpleaños Feliz" to a proud Esteban.

Fifth Graders Share with Younger Buddies

As Jessie Michaels' fifth graders entered their new classroom on the first day of school, they were surprised by the large assortment of picture books displayed on the shelves of the classroom library, standing on tables, and lining the ledges at the front of the room. Posters featuring picture books and their authors were exhibited on walls and bulletin boards.

Many of the students rolled their eyes at one another questioningly. There were whispered remarks about being "back in kindergarten" and "Looks like we're gonna cruise this year." Jorge backed out the door to check the number of the classroom, saying, "This is fifth grade, isn't it?"

After the students settled into desks and the morning business had been handled, Jessie explained. "Mrs. Simmons asked if we and her kindergartners might team up this school year as 'buddy classes.' She thinks that her students will benefit from sharing reading and writing experiences with some older students from time to time throughout the school year. I agreed, and thought that as fifth graders this might be an interesting learning experience for you as well. So, the books I chose to bring in today will get us started on this project."

Jessie went on to explain that she and Mrs. Simmons thought the two classes would try to get together every other week, and during the sessions each fifth grader would read a picture storybook to a kindergartner. The ways they share during the buddy meetings would probably change over time, and Jessie suggested that after their first session they would discuss some possibilities.

For now, Jessie said, the students would be expected to choose a picture book that they were particularly fond of and one they thought would appeal to a kindergarten child. She suggested that they spend the next hour perusing the books, and said it would be helpful if they used their journals to make notes.

The students explored the books, choosing those they wanted to read individually or share with a classmate. There was a great deal of interaction as books were shared and exchanged. As the students read, Jessie circulated among them responding to their comments, sometimes offering a suggestion. After about 40 minutes, Jessie reflected on the group's involvement. She noted that everyone in this new class of students was actively, purposefully engaged in reading—and they were less than two hours into the day. "What a great start to a new school year," she thought to herself.

At the end of the hour Jessie called the group together to share their findings. Many children were delighted to discover old favorites, books that had been special to them when they were younger. Other children were excited and eager to talk about new finds. Some of the students, like Tonya and Vanessa, had paired up to share their individual favorites with one another. Often the students had used their journals to list a few of the picture book titles. Robyn and Travis had numbered theirs in order of preference.

After their sharing, Jessie showed her fifth graders the cover of *Chicken Sunday* (Polacco, 1992). She asked, "What do you think 'chicken Sunday' might mean?" After several students responded, Jessie began reading, holding the book so her students could view the pictures. When she got to the part where Miss Eula tells the children that they need to show Mr. Kodinski that they are good people, she asked, "What might the children do?" At the end she said, "What did you think of the story? Did it make you think of anything that's ever happened to you?"

Next Jessie asked, "What did you notice about the way I shared *Chicken Sunday*?" The students recognized that their teacher had provided a good model for them to consider in planning to read aloud to the kindergartners. Jessie listed their comments on chart paper:

Know the story and the words

Read clearly

Be expressive

Ask a few questions

Show the pictures

Jessie told her students that tomorrow she would show them examples of particular kinds of picture books, discussing their characteristics and appeal for young children. She said that before they read with the kindergartners they would practice reading their selections to their own classmates, talk about effective techniques for reading aloud, think about how to involve the kindergartners, perhaps by planning to ask some good questions, and consider how to evaluate the success of the experience. "Maybe we *can* learn something from picture books," said Jorge.

KEY CONCEPT 1   STUDENTS SHOULD GROW TOWARD INDEPENDENCE IN LITERACY AS TEACHERS GRADUALLY RELEASE RESPONSIBILITY TO THEM.

LEADING STUDENTS TOWARD INDEPENDENCE

In Chapter 1 we discussed the importance of literacy for functioning in a complex society. Teachers, like those we have discussed, recognize their responsibility in providing students with appropriate guidance so that, as adults, they can function independently at adept and advanced levels of literacy. These teachers know the importance of building a foundation for lifelong literacy.

Teachers should take certain steps to help their students gain independence in the use of reading and writing strategies they have been taught. They know their aim has been accomplished if students can apply reading and writing strategies on their own in school and also can use these strategies outside school.

We saw how teachers like Joyce Souza help their students reach the goal of independence by gradually releasing responsibility. As discussed in Chapter 1, the idea is gradually to turn control of strategy use over to the students. The teacher should be doing less and less, while the students are doing more and more.

In Chapter 7 you saw how Joyce Souza helped a group of students who were struggling to summarize informational text to gain independence. First she modeled the strategy herself. Then the students engaged in a variety of guided practice activities with Joyce's support and the support of one another. Over time, the students began to independently apply the strategy of summarizing using text material appropriate to their independent reading levels.

Annemarie Palincsar and Kathryn Ransom (1988) believe that *guided practice* is a critical step for bringing strategies under full control of students, and especially critical for poor readers. Guided practice differs from ordinary practice because it involves collaboration between the teacher and student. In Pearson's model (1985) of the gradual release of responsibility (see Chapter 1), it is an intermediate step in leading students to independence. The teacher and student carry out the strategy together, with the teacher tailoring the amount of assistance to the needs of the individual. The teacher gives just enough help to enable the student to carry out the strategy successfully—and no more.

After guided practice, Palincsar and Ransom recommend that students be given *independent practice*—the opportunity to execute the strategy on their own. Independent practice builds students' proficiency in using the strategy and encourages them to transfer it to other situations. This means having students extend use of the strategy to other settings and to other texts. Joyce Souza's students had such opportunities as they independently read and summarized information for their research on birds.

Palincsar and Ransom stress the importance throughout strategy instruction of having students monitor their own success in learning and applying the strategy. One way to do this is to have students compare their performance during initial learning with their present performance. Joyce Souza's students evaluate their progress as they set their own learning goals and monitor their success with the work they select for their portfolios.

Guidelines

Peter Johnston (1985) reminds us that the goal of strategy instruction is "to have students (a) recognize the strategy, (b) find it effective in attaining a desired goal, (c) adopt the strategy for their own use, and (d) generalize it to other situations" (p. 639). He makes several specific recommendations for meeting this goal.

1. *Have students describe the procedure in their own words.* This idea comes from research on teaching students to make inferences about text (Hansen & Pearson, 1983). As Jessie Michaels' and Joyce Souza's students gained experience with instructional approaches such as experience-text-relationship (Chapter 3) and concept-text-application (Chapter 4) the teachers asked, "What is it that we do when we meet to begin a new story?" Typical answers are "We talk about our lives and we predict what will happen in the stories," and "We think about what we know and what we want to learn."

Jessie Michaels and Joyce Souza have found that their students are often unaware of the procedures they use during instruction, so they regularly engage the children in reflections of this nature. As students verbalize the procedures they gain greater awareness of their own mental processes.

2. *Have students discuss why the strategy is useful.* Jessie Michaels and Joyce Souza follow their students' responses with the question, "Why do we do that?" Their students realize that "it helps us to understand what we'll be reading." Johnston points out that questions like these help students to transfer or generalize the strategy, because they have come to an understanding of the overall goals of instruction and how the strategy can be useful to them.

3. *Help students see how the strategy can be useful in a variety of situations.* Another kind of question teachers can ask is one promoting connection making. Joyce Souza said to her third graders, "Remember when we began reading the informational book about tigers? Before we begin this story about the peregrine falcon, what might we do?" When helping students learn to summarize text information, she asked them to consider the similarity of the task across different genres. Questions of this kind promote generalization by helping students see how a strategy may be useful in different situations with different texts.

4. *Promote self-monitoring.* It is important that students monitor their own performance. Jessie Michaels has worked to modify the kind of feedback she gives to her students. She knows how easy it is to simply tell students whether their answers are correct and she also knows that they then come to rely on her rather than themselves. Now, whether the students' responses are right or wrong, she more frequently responds with questions: "Do you think your answer is correct? How do you know? Does that answer make sense to you? Why or why not?"

Joan Lyons also encourages her beginning readers to monitor themselves. "Look at the picture; it should help you. Look at how that word begins. Does that make sense? What might you do to help yourself?"

Activities

Another important step in leading students toward independence is to give them the opportunity to use their own judgment in independent assignments. In Chapter 3 you saw that Jessie Michaels introduced her fifth graders to a variety of formats they could choose from when writing in response to literature.

Students also enjoy selecting and developing other ways for sharing their responses to literature with others. Here are some possibilities that students have found interesting (adapted from Short & Pierce, 1990, pp. 150–151):

Develop a skit or play based on events or characters from the story.

Produce a readers' theater script to highlight events from one story or to show similarities and differences between stories.

Write a new story using the same theme or involving the same characters.

Create a chart, web, or poster to share specific aspects of the book or to compare books with similar themes.

Continue learning through doing more research on a topic.

Invent a game or learning center incorporating the book's characters or events.

Create a work of art, such as a quilt, mural, diorama, mobile, or collage, based on the book.

Advertise books with poster sandwiches (posters that children hang over their shoulders—one in front, one in back).

Create poems or songs to share information or reflect feelings.

Our teachers recognize that these guidelines and activities strengthen their students' literacy development and independence. Yet they have all had students who can read well but who are not willing to do much reading on their own. In the next key concept, we will look at ways to help students to develop an interest in voluntary reading.

KEY CONCEPT **2** STUDENTS SHOULD HAVE OPPORTUNITIES TO READ INDEPENDENTLY FOR THEIR OWN ENJOYMENT AND INFORMATION.

ENCOURAGING VOLUNTARY READING

The teachers we have highlighted throughout this book recognize the value of voluntary or independent reading in which students have opportunities and the motivation (see Chapters 5 and 6) to read self-selected books. They consider reading a valuable and pleasurable leisure-time activity in and of itself. They also know that time spent reading books at home has been found to be the best predictor of children's growth as readers from second to fifth grade (Anderson, Wilson, & Fielding, 1988).

However, these teachers are aware of the reality of competing activities that take time away from reading: playing sports, watching television, and socializing. Elementary school students spend an average of 10 to 15 minutes per day reading at home (Taylor, Frye, & Maruyama, 1990).

These teachers are also aware that in many elementary classrooms students spend no more time engaged in reading *during* the school day. Studies suggest that students spend only from 8 to 15 minutes per day in silent reading (Taylor, Frye, & Maruyama, 1990). Joyce Souza recalls that there was a time when this was true in her classroom. Her children spent most of their time with worksheets, in writing answers to questions from their textbooks. "When you finish your work you may get a book to read," is what she used to say. Now, reading books is central to her program.

Teachers like Susan Meyer and Joyce Souza understand the importance of voluntary reading and include it as an aspect of literacy in their curriculum framework (see Chapter 1). They recognize the pleasure students gain from reading as well as the contribution voluntary reading makes to their development as readers and writers.

Their goal is to encourage students to do more reading both in school and at home. They support this goal by making books available, establishing time for reading, and developing a community of readers within their classrooms. They also work with their students to assess their attitude and development as independent readers.

Making Books Accessible

CLASSROOM LIBRARIES. In Chapter 4 we discussed the classroom library that Joyce Souza and her students organize and maintain. She estimates that at any one time the library houses at least 250 titles. As pointed out in Chapter 5, all our teachers believe that a well-stocked classroom library is essential in promoting children's independent reading of books. Their libraries include a variety of genres, old favorites as well as new titles, and the books come from many sources. Often teachers build personal collections that they supplement with materials borrowed from school and community libraries. Their students, too, enjoy sharing books from their home collections. Books are rotated in and out of the classroom on a regular basis.

Teachers make sure that the books they include represent the full range of their students' interests and abilities. They draw on informal assessments about students' interests in particular topics or literature as well as their favorite books and authors (as described in Chapter 7) to guide the selection of materials for their classroom libraries. They also rely on specific book and author recommendations that students make over the school year.

SUMMER MAILING PROGRAM. Summer loss of reading proficiency is sometimes of concern to teachers, particularly those who work with children from low-income families. Doris Crowell and Tom Klein

(1981) suggest that giving these children access to books over the summer vacation is one answer. They designed a program that involved mailing paperback books to children who had just completed the first and second grades. The children received books at their independent reading levels. One book was mailed each week for ten weeks during the summer vacation, and the children were allowed to keep the books. All the children appeared to benefit from the accessibility of books throughout the summer.

GUIDING SELECTION. When considering the accessibility of books, teachers are often concerned with guiding students in the selection process. You may recall that when Susan Meyer observed Jennifer's and Brenda's regular reading of Baby-sitters' Club books, she thought she might intervene to provide other suggestions (Chapter 1). Our other teachers are also attentive to their students' book selections. When Joan Lyons noticed that Laticia and Verner had selected books beyond their independent level, she nearly said, "Those books are too hard for you." Instead, she sent a note to their parents suggesting that the books might need to be read aloud to the children and planned to monitor their future choices to decide whether to intervene.

Teachers like Susan Meyer and Joan Lyons believe that their students should be allowed to choose the books they like, yet they know it is important for children to read extensively at their independent level (Chapter 7) to promote comprehension, vocabulary development, fluency, and overall reading facility. Teachers know that because children will have difficulty understanding books that are too challenging for them they should offer guidance; at the same time, children need to learn to make appropriate selections for themselves. When students continually choose light reading, their teachers try to remember that adults, too, find pleasure in an "easy read." Teachers will want to continually assess their students and use their professional judgment in guiding their selection of appropriate books and higher quality literature (Routman, 1991, pp. 43–44).

Establishing Time for Reading

INDEPENDENT READING IN THE CLASSROOM. Most teachers establish regular times and routines for independent reading. At the beginning of this chapter, we described independent reading in Joan Lyons' first grade. Susan Meyer reminded her third graders to take out the books they would read during the special time she set aside each school day for reading independently and sharing books together (Chapter 1). Jessie Michaels told her fifth-grade students that they might read from the books they had chosen after completing their written responses to literature (Chapter 3). Teachers recognize the importance

The teacher in this classroom has set aside a special time during the day for sustained silent reading. All students read self-selected books, then engage in some type of informal sharing at the end of the reading period.

of allotting time each day for students to read self-selected books. They know that students must have numerous opportunities to engage with books, if they are going to make reading a habit. They also recognize the importance of sharing to a successful independent reading program. Therefore, the teachers include regular times for students to share their books with partners, in small groups, or with the whole class.

Teachers often include a special time each day in which everyone engages in voluntary reading. Joyce Souza has set aside time after lunch that she calls SSR (sustained silent reading). Some teachers use other terms such as RR (recreational reading), DEAR (drop everything and read), and OTTER (our time to enjoy reading). Near the beginning of the year Joyce talked with her students about how they would use this time.

> *Teacher:* This will be a quiet time in which we will all choose to read books that are of special interest to us. I know most of you had SSR time when you were in second grade. How do you decide on a book to read?
>
> *Jermaine:* I look at the pictures.
>
> *Teacher:* How does that help you?
>
> *Jermaine:* I can tell what the book will be about.

Camela: I like to read books by Beverly Cleary so I look for books she wrote.

Teacher: (after further responses) I see that many of you make choices because you think you will enjoy the story. I wonder if you think about whether you can read the book on you own. How might you know if you can read it easily?

Karl: If it's a thick book, it's too hard!

Ryan: I look at how many words are on the page. If it has lots of words, it's a hard book.

Sui-lyn: Last year we learned to read the first page of the book. If I don't have trouble, and if it sounds interesting, I pick it to read.

Joyce then suggested that they might want some rules for their SSR time. Based on their past experiences as second graders, the students suggested:

1. No talking; no walking.
2. Stick with your book until the end of SSR.
3. At the end of SSR use your book log to record the date, title, and page you stopped reading.

Joyce begins each SSR period by setting a timer. She usually starts the year with a 5- to 10-minute period and gradually increases it until students are reading 15 to 20 minutes. This year she decided to involve the children in the decision making.

Teacher: How long do you think our SSR period should be? Our schedule could allow us between 5 and 30 minutes.

As expected, the children's suggestions differed. Many favored a 30-minute period. They compromised on a 10-minute allotment and decided to evaluate their sustained involvement at the end of the SSR period. Then they would decide if they wanted to adjust the time for the next day. Joyce was pleased by the thoughtful consideration her students showed in planning this time for themselves. She knows that students will be more committed to independent reading when they participate in the planning and evaluation.

INDEPENDENT READING OUTSIDE THE CLASSROOM. All the teachers we have discussed have programs for encouraging their students to read outside school. Joan Lyons' first graders check out a book each day to read at home to a family member. Their system is simple. The children have special envelopes printed with their names, school, and room number for carrying the books they choose. Also on the outside of the envelope is a form with spaces for the date, title of book, and the initials of the person who listened to them read. Each book in the classroom library contains a card showing the book's title.

CHECK IT OUT

FIGURE 8.1
Pockets for Library Cards

Joan made a wall chart with book pockets for each student (see Figure 8.1). When children check out a book from the classroom, they remove its card and place it into their pocket on the chart. When they return the book, they remove the card and replace it in the book. Joan can quickly scan the chart before the children go home to see that everyone has a book and to note their selections. She, or a student helper, also makes a quick check in the morning to be sure that books have been returned.

Many teachers use room displays to track students' independent reading. Bookworms grow around some classroom walls as students write their names and the titles of each book they read on a construction-paper circle that becomes a new addition to the worm's body. Colorful bulletin-board displays such as the one shown on the next page are frequently used to highlight students' independent reading.

Some teachers offer incentives to increase their students' enthusiasm for reading. Other teachers are uncomfortable with the idea of extrinsic motivators; they believe that the pleasure gained from a good book should be the reward. Those teachers who offer incentives, such as pencils or books after children read a designated number of books, hope the extra motivation will eventually lead their students to become self-directed readers. Most teachers view the incentives as a way to get students started, and then they present ways to maintain the habit of reading for its intrinsic benefits, the enjoyment of reading. Sometimes teachers set up a special event or party when the cumulative number of books read by all class members reaches a certain total.

Seeing their balloons move higher into the clouds on this chart reminds fourth graders of how much voluntary reading they have done. The chart is one of several ways the teacher promotes voluntary reading.

Because books differ in length and difficulty, some teachers, especially those of older children, ask students to tally numbers of pages or the number of minutes spent in voluntary reading, rather than counting numbers of books.

Often corporations and charitable organizations encourage children's independent reading through incentives and fund raisers. These offers are regularly sent to school personnel; teachers and students participate in as many or as few as they choose. Again, these are extrinsic motivators and teachers must be cautious. However, young children are usually enthusiastic about such programs and are often motivated to read more than usual.

For students who receive little home support, teachers often find an adult or an older student within the school to "buddy" with these children. Then everyone is given the opportunity to participate.

Developing the Classroom Community

Access to a wide range of books and opportunities to read are certainly necessities for a successful voluntary reading program. However, our teachers have discovered that the social support within the classroom provides the essential key to assure students' continued interest in reading. When teacher and students regularly interact around books, a network of readers is formed that furthers all members' active participation.

When Joyce Souza sets the timer for the SSR period, she always reads her own book along with her students. She recognizes the importance of sharing her own pleasure in reading. How could she tell her students that reading is enjoyable and not model her own involvement?

Joyce also talks with her students about the books she reads both in and out of the classroom.

> *Teacher:* (as the timer sounds to signal the end of SSR) Goodness, I hate to stop reading. I'm in the midst of this great mystery which I began reading during the weekend. My husband had just finished it and he said, "I know you'll enjoy this." And I do. I keep questioning him about the ending, but he won't tell me if I'm guessing right.

Joyce sees herself as a member of the classroom community of readers and regularly talks of her own reading experiences. She shares such things as her feelings about a story, connections she makes to her own life, interesting information she learns, the author's writing style, or why she chose the book. She also reads from a variety of genres during the SSR period—fiction, informational books, professional books, and children's literature.

Fielding, Wilson, and Anderson (1986) looked at the question of why some children become avid readers. They found that avid readers often mentioned their teachers' influence on their reading habits. They spoke of teachers having books available in the classroom, reading out loud to the class, recommending books to them, talking to them about books they had read, requiring them to read a certain number of books in a grading period, or just being such good teachers that children came to love reading by being in their classes. According to the children themselves, teachers can have a significant influence on the development of avid reading.

Teachers might need to take an explicit approach with some students to ensure that they become participants within the classroom community of readers. In their study of fifth-grade students, Kathryn Au, Michelle Kunitake, and Karen Blake (1992) found that most of them had unsophisticated or haphazard methods for getting ideas of what to read. Au and colleagues recommend that teachers teach students reliable strategies for selecting books to read independently such as reading book jackets or browsing through them. In addition, teachers could give students experience with a wide variety of genres and topics through class read-alouds. Students would become aware of the options available to them, especially if the teacher makes explicit the connection between books read aloud and books they might choose for themselves.

You saw that Joyce Souza sometimes shares at the end of the SSR period. She also encourages the children to share about the books they are reading. Some teachers, like Susan Meyer, promote sharing of the books students read outside their classroom. Susan expects the students to read for at least 15 minutes every day after school. Then, within the daily language arts period, she schedules time for them to talk about their independent reading with one another.

Some teachers suggest that students share their books through writing or other types of expressive presentations. We offer a variety of possibilities in Key Concept 1. Dixie Lee Spiegel (1981) argues convincingly that students not be *required* to share the reading they have done through book reports or other projects. She believes the motivation for voluntary reading should be the students' own interest in reading, rather than external forces such as teachers' requirements. On the other hand, she strongly recommends voluntary sharing, because many students enjoy sharing their reading experiences with other children and with adults. Encouraging voluntary sharing contributes to the development of a community of readers within the classroom.

Spiegel offers two sensible guidelines for voluntary sharing. First, teachers should be sure that the amount of time the student spends on a sharing project is much less than that spent reading the material. Art projects such as murals or models based on the reading frequently take up a great deal of time. Even though students often enjoy these projects, Spiegel points out that the projects may have more to do with artistic expression than with developing the habit of voluntary reading.

The second guideline is that teachers have children use techniques for sharing that promote the voluntary reading of other students. One way to do this is to have the children add pages to a catalogue of recommended books (Criscuolo, 1977, cited in Spiegel, 1981). When children have read a book they think will be interesting to their classmates, they write a synopsis or advertisement for it, perhaps including an illustration. The teacher makes sure the children include information such as the title, author, and where the book may be found (school or classroom library).

READING LOG

NAME Danaelle _____

DATE _____

DATE	TITLE & AUTHOR	RATING (1-5)	TYPE OF BOOK	INTERESTING WORDS
9-1	The cat in the hat	5	Funny	
9-5	Bread and Jam	3	Animal	
9-13	Tell me some more	4		
10-3	Nate the Great	3	Detective	nightcap rummage
10-7	Berenstain Bears In the Dark	4	Bear	
10-9	Betty Bear's Birthday	2	Bear	

FIGURE 8.2
A Reading Log, Partially Filled Out

Assessing Interest and Involvement

Teachers who value voluntary reading as an important aspect of their literacy curriculum will want to include it in their ongoing assessment of students' literacy development. Earlier we considered how beginning-of-the-year inventories help teachers learn of the books, authors, and topics in which their students are interested. This information helps them select materials for their classroom libraries.

Students' reading logs (Figure 8.2), where they list the books they have read, provide assessment information for teachers in setting instructional goals and students in setting personal goals.

The fifth graders in Jessie Michaels' classroom add information to their logs at the end of each school day. Jessie sets aside a daily SSR period, and she encourages her students to read during their free time in class as well as after school. Each month she asks her students to list one goal they would like to meet through their inde-

VOLUNTARY READING
(O or N)

Voluntary Reading Evaluation
+ = All 3 settings
3 = Any 2 settings
− = Less than 2 settings
O = Observed   N = Not observed
(P) = Probe question asked

Child reads
regularly in
these settings:

STUDENT NAMES	Free class time	SSR	Outside class	EVALUATION [+, ✓, −]	New or interesting words noted (3)	COMMENTS
Danaelle	O	O	N	✓	O	Asked about <u>rummage</u> and <u>nightcap</u> during a discussion following SSR time.

FIGURE 8.3
Voluntary Reading Checklist
Source: Carroll, 1992.

pendent reading, and every week they consider what they are doing to work toward their goals. The students' goals are varied:

Tonya: I will read Beverly Cleary's autobiography, *A Girl from Yamhill: A Memoir.*

Darrah: I will try to finish a whole book this month.

Sharita: I will find and read more information about Kwanzaa.

As Jessie reviews the students' logs she notes that a few of the children have selected other works by the authors whose books they are reading in their current thematic unit. She also discovers that several students seem to be consistently reading books on only one topic (horses are Tammy's choice), by the same author, or of the same genre. Jessie plans to continue presenting a variety of literature to the discussion groups and through her read-alouds. It is early in the school year. For now she will trust that all her students will branch out. She will make a reevaluation next month to decide if she needs to be more explicit.

To assess voluntary reading, some teachers periodically complete checklists based on their observational notes, student goals, and students' reading logs (see Figure 8.3). Kindergarten teachers may simply be interested in noting whether or not their students enjoy looking through books and forming their own stories based on pictures. Teachers of older students have found it helpful to monitor students' independent reading during SSR, free time in school, and outside school. By evaluating information of this kind, teachers can identify children who need extra attention to become involved in voluntary reading.

KEY CONCEPT **3**   STUDENTS SHOULD HAVE OPPORTUNITIES TO SUPPORT ONE ANOTHER'S LITERACY DEVELOPMENT AS MEMBERS OF AN EXTENDED COMMUNITY.

THE COMMUNITY OF READERS

In Key Concept 2 we discussed how students' literacy development is enhanced by sharing independent reading within the classroom community. Teachers will want to explore other ways students can participate in literate communities beyond, as well as within, their classrooms.

Throughout this book you have been introduced to students who are actively involved in supporting one another as readers and writers. You have seen children coming together in pairs, small groups, and as a whole class to exchange personal views about books. Less able readers have been paired with more able peers so that they too can participate in a group's literature discussions.

Student writers have helped one another explore topics and refine pieces of writing through peer conferences. Work on research projects has been shared so that all students could experience success. Students have reflected upon one another's literacy growth as they engaged in the assessment process together. The teachers value the support for learning that students can provide to one another, and they continually seek ways to encourage the active participation of all students.

As in the development of literacy skills, children need guided practice if they are to work together in productive ways. Regie Routman (1991) cautions us that teachers cannot simply put children together and expect that productive learning will occur. She discusses the effectiveness of pairing children to read together when it is carefully organized by the teacher so that students know how to proceed. The kind of guidance that teachers provide should be determined by their purpose for the pairing. When teachers want to ensure that less able students have access to literature selections, they may pair children of different reading levels. Then the more able student reads the text aloud while the less able follows along visually, or the students read out loud together with the more able student taking the lead. If the purpose is to share enjoyment of independent reading, the student pairs will participate more equally in the reading.

Shelley Harwayne (1992) also emphasizes the need for teacher guidance if students are to work together in supportive, productive ways. She describes how a literate classroom community formed as fifth-grade students came together each day to explore a variety of literature. One morning early in the school year, after the class had shared poetry selections together, she distributed a copy of a poem to each small table group of students. She asked the groups to use the next 20 minutes to prepare a choral performance of the poem for presentation to the whole class. As the children worked, Harwayne and the classroom teacher visited each group, offering their support, observing, and making notes about student interactions.

Harwayne points out that this activity set the tone for future student response groups. "Here was their opportunity, to be repeated many times during the first weeks of school, to come together in small social communities. The students got to know one another. They learned to negotiate and take turns. They learned to revise, critique, and compliment one another. They learned to rehearse, modify, and clarify their ideas. They also learned to encourage one another, to take pride in one another, and to perform in front of one another. All of these were skills they would later need to respond to one another's writing" (p. 16).

Once children feel a part of the classroom community, teachers often seek to extend their experiences beyond the classroom walls. You learned at the beginning of this chapter of a partnership between kindergartners and fifth graders who meet regularly to share literacy experiences.

Routman (1991, p. 477) and Harwayne (1992, pp. 17–18) again remind us that successful sharing among students, including those of different ages, does not occur automatically. Routman describes how fourth graders were paired to read with at-risk first graders. Before the older students began reading with the younger children, their teachers carefully considered which children would be likely to work well together. The fourth graders were shown how to introduce books, how to guide the reading, and how to record information in the first graders' reading folders.

Likewise, when Harwayne's fifth graders decided to share poetry with first graders they carefully researched and planned their lessons. That, however, was not enough. During their first lesson together, Harwayne was surprised with the impatience and manner of the older students. She realized that she had neglected to guide them in how to teach. She remedied this by giving the fifth graders opportunities to observe the first graders and their teacher during shared reading. When the fifth graders returned the next month with their new poems, they were much better prepared to be teachers.

Connie Morrice and Maureen Simmons (1991) describe a year-long buddies program they developed for their first- and fifth-grade classes. They termed their program Beyond Reading Buddies because they included writing, speaking, listening, and drama as well as reading. They set aside large blocks of time throughout the year to explore literacy activities centered on big books, special holidays, and outdoor science. As the buddies read, wrote, and shared texts together a network of mutual support developed among the students.

An important component of this cross-age program was goal setting and evaluation. The teachers helped their students understand the overall goals for the program and for each session. Peer and self-evaluations helped the children consider what went well and what needed working on, and the teachers' observational notes helped them support each pair of students as well as evaluate the overall effectiveness of the program.

The teachers concluded that their students benefitted from opportunities to extend their exploration of literacy and to gain greater control over their own learning. First graders and fifth graders came to participate more fully as members of the literate community.

Often whole schools, including nonteaching personnel, join together to promote the development of a literary community among students and adults. A schoolwide SSR program has been put into place in many schools. This approach sends the message that reading is important, and the message takes on greater importance when backed by the entire school. During the school day a block of time is set aside, usually 10 to 20 minutes, in which everyone reads—all students, all staff. Often non-classroom–based staff members will enter classrooms to read during the SSR period. The school principal may be found in kindergarten and the custodian in a fifth-grade classroom.

Jim Trelease (1989, pp. 145–146) shares a principal's explanation of the purpose of SSR, which was sent to parents in a newsletter:

> It is a serious effort to raise the student's awareness of reading. All in the school participate. Please do not call or come to school during that fifteen-minute span.

Trelease describes another school where the daily SSR period begins with a student sharing over the intercom system. The student tells what he or she is reading and gives a brief synopsis of the book.

Other schools use a large hallway bulletin board to share the reading done by the students and adults within the school. When members of a school join together as a larger community of readers, their enjoyment and knowledge of books are enhanced and extended.

An author study, suggested by Sharron McElmeel (1988), is another way to form a school community of readers. McElmeel proposes that for a designated length of time the entire school focus on an author's or illustrator's body of work. The school library becomes the center for the study. The author's books are highlighted along with information about the author. Activities are explored and classroom projects are displayed.

McElmeel discusses ways authors' works can be appreciated by all students within the school. She points out that students of different ages can appreciate the same book, though at different levels. For example, during a study of author Beatrice deRegniers, kindergartners through sixth graders were able to compare and contrast film and text versions of *Little Sister and the Month Brothers* (1976) and explore the genre of folk literature. The older children also compared and contrasted a third version of the folktale and then extended their study by examining deRegniers' life in relation to her writing. Books written by some authors span a range of different ages. Arnold Lobel's *Frog and Toad* books are usually considered most appropriate for first-grade readers. However, the humor of "The Bad Kangaroo" in Lobel's *Fables* is sophisticated enough for adults.

McElmeel believes that a schoolwide author study provides students and teachers opportunities to explore the connections between and across works of literature. We can recognize, too, the potential of an author study for creating a larger literacy community in which students and teachers of all grade levels come together to share and appreciate their discoveries.

Book swaps are another way to extend the school's community. When children bring in a book to trade (often in the school library), they are given a coupon that entitles them to receive another book in exchange. A bulletin board near the trading area allows children to advertise for books they would like to exchange with others.

It is important that school personnel work together to promote the social aspects of literacy. A school culture embracing a total commitment to book reading will encourage students to value membership within an ever-expanding community of readers and writers.

KEY CONCEPT 4   STUDENTS' PROFICIENCY AND INTEREST IN LITERACY SHOULD BE STRENGTHENED THROUGH CONNECTIONS BETWEEN HOME AND SCHOOL.

HOME-SCHOOL CONNECTIONS

Earlier in this chapter we saw an example of how parents were involved with their children's literacy learning in Susan Meyer's third-grade classroom. Research across diverse populations of students shows that "parent involvement in almost any form appears to produce measurable gains in student achievement" (Henderson, 1988, p. 150). When we consider the importance of developing supportive literate communities, we must include our students' families as well.

Hally Simmons began involving her students' parents before the first day of school. A few weeks before school began she sent a letter addressed to each child. In the letter she introduced herself to the students, told them of some new books she had chosen for the classroom library, and expressed her enthusiasm for learning with them throughout the coming school year. She also invited them to bring a favorite book to share with their classmates on the first day of school.

Attached to the children's letter was one for their parents. Hally Simmons welcomed the parents' collaboration and participation. She invited them into the classroom to read with children, help with writing, share an interest or a talent, and participate in field trips. She also encouraged the parents to attend a beginning-of-the-year open house and told them that she would be sending a weekly newsletter to keep them informed of classroom happenings. She suggested that they might like to respond to the newsletters with their own comments or questions.

Hally Simmons recognizes the importance of involving parents as members of the school community. In addition, she values the literacy community of the child's home. During the first month of school she asked parents to complete a questionnaire telling about their children's involvement in literacy activities, interests, unique characteristics, and family circumstances. This information helped Hally appreciate her students' literacy backgrounds and family circumstances. She discovered that Marco's family corresponds regularly with family members in Mexico and that Bronson's grandmother is the family member who reads stories aloud to him. Hally Simmons also learned that a few children had little home support with reading or writing. She would plan to offer opportunities to their families and, in the meantime, she would provide these students with an extra dose of her attention.

Teachers often use two major means to strengthen the connections between school and home for the purpose of improving children's literacy development: communicating with parents and enlisting parents' participation in their children's literacy activities. We now discuss ideas for parent involvement within these two areas. Many of the ideas can be easily adapted to situations where the teacher is working with a family member other than the child's parents.

This second grader works on a newsletter designed to keep her parents informed about her learning. Her teacher will also add comments.

Communicating with Parents

WRITTEN COMMUNICATION. You will remember examples throughout this book in which teachers shared information with parents through writing. Often teachers begin the school year with a letter to parents describing the overall goals of the classroom program and the types of activities in which their children will be engaged. Regular newsletters, often with contributions by the students, continue throughout the school year, sharing more specific goals and keeping parents involved in the learning process. Monthly newsletters can communicate classroom routines, special events, themes being studied, and strategies being taught. Some teachers leave space within the newsletter for students to write a personal message to their own parents. Other teachers make the newsletter an authentic writing project, involving the whole class in its production.

Schools have generally relied on report cards as the chief means of communicating with parents about children's progress.

Report cards generally can provide only a very broad overview of children's accomplishments; there are more informative means.

Some teachers regularly send the portfolios home with their students. They include a letter asking parents to study the contents along with their children, write positive comments about the work, and return the portfolio within a designated time. The letter also invites parents to contact the teacher directly with any concerns (Tierney, 1991). To accompany the portfolios, some teachers have their students write a letter to their parents telling why they are proud of the work that has been selected and how it shows progress toward their goals.

Another option for sharing student growth is progress letters. In these letters teachers can describe in detail the kinds of text selections the child is able to comprehend, some of the areas in which new vocabulary has been learned, and the kinds of books the child seems interested in reading on his or her own. Brief notes may be sent home with certain children on days when they have accomplished something special (for example, read their first published book to the class).

CONFERENCES AND OPEN HOUSES. Parents or other family members usually make time to attend school conferences and open houses. In many schools, parent conferences are scheduled twice during the year. Teachers should invite parents' active participation in the conferences by encouraging them to ask questions about their child's progress and to share their own unique insights concerning their child's development.

Student portfolios are often the focal point of parent conferences. As parents examine samples of the selections their child is reading and of the child's writing, and compare them with earlier work, they gain a better idea of how the child is progressing. Some teachers, like Susan Meyer, send the portfolios home to be shared by their students before the parents come for their conferences. Students and parents have time to talk together about the children's goals, evaluation, and work products. Parents come to the conference better prepared, with additional insights into their child's strengths and needs and a view of their child as an individual with unique abilities and interests in reading and writing.

Open houses can serve as an occasion for the teacher to explain her approach to literacy instruction to the parents as a group. Teachers have found that parents usually enjoy being involved with the materials and activities of the classroom, so they display student writing on their bulletin boards and make a variety of reading materials available for parents to peruse. Some teachers invite the parents to experience reading and writing instruction in much the same way their children do each day. For example, they may choose a literature piece for the parents to read, respond to in writing, and discuss with one another. The teacher then explains her daily reading instruction in terms of the adults' experiences. Teachers find that when parents experience active involvement they gain a deeper understanding of the classroom program. In addition, they have acquired a more refined model for reading and writing with their children at home.

Enlisting Parents' Participation

Fielding, Wilson, and Anderson (1986) found that the parents of avid readers create home environments where reading seems attractive to children but otherwise do not worry too much about it. For example, parents make sure there are many books in the home and act as models because they enjoy reading. Parents who read the newspaper, make shopping lists, write letters, or talk about favorite books are creating a literate home environment. Teachers can help parents understand that participation in daily, routine literacy activities will further their children's development and interest more than if they were to schedule special reading and writing events.

PARENTS' READING ALOUD TO CHILDREN. Reading aloud to children, or listening to their children read, is probably the most common pattern of parent involvement (Epstein & Becker, 1982). Families will differ in their manners and routines for sharing books. Rather than recommending specific procedures that parents should follow, or a particular schedule or amount of reading to be done, teachers might best support home reading by offering parents suggestions about books they and their children are likely to enjoy together. Parents of students in upper grades need this support in particular, as often they do not recognize the value of sharing reading with older children.

A good reference appears annually in *The Reading Teacher,* which lists the new books children reported liking best. *The New Read-Aloud Handbook* (Trelease, 1989) and *The New York Times Parent's Guide to the Best Books for Children* are also valuable resources.

Many teachers send book club information home so that students may order books inexpensively. Parents find it helpful when teachers include recommendations of the books they think the children will most enjoy. Teachers often use their newsletters to recommend favorite authors, titles, and magazines for families to locate and share together.

MAKING USE OF THE LIBRARY. When teachers suggest specific titles and types of books, they can encourage parents to take their children to look for them at the library. Because many communities do not have public libraries, and nonmainstream families often find libraries inaccessible, teachers cannot rely upon their students' acquisition of library materials. As much as possible, however, teachers should promote library use. Teachers might introduce children and parents to public libraries through field trips, collect applications for library cards, provide parents with information on the location and hours of public libraries, and pass on announcements of special events such as story hours.

Most public libraries offer summer reading programs. Routman (1991) suggests that teachers invite the local librarian into their classrooms to talk about summer reading and their programs. The librarian can distribute an annotated reading list that offers students and their parents guidance in making their summer selections.

VOLUNTARY READING PROGRAM. Spiegel (1981) points out that asking parents to support voluntary reading gives them a positive, pleasant, and low-pressure way of helping their children at home. Earlier we suggested that teachers should discuss their literacy programs with parents during school open houses and conferences. During these occasions teachers will help parents understand the value of voluntary reading in children's literacy development. To further parents' support and cooperation, Spiegel suggests a series of short newsletters, sent home every two days or so, explaining the reasons for having a voluntary reading program and how it will work. This introductory set of newsletters could go out during the first two weeks of school.

> *Newsletter 1:* Explain what a voluntary reading program is and how it will work in your class. Include a schedule of what information will be contained in subsequent newsletters.
> *Newsletter 2:* Provide the rationale for having a voluntary reading program, with emphasis on how it fits into the basic curriculum. Include a short statement of support from your principal and reading teacher.
> *Newsletter 3:* List suggestions for ways parents can help support the program through their efforts at home.
> *Newsletter 4:* List ways parents can volunteer their time in the classroom to support the program (p. 58; *voluntary* substituted for the word *recreational*).

Teachers can follow up on the suggestions offered in Newsletters 3 and 4 within their regular weekly or monthly newsletters throughout the school year.

HOMEWORK. Many parents want even their primary-grade children to be given homework assignments and are happy to help with homework. Teachers should be certain to design homework to support the major goals of the classroom program, not to serve as busywork, and to help parents understand the reasons for giving certain kinds of homework assignments rather than others.

Homework will generally prove most valuable if it encourages children to use reading and writing in authentic ways and provides opportunities for problem solving that are relevant to their lives. Independent reading of a book chosen by the child and reading the newspaper for particular kinds of information are sound homework activities. Corresponding with pen pals, relatives, and friends is an important use of literacy that parents can be encouraged to support. Another possibility is to involve parents and children in journal writing to document important events in their family lives.

Betty Shockley (1993) describes a home journal project involving her first graders and their families, centered around books the children chose to take home from the classroom library. Throughout the school year, family members shared the books and responded in their journals in ways that were unique and meaningful to each family. Shockley added her own personal responses to each family's journal. Students, parents, and teacher learned from one another through the authentic school-to-home and home-to-school literacy experiences this project encouraged.

PARENT VOLUNTEERS. As we saw in Susan Meyer's third grade, parents are usually welcome additions to the classroom community as observers and participants. By visiting the classroom, parents come to understand, support, and reinforce their child's literacy development. They can also provide assistance and serve as resources within a busy classroom. When parents are not available, other family members or friends often serve as substitutes.

When adults work directly with students, teachers should be sure they clearly understand the literacy program and know how they can be of help. Sometimes teachers schedule a special orientation session for their regular volunteers or arrange time to talk informally with parents and answer their questions.

Parent volunteers often are used to listen to individual children read, to confer with children during writers' workshop, to help students publish their books, and to support special projects.

Routman (1988) tells of a first-grade teacher who uses parents to help broaden the classroom curriculum. Each week, one student invites a family member to share something about his or her job or a hobby. The children listen, ask questions, and respond in their journals. After the visits the children write thank-you letters and read and discuss related books. Parents become more involved in the classroom community, and the children's understanding of the literate community is broadened.

SUMMARY

We opened this chapter with glimpses into three classrooms to illustrate how teachers can foster a love of reading by inviting students' participation in an ever-expanding literate community. In the first key concept we addressed the issue of how teachers can lead students toward greater independence in using reading and writing strategies. We described the concepts of guided and independent practice, and again mentioned the importance of teaching students to monitor their own comprehension. In the second key concept we turned to voluntary reading and discussed approaches teachers might use to develop students' interest in books. We also showed the importance of the classroom community in supporting a love of reading.

In the third key concept we extended students' literate community both within and beyond the walls of the classroom. We discussed how children can learn from one another in their development as readers and writers. Our fourth key concept emphasized the importance of the home in children's literacy development. We suggested that teachers keep parents informed about classroom activities and their children's learning and invite parents to participate in the process. Students will be well served when teachers help them appreciate the value of membership in the greater community of literacy users.

◀ **ACTIVITIES**

Reflecting on Your Own Literacy

Consider your own development as a reader. Think of times when others supported your interest in books. Write a brief reflection about one of your memories. Form a group with two or three others to share your thoughts. Do you notice any similarities or patterns among the reflections of the members in your group?

Applying What You Have Learned to the Classroom

Visit both primary- and intermediate-grade classrooms to discover how students' love of reading is being fostered. Note the classroom environments. Talk with the teachers to learn what they do to support their students. Record your findings. What similarities and differences do you note among the classrooms?

BIBLIOGRAPHY

References

Anderson, R. C., Wilson, P. T., & Fielding, L. G. (1988). Growth in reading and how children spend their time outside of school. *Reading Research Quarterly, 23*(3), 285–303.

Au, K. H., Kunitake, M. M., & Blake, K. M. (1992). Students' perceptions of how they became interested in reading. Paper prepared for the symposium, "Exploring children's disposition to learn: The role of motivation and interest in reading," annual meeting of the National Reading Conference, San Antonio, December 1992.

Carlsen, G. R., & Sherrill, A. (1988). *Voices of readers: How we come to love books.* Urbana, IL: National Council of Teachers of English.

Carroll, J., (Ed.). (1992). *Literacy curriculum guide.* Honolulu, HI: Kamehameha Schools/Bernice Pauahi Bishop Estate, Early Education Division.

Crowell, D. C., & Klein, T. W. (1981). Preventing summer loss of reading skills among primary children. *The Reading Teacher, 34*(5), 561–564.

Epstein, J. L., & Becker, H. J. (1982). Teachers' reported practices of parent involvement: Problems and possibilities. *Elementary School Journal, 83*(2), 103–113.

Fielding, L., Wilson, P., & Anderson, R. C. (1986). A focus on free reading: The role of tradebooks in reading instruction. In T. E. Raphael (Ed.), *Contexts of school-based literacy.* New York: Random House.

Hansen, J., & Pearson, P. D. (1983). An instructional study: Improving the inferential comprehension of good and poor fourth-grade readers. *Journal of Educational Psychology, 75,* 821–829.

Harwayne, S. (1992). *Lasting impressions: Weaving literature into the writing workshop.* Portsmouth, NH: Heinemann.

Henderson, A. T. (1988, October). "Parents are a school's best friend." *Phi Delta Kappan,* pp. 149–153.

Johnston, P. (1985). Teaching students to apply strategies that improve reading comprehension. *Elementary School Journal, 85*(5), 635–645.

Lipson, E. R., compiler. 1988. *The New York Times Parent's Guide to the Best Books for Children.* New York: Times Books.

McElmeel, S. L. (1988). *An author a month (for pennies).* Englewood, CO: Libraries Unlimited.

Morrice, C., & Simmons, M. (1991). Beyond reading buddies: A whole language cross-age program. *The Reading Teacher, 44*(8), 572–577.

Palincsar, A. S., & Ransom, K. (1988). From the mystery spot to the thoughtful spot: The instruction of metacognitive strategies. *The Reading Teacher, 41*(8), 784–789.

Pearson, P. D. (1985). Changing the face of reading comprehension instruction. *The Reading Teacher, 38*(6), 724–738.

Routman, R. (1988). *Transitions: From literature to literacy.* Portsmouth, NH: Heinemann.

Routman, R. (1991). *Invitations: Changing as teachers and learners K-12.* Portsmouth, NH: Heinemann.

Shockley, B. (1993). Extending the literate community: Reading and writing with families. *The New Advocate, 6*(1), 11–23.

Short, K. G., & Pierce, K. M. (1990). *Talking about books: Creating literate communities.* Portsmouth, NH: Heinemann.

Spiegel, D. L. (1981). *Reading for pleasure: Guidelines.* Newark, DE: International Reading Association.

Taylor, B. M., Frye, B. J., & Maruyama, G.M. (1990). Time spent reading and reading growth. *American Educational Research Journal, 27*(2), 351–362.

Tierney, R. J. (1991). *Portfolio assessment in the reading-writing classroom.* Norwood, MA: Christopher-Gordon Publishers, Inc.

Trelease, J. (1989). *The new read-aloud handbook.* New York: Penguin Books.

Suggested Classroom Resources

Cleary, B. (1988). *A girl from Yamhill: A memoir.* New York: William Morrow.

Cowley, J. (1986). *Ice cream.* Bothell, WA: The Wright Group.

Cowley, J. (1987). *Grandpa, Grandpa.* Bothell; WA: The Wright Group.

Cowley, J. (1990). *Noise.* Bothell, WA: The Wright Group.

deRegniers, B.S. (1976). *Little sister and the month brothers.* New York: Clarion.

Lionni, L. (1983). *Swimmy.* New York: Pantheon.

Lobel, A. (1980). *Fables.* New York: Harper & Row.

Lobel, A. *Frog and toad* series. New York: Harper & Row.

Paterson, D. (1975). *Eat.* New York: The Dial Press.

Polacco, P. (1992). *Chicken Sunday.* New York: Philomel Books.

Seuss, Dr. (1983). *Hop on Pop.* New York: Random House.

Soto, G. (1987). *The cat's meow.* San Francisco: Strawberry Hill Press.

Further Readings

Handel, R. D. (1992). The partnership for family reading: Benefits for families and schools. *The Reading Teacher, 46*(2), 116–126.

Hansen, J. (1993). Synergism of classroom and school libraries. *The New Advocate, 6*(3), 201–211.

Leland, C., & Fitzpatrick, R. (1994). Cross-age interaction builds enthusiasm for reading and writing. *The Reading Teacher, 47*(4), 292–301.

O'Masta, G. A., & Wolf, J. M. (1991). Encouraging independent reading through the reading millionaires project. *The Reading Teacher, 44*(9), 656–662.

Video Tapes

Reading to your children (1992). North Billerica, MA: Curriculum Associates.

9 TEACHING STUDENTS WITH SPECIAL NEEDS

Kyoung Suk, a second grader from Korea, likes to make "little books" by stapling combinations of five-by-five lined and unlined paper together and adding laminated construction paper covers. He particularly enjoys making books based on the Mr. Men series by Roger Hargreaves (1978). After Kyoung discovered the books, he asked me to read them to him. Even though he didn't understand many of the details of the stories, their illustrations and my dramatization of the actions enabled him to follow the main story line. Today he is working on a new little book, which he entitled *Mr. Snow*. Sheh Mai, another Korean student in the class who is more familiar with English, helps translate for Kyoung Suk. Kyoung relays a sentence in Korean to this friend, who then translates to me: "Mr. Snow is a fat man who likes to live in cold weather." . . . Regardless of the age or English capability of the children, their message should be rendered in complete thoughts rather than only doled out in short, choppy phrases. While many would predict that short phrases would be easier to remember, I have found that complete, lengthier sentences are best because they more closely reflect the students' original intention. (Ridley, 1990, p. 215)

◀ OVERVIEW

In this chapter we pay a final visit to three classrooms: Joan Lyons' first grade, Susan Meyer's third grade, and Jessie Michaels' fifth grade. We highlight the approaches these teachers use to develop the literacy ability of students with special needs. In the first key concept we look at what teachers can do to develop these students' ownership of literacy. With ownership as the starting point, we then look at instructional strategies teachers can use to promote students' ability to construct meaning from text. The second key concept focuses on reading comprehension strategies and highlights small-group lessons following two approaches: instructional conversations and reciprocal teaching. The third key concept addresses word-reading strategies. Writing can play an important role, along with other activities that call students' attention to spelling patterns. In the fourth key concept we look at how the classroom teacher can promote the literacy development of students with special needs by

281

providing them with a system of consistent support, making use of the resources of the home as well as the school.

KEY CONCEPT 1: Teachers should make sure that students with special needs develop ownership of literacy and become part of the classroom community of learners.

KEY CONCEPT 2: Teachers should use instructional strategies that develop students' text comprehension ability.

KEY CONCEPT 3: Teachers should use instructional strategies that develop students' ability to identify words with accuracy and fluency.

KEY CONCEPT 4: Teachers should engage in a consistent effort to provide high-quality instruction to students with special needs, creating systems of social support involving other teachers, classmates, and family members.

◀ **PERSPECTIVE**

Approaches for Teaching Students with Special Needs

We use the term "students with special needs" to refer to students who, for whatever reason, have special needs in learning to read and write. Some students may have received low-quality instruction in their first years in school and have fallen behind their peers. Others may speak a home language other than standard English and be in classrooms where teachers do not know or appreciate their language. Some may come from a cultural background with different values and norms from those of the school. Some may simply find it difficult to learn to read and write, just as others find it difficult to learn to draw or to carry a tune.

Our approach to teaching reading to students with special needs is straightforward. We will not spend time trying to pigeonhole these students by giving them labels such as "poor reader," "limited English proficient," "learning disabled," or "culturally deprived." We believe that too much time has been spent labeling students and too little time strengthening their learning situations. As you read the classroom descriptions below, notice the steps the three teachers have taken to strengthen the learning situations in their classrooms, to make sure that students with special needs do learn to read and write well.

Supporting Students with Special Needs in a First-Grade Classroom

The children in Joan Lyons's first-grade classroom speak a variety of languages at home, including Spanish, Chinese, and black English, and their background experiences are as diverse as their home languages. Some children come from families that have lived in the United States for generations, while others have recently immigrated from Southeast Asia, Mexico, and Eastern Europe. Joan wants to celebrate the diversity in her students' backgrounds while also bringing them together as a community of learners.

From the beginning of the school year, Joan conducted a writers' workshop in which the children wrote on self-selected topics. She encouraged them to use invented spelling in their drafts and then worked with them on conventional spelling when the time came to edit their pieces. As children sat in the author's chair and shared their drafts and published pieces, others in the class came to appreciate their classmates' unique experiences. For example, Rosenda read a piece about visiting her uncle's prawn farm in the Philippines. Children also learned about the emotions that they all shared. When Taylor read a piece about his sister going to the hospital, his classmates could understand his fears.

Right from the start, Joan encouraged all the children to write, not just those who could speak English well. Rosenda, for example, spoke Ilokano at home and was just starting to become comfortable with English. Taylor's first language was black English, but he was sensitive to the differences between his own oral language and the written language he heard in books, and his writing was almost entirely in standard English. Because of their language backgrounds, both Rosenda and Taylor might be considered students with special needs. However, both prospered during the writers' workshop.

When Joan noticed that several children needed help with the same skill, such as adding more information to their stories, she addressed this need through mini-lessons taught to the whole class or to a small group. In individual writing conferences, Joan could meet the special needs shown by each child. During the readers' workshop, Joan used different forms of grouping (see Chapter 6). Most of the time, she divided the class into three small groups for reading instruction, sometimes by reading ability, and at other times on the basis of their interest in a particular book. In first grade, Joan had discovered, many children need help understanding story elements, such as the problem and solution in the story, or developing effective word-reading strategies.

By grouping children by reading ability, Joan was able to target the comprehension and word-reading strategies needed by a particular group. For example, in November one group of children was able

Displaying words written in both Spanish and English is one way of showing students that their Spanish-language skills are valued in the classroom.

to read picture storybooks such as *I Need a Lunch Box* by Jeanette Caines (1988). Joan gave these children instruction about the problem and solution in the story, as well as about root words and endings, such as *-ed* and *-ing.*

The literacy of children in another group was still emergent. With this group, Joan engaged in the shared reading of big books, such as *Grandpa, Grandpa* (Cowley, 1990). As discussed in Chapter 2, these books are easier for children to read because they often have predictable text and few words on a page. Joan provided this group with instruction in comprehension skills such as the sequence of events, concepts about print such as word matching, and word-reading skills such as beginning consonant sounds. One day, Joan handed each child a sentence strip describing an event in the story. With her help, each child read his or her sentence strip. Joan had the children look for words that appeared in more than one sentence and for words that started with the same letter. In the spring, Joan used an instructional strategy called Making Words (described under Key Concept 3) with these children. These lessons built on the phonics skills they were starting to develop through invented spelling and taught them more about the way letters go together to form words.

In short, because of the range of reading ability in her classroom, Joan often found it convenient to group the children for instruction. However, she was also concerned about the children's self-esteem as readers (for further information on self-esteem and motivation, refer to Chapter 6). She wanted to make sure that, although some had considerably more skill than others, they all came to love books and to regard themselves as capable readers. Joan read aloud to the class every day, so there were many works of literature that all the children knew. Also, Joan often departed from her format of three reading groups. Every few weeks she had the children choose one of three picture storybooks to read, so groups were formed on the basis of interest instead of reading ability. She conducted experience-text-relationship lessons with each group, as described in Chapter 3. In the spring she had the children do research on animals, and for this unit she let them choose their own groups, depending on the animal they wanted to study.

Whenever she used interest groups, Joan took special care to monitor the progress of the children who might encounter difficulty. Daily, she gathered five or six children (not always the same ones) together for an extra small-group reading lesson. By using flexible skills groups, Joan could help children with special needs develop the reading comprehension and word-identification skills that many of their classmates had already acquired. (For more information about grouping, refer to Chapter 6.)

Sometimes Joan read this group of children a story they could not have read on their own, such as *Tar Beach* (Ringgold, 1991) or *Lon Po Po* (Young, 1989), and then engaged them in an instructional conversation about it (for more information about instructional conversations, see Key Concept 2). This gave the children the experience of thinking about and discussing text more complex than that they could read on their own. In these lessons Joan discovered that Taylor was better at reasoning about text than many of the other students whose word-reading strategies were stronger than his.

Over the course of the school year, several of the least able readers in Joan's class would participate in the Reading Recovery program (for more information, see Clay, 1985; Pinnell, Fried, & Estice, 1990). These children received a half hour of individual daily instruction with a teacher specially trained to teach the program. This intensive individual instruction allowed these children to keep pace with their peers.

Each day, Joan set aside time for independent reading. She called this OTTER time—"our time to enjoy reading." Some children chose to read alone, but most preferred to read with a partner. The partners found a place where they could sit and take turns reading pages of the book aloud. Joan made sure that Rosenda and Taylor were always paired up with children who could help them with their reading. Joan wanted all of her students, including those with special needs, to come to enjoy reading and to love books. Every child took a book home every evening, and Joan knew that over half the children had a parent, older sibling, or other family member reading with them every night.

Rosenda, Taylor, and several other children in the class also had reading buddies from Carol Chang's sixth-grade class. Every other week, their reading buddies came to share a new picture storybook with them, and the children looked forward to these visits.

Supporting Students with Special Needs in a Third-Grade Classroom

Like Joan Lyons, Susan Meyer conducted both a writers' and a readers' workshop involving all of the students in her third-grade class. Susan's students were also from many different language and ethnic backgrounds, and they represented an even wider range of literacy achievement. Some could read books written at the sixth-grade level, while others found it challenging to read stories written at the first-grade level.

Susan tried to find a way for every student in the class to be recognized for solid achievement in literacy. In the writers' workshop, Susan found that some of the most creative writers were the students who struggled the most with reading. Through teacher and peer conferences, she made sure these students received the help they required to get their ideas down on paper. When these students shared their writing with the class from the author's chair, they received the recognition they needed to persevere. For example, Bobby's first book, an adventure story entitled "The Scariest Halloween," won the admiration of his classmates. Bobby needed this boost, since he was one of the students still reading at the first-grade level.

During the readers' workshop, Susan received the support of one of the school's Title 1 teachers, Carla Hernandez. Title 1 is a federally funded program that assists low-achieving students enrolled in schools in low-income communities. Carla came into the classroom to provide the Title 1 students, including Bobby, with small-group instruction. She did not follow the usual "pull out" procedure of having students leave the classroom for Title 1 instruction.

Each week, Susan and Carla met to discuss the reading instruction they would be providing to students. They agreed that they would both be using instructional conversations (see Key Concept 2) and the experience-text-relationship approach (see Chapter 3) to develop the students' reading comprehension ability. They also agreed that the Title 1 students would benefit from repeated reading (see Key Concept 3). After Susan had introduced the students to the procedures for repeated reading, Carla took over. She familiarized the Title 1 students with the texts they would be reading and helped them keep records of how quickly they were reading.

To blur the lines between the Title 1 students and others, Carla also included in her instructional conversations one or two students who did not qualify for Title 1. These other students served as models and also benefited from the extra attention Carla gave them. At one time or another, all of the students in the class participated in Carla's lessons, so there was not a hard-and-fast line between the Title 1 students and everyone else in the class.

When she was not conducting a lesson or helping students with repeated reading, Carla assisted students with the reading assignments Susan had given them. While she targeted the Title 1 students, Carla would interact with any student who requested help. While Bobby and the other Title 1 students benefitted from consistent, well-coordinated instruction to boost their ability to construct meaning from text, in fact the whole class gained from Carla's presence.

Like Joan Lyons, Susan Meyer used different reading group arrangements. Most of the time, she had the students form three groups on the basis of their interest in reading a particular storybook or novel. At other times, she made the decision about the children who would be in each group and the novel each group would read. She did this so that students would have the opportunity to work with a mix of classmates and to read literature that they might not have chosen on their own. For example, Susan decided to broaden Bobby's experiences by placing him in the group that would be reading *Sarah, Plain and Tall* (MaLachlan, 1985), a book unlike the humorous or action-packed stories he preferred. As it turned out, Bobby, who lived with his mother and stepfather, brought to the small-group discussions many insights about what it was like to adjust to changes within a family.

Susan was grateful to have Carla's help, but she knew that it was still her responsibility, as the classroom teacher, to help Bobby and the other Title 1 students learn to read. Therefore, she included the Title 1 students in all the same readers' workshop activities experienced by the other students. Along with everyone else, Bobby and the other Title 1 students learned to discuss their personal responses to stories, to write story summaries, to spot new and interesting words in their reading, and to see relationships among works of literature.

Like Joan Lyons, Susan Meyer recognized the importance of developing her students' love of books. By third grade, many students are developing their own tastes and interests as readers. Each day, at the end of the time for sustained silent reading, one or two of Susan's students gave talks about books they had recently finished reading. As part of their book talks, students mentioned the names of classmates they thought would especially enjoy the book. For example, Tamekia thought Esteban, who liked science, would enjoy reading her book about astronaut Sally Ride.

Susan also had a home reading program. While Joan Lyons did not specify any particular amount of time for her first graders' reading at home, Susan asked her students to read for 15 minutes each weekday evening.

Supporting Students with Special Needs in a Fifth-Grade Classroom

By the fifth grade, the typical class exhibits a wide range of reading achievement, and Jessie Michaels' class was no exception. While three of her monolingual, English-speaking students appeared to be reading at the second-grade level, another three could read books written for teenagers. Some students did not fit neatly into any category. Jun, who had just moved to the United States from Japan, could read and write in Japanese but knew little English. Marissa could read and write in both Spanish and English, although her Spanish literacy was stronger.

Like the other two teachers, Jessie felt that all her students would grow as readers and writers once the classroom had become a community of learners. To build a classroom community, Jessie organized writers' and readers' workshops in much the same way that Susan Meyer did. She conducted a writers' workshop four times a week, because her schedule did not permit her to hold one daily. Jessie put an emphasis on expanding students' writing horizons, and her students tried their hand at writing everything from science fiction to poetry. Jessie's students were able to conduct effective peer conferences, although she always had to remind them to say something positive to the author before jumping in with questions and suggestions for revision.

Because Jessie had repeatedly stressed the importance of the students helping one another and of learning and growing together as a class, students with special needs could always find a classmate to assist them. Sometimes Jessie was surprised by what the students were able to teach one another. For example, Roy taught Tony to use a web to organize the information he had collected for a report on sharks. Jessie offered the students with special needs as much help as she could, but she wanted to make sure that they were becoming independent readers and writers. For this reason, she taught them first to think for themselves, second to turn to a classmate, and third to seek out the teacher.

During the readers' workshop, Jessie used a combination of teacher-led discussions and peer-guided discussions. The class was organized into four reading groups, and she met with two groups a day while the other two groups held discussions on their own. Jessie did not use ability grouping; each group consisted of students with a wide range of reading ability, including Title 1 students, bilingual students, and students in special education, as well as students reading at or above grade level.

Carla Hernandez was also the Title 1 teacher for Jessie's class. Carla met with Jessie, as she did with Susan Meyer, to coordinate the instruction they provided the students. Carla sat at a table at the side of the room, and Title 1 students joined her there to receive lessons and to consult with her about their reading and written responses to literature. Again, because Carla wanted to blur the lines between the Title 1 students and others, she invited other students to join her. Over the course of the year, all the students in the class learned that they were welcome at Carla's table.

Jessie discovered that the students with special needs in her class needed a great deal of help with the comprehension of informational text in particular. For this reason, Jessie and Carla decided to use an approach called reciprocal teaching (to be described in Key Concept 2). In reciprocal teaching, students learn to comprehend informational text through strategies such as self-monitoring and summarizing, which prepare them for activities such as note taking.

Jessie also asked Carla to work on vocabulary-building activities. Carla introduced a Word Wizard chart for the Title 1 students (see Figure 5.6), and soon nearly everyone in the class wanted to be included. Carla taught the students to make lists of the new and interesting words in their novels, and by November students were making lists of their own, not only for their reading-group novels but also for the books they were reading independently. Carla involved the ESL students, including Jun and Marissa, by having them write the word in their home language just below the English word. The other students were fascinated to see words written in Russian, Japanese, and other languages that do not use the Roman alphabet.

Like Susan Meyer, Jessie Michaels had a daily time for sustained silent reading. She found that while most students enjoyed hearing book talks by other students, there were a few students who did not like to read. Some of them had become discouraged because they experienced so much difficulty in learning to read. Others could read but preferred to do something else, such as draw or chat with friends. Jessie took up the challenge of figuring out which books these students might enjoy. Marissa finally got "hooked on books" when Jessie brought her a book from her own personal library.

Jessie asked her students to read for 20 minutes at home every day, including weekends. By looking at students' independent reading logs, and through reading conferences, Jessie was quite sure that all were reading at home on weekdays and that most were also reading on weekends. Jessie encouraged her students to discuss their reading with their parents, and she suggested that parents ask their children an open-ended question or two, such as "What did you like best about this book?" She also suggested that parents try to read when their children were reading, although she knew this would be difficult given the busy schedules of many families. However, one mother came in to tell Jessie that she had instituted a home reading time. Now relatives and other visitors knew that they should bring something to read with them if they dropped in after dinner.

In short, Joan Lyons, Susan Meyer, and Jessie Michaels all followed a similar overall approach to develop the literacy of students with special needs. They set the foundation for literacy learning by creating a classroom community of learners, with both a writers' and a readers' workshop. They made sure that students with special needs were involved in all of the same activities as the other students in the class. In addition, they took extra care to monitor the progress being made by students with special needs and gave them extra attention and instruction. In Key Concepts 2 and 3, we will look at the nature of this extra instruction.

Perhaps most important of all, Joan, Susan, and Jessie took responsibility for the learning of students with special needs, even when resource teachers were available. All took the time to coordinate ongoing classroom instruction with the resource teachers from the Reading Recovery and Title 1 programs. All three teachers also built a network of support around students with special needs, by linking them with classmates who could help and by communicating to parents the importance of home support for reading and writing.

KEY CONCEPT 1

TEACHERS SHOULD MAKE SURE THAT STUDENTS WITH SPECIAL NEEDS DEVELOP OWNERSHIP OF LITERACY AND BECOME PART OF THE CLASSROOM COMMUNITY OF LEARNERS.

OWNERSHIP AND THE CLASSROOM COMMUNITY

You have seen that Joan Lyons, Susan Meyer, and Jessie Michaels share many of the same beliefs about how to help students with special needs become proficient readers and writers. These beliefs center around the idea that students with special needs must first develop ownership of literacy. Ownership of literacy—valuing literacy as part of one's own life—is the foundation for becoming literate and developing the specific skills and strategies required to read and write.

Assessment of Students' Ownership of Literacy

At all grade levels, teachers will often find it useful to begin the year by assessing students' understanding of reading, goals for reading, and ownership of literacy. As discussed in Chapter 7, this assessment will be carried out with all students in the class, but it will prove especially useful as the basis for future work with students with special needs. For example, Joan Lyons and Susan Meyer often find that students with special needs think that reading is pronouncing all the words correctly, rather than understanding the meaning of the text. Jessie Michaels usually finds that students with special needs have not yet discovered the joys of reading a good book.

With some teacher assistance, students in the third grade and above can be asked to respond in writing to the following questions:

What is reading?

What do good readers do?

How do you feel about reading?

As a reader, what are some things you are good at doing?

As a reader, what are some things that you would like to become better at doing?

What is one goal that you have for yourself as a reader this year?

Parallel questions may be asked about writing. As suggested in Chapter 7, students' answers to these questions can go into their portfolios. During conferences on portfolios, students can discuss with the teacher how well they are meeting their goals and whether new goals should be set.

Often students with special needs benefit from setting specific goals for themselves, associated with a particular book or project: finishing a book within a certain period of time, reading a passage from a book fluently and accurately, looking up information in the encyclopedia and taking notes, completing the draft of a story, or editing a piece independently.

In the case of students with special needs, group and individual conferences on students' responses to the assessment questions will be particularly important. Students with special needs often struggle with reading and writing in ways that other students do not, so it is not unusual for them to state that reading is boring (Robb, 1993), not to recognize that they have strengths as readers, and to have no reading goals or only narrow goals. For example, Jessie Michaels finds that while an able reader in the fifth grade may have the goal of reading books in a new genre, such as historical fiction, a student who struggles with reading may simply have the goal of knowing how to read more words. While this goal suggests that the student is aware of his or her own difficulties as a reader, it also suggests that the student needs a broader view of literacy.

In her work as a resource teacher of seventh- and eighth-grade students who were reading far below grade level, Robb (1993, p. 26) addressed issues of reading ownership by having students discuss the following questions in individual interviews:

> How do you feel about reading?
> Do you read for pleasure? If yes, I asked them to tell me what they read.
> Do you own a public library card?
> Do you use your community library? The school library?
> How do you think you can improve your reading?
> Does anyone read aloud to you?

The students told Robb that reading was boring, that it took too long, and that the words were difficult to understand. They did not do much reading on their own and did not have specific ideas about how to improve their reading. Robb found no one was reading aloud to these students at home or at school, and so she decided to start the year by reading aloud to them. Her experience serves as a reminder that students, especially those who struggle with reading, are never too old to be read aloud to, as a way of becoming "hooked on books."

Linking Students with Books

Students with special needs often have not had the chance to become "hooked on books." As discussed in Chapter 8, one of the main things teachers can do to help students with special needs develop ownership is to give them a sense of the excitement and enjoyment that can come from reading.

Linda Fielding and Cathy Roller (1992) found that students with special needs disliked easy books. Although they could read these books on their own, they deemed them boring. The primary reasons for this attitude seemed to be a real or imagined pressure to keep up with peers and a sincere lack of interest in the content of the easy books. As students with special needs progress through the grades, this problem worsens. According to Fielding and Roller, part of the solution is to find ways of making difficult books accessible.

To accomplish that, Fielding and Roller recommend giving students with special needs time to read difficult books independently. Although the students may not actually be able to read much of the text, often they can read enough to find out what they want to know and to participate in group discussions. Contrary to teachers' expectations, students may in fact be able to gather considerable information about particular subjects, for example, for a report on sharks.

A second approach, reading aloud, was mentioned earlier and will be discussed further under Key Concept 2. This approach has the benefit of allowing students with special needs to have access to

All students benefit from having easy access to books and the opportunity to share reading with others.

stories, concepts, and vocabulary that they would not be able to read on their own. When the teacher reads aloud, students gain a sense of the world of books that they might otherwise lack.

A third approach recommended by Fielding and Roller is partner reading. Joan Lyons, our first-grade teacher, used partner reading to help students with special needs by pairing them with a more capable reader.

A fourth approach is rereading. Rereading builds students' fluency and comfort with a text and also helps them to read other texts of similar difficulty with greater fluency (Herman, 1985; Samuels, 1979). We will have more to say about repeated reading in Key Concept 3.

A final approach for making difficult books accessible is to start with easier ones. Fielding and Roller suggest that easier books prime students to read more difficult ones. In the case of a content-area topic, the easier books remind students of prior knowledge of the topic and introduce them to some of the technical vocabulary they will need to know. In the case of fiction, the easier books familiarize students with the characteristics of the genre as well as with vocabulary. For example, students might read *Wagon Wheels* (Brenner, 1978), a book written at about the first-grade level, before *Cassie's*

Journey: Going West in the 1860's (Harvey, 1988), written at about the third-grade level.

Fielding and Roller suggest that students be encouraged to stick with a book they really want to read, despite its difficulty. Tell students that as they get further into the book, they are likely to find it easier and easier to read because they will have learned something about the vocabulary, style of language, and patterns of events.

Inclusion in the Classroom Community

One of the ways that students develop ownership of literacy is through membership in a classroom community in which reading and writing are highly valued activities. Joan, Susan, and Jessie took great care to make sure that students with special needs were full participants in the classroom community.

When students are constantly singled out, through being placed in the "bottom group" or through participation in Title 1 or other remedial reading programs, they are stigmatized and may lose confidence in their ability to learn to read (Shepard, 1991). Furthermore, other students come to regard them as failures. To prevent this division between the reading haves and have-nots, it is important for teachers to take steps to blur the lines among students at differing levels.

Joan, Susan, and Jessie blurred the distinctions by not having fixed ability groups and by including students with special needs in reading groups with other students. Students received extra instruction through Carla's work with the Title 1 program, and they did not have to leave the classroom for these services. Also, because Carla at times included other students in her lessons, the Title 1 students were not isolated from others.

The three teachers encouraged a classroom atmosphere of cooperation rather than competition and taught their students to support one another's progress, as discussed also in Chapter 6. They made every student feel welcome in adding to the classroom's literacy resources. Students could contribute in a variety of ways, such as by using writing to share unique experiences, as Rosenda did, or by using reading to discover a book that another classmate might enjoy, as Tamekia did.

Classroom rules and values reflected this emphasis on cooperation and celebration of the accomplishments of all. Joan Lyons discussed with her first graders how they too could be teachers by sharing what they knew when approached by another child. At the end of the morning, Joan had a time when the children evaluated how the writers' and readers' workshops had gone that day. During this evaluation, Joan told about instances of cooperation that she had seen, and she asked children to share what they had done to help someone else or how someone had been a good friend by helping them.

In her fifth-grade class, Jessie Michaels had a rule: "Helpful comments only; no putdowns." This meant that students were not allowed to ridicule anyone. Instead, they were first supposed to say what they appreciated about someone else's efforts. They were allowed to criticize or complain only if they could provide a suggestion about what the other person could do to improve his or her work or behavior. Jessie's fifth-grade students spent quite a bit of time working in small groups without the teacher, for example to discuss the novels they were reading and to give feedback about one another's writing. In these small groups, students needed to learn how to manage conflict and to work productively with one another. Students with special needs often had to work hard to keep up with their peers, but they benefitted from participating in group discussions and from receiving feedback about their work from their classmates as well as the teacher.

In short, there is much teachers can do to develop the ownership of literacy of students with special needs. Teachers can begin by assessing students' ownership through written responses or, if time permits, individual interviews. Teachers can help students with special needs to become "hooked on books" through reading aloud and helping them to find books they will enjoy reading on their own. Finally, teachers must create an atmosphere of cooperation so that students with special needs are supported and motivated to become part of the classroom community. Instruction in particular skills and strategies will be much more effective if students already have the motivation to read on their own. Once students with special needs have reasons for reading, they will *want* to develop the skills and strategies they need, and the teacher's job will be much easier.

KEY CONCEPT 2 | TEACHERS SHOULD USE INSTRUCTIONAL STRATEGIES THAT DEVELOP STUDENTS' TEXT COMPREHENSION ABILITY.

BUILDING COMPREHENSION ABILITY

Small-Group Discussions: Cultural and Linguistic Issues

No approach appears more effective in developing students' text comprehension ability than small-group, teacher-led discussions. Only in small-group discussions do students have the opportunity both to engage in extended conversation about complex ideas and to have their understandings deepened by the ideas of their peers. And it is only when the teacher leads these discussions that students' thinking about text can be improved through interaction with a mature reader.

As we have discussed elsewhere in this textbook, the literature selected for discussion must have sufficient depth and interest for students to merit the time being spent on it. High-quality children's literature, of the type discussed in Chapter 3, should be used with students with special needs as with all other students. Students with special needs may benefit in particular from the opportunity to read multicultural literature, especially works that will give them pride in their own heritage and that can inspire them to write about their own experiences (Harris, 1992).

Teachers will want to be aware of managing the dynamics of small-group discussions in ways comfortable for students of diverse backgrounds. In the traditional form of classroom recitation the teacher calls on an individual student, that student responds, and the teacher then evaluates the student's response (Mehan, 1979; Cazden, 1988). This is often called the IRE pattern:

I = teacher initiation
R = student response
E = teacher evaluation

Discussions following the IRE pattern tend to be stilted, with teachers asking questions about details and students giving brief responses of only a few words. Students of some cultural backgrounds, such as Native Americans (Philips, 1983), may not be comfortable with being singled out to perform before a group in the manner demanded in the IRE pattern.

In general, teachers will want to conduct small-group discussions in a manner that promotes extended, thoughtful conversation about text and that gives students the opportunity to determine when they will contribute. An alternative to the IRE pattern was discussed in Chapter 1: the talk-story style of the Native Hawaiians. Discussion following the talk-story style might look something like this:

I = teacher initiation
R1 = response of first student
R2 = addition by second student
R1 = addition by first student
R3 = addition by third student
S = teacher summary

The teacher simply asks a question and waits for students to begin responding. The students themselves, rather than the teacher, decide if they have something to add to the discussion.

While there is no one pattern of interaction in small-group discussions that will work well with all students all the time, teachers should be aware of the possible need to change the way they manage interaction, to allow discussion to flow freely. Once ideas are flowing comfortably, teachers have a chance to sharpen students' thinking about text and improve their comprehension.

Another factor teachers need to consider when working with students with special needs is the students' language background. Teachers may wonder whether conversations about literature are an appropriate activity when students are not yet able to speak much English. However, research suggests that students may benefit from both teacher- and student-led discussions even though they are not yet fluent in English.

Luis Moll and Esteban Diaz (1985) studied Spanish-speaking students who were reading stories written in English. When the classroom teacher discussed a story with students in English, it seemed that the students did not have a good understanding. However, when students were allowed to discuss the story in Spanish, they showed a great deal of understanding. In general, ESL students understand more of what they read in English than they are able to express orally or in writing. Many studies show that students' literacy develops best when they are allowed to build on strengths in their home language (Au, 1993). In short, the strongest text comprehension discussions will probably occur when students can discuss the story in their home language.

In practice, however, most classroom discussions occur in English, either because the teacher cannot speak the students' home language or because the students are from several different language backgrounds. Yet, even with a discussion conducted in English, there are still things the teacher can do to use students' existing ability in the home language as well as English. For example, she should let students know that it is the quality of one's thinking that is important and that it is all right to present ideas in less-than-perfect English or even in a mixture of English and the student's home language. It then becomes the teacher's job to respond to the content of the student's message, regardless of linguistic code or grammatical errors. Or the teacher may have the student give her ideas in her home language and ask another student with the same language background, but who is more fluent in English, to translate. These procedures require both teacher and student to take a risk, but they have the advantage of involving students of diverse language backgrounds in discussions of text right from the beginning, rather than waiting until the students have become completely fluent in spoken English. Needless to say, students are more likely to be willing to speak in small groups than in front of the whole class.

Instructional Conversations

In the rest of this key concept we discuss two approaches for developing students' text comprehension ability: instructional conversations and reciprocal teaching. These approaches are consistent with the ideas presented in Chapters 3 and 4 and are ways of providing students with special needs with additional scaffolding and strategy instruction.

Claude Goldenberg (1993) advocates the instructional conversation as a way of helping students with special needs reason about and understand important text ideas (see also Tharp & Gallimore, 1988, 1989). The metaphor of weaving captures the spirit of what the teacher is trying to accomplish in instructional conversations. At one level the teacher is weaving together the contributions made by different students with the concepts she wants to have students explore. The teacher is also weaving the students' background knowledge and experiences with the new knowledge presented in the text.

Goldenberg recommends following these steps in planning for an instructional conversation around a book or story.

1. Choose a book or story suitable for instruction. Good stories can come from many sources, including trade books and basal readers.
2. Read and reread the story until you have a good grasp of it. If you can, discuss the story with colleagues or other adults to see if it has aspects you didn't notice.
3. Decide on the theme that you will use to focus the discussion, at least in the beginning. Most good stories have several possible themes, so select the one that makes the most sense to you and that you think will also make sense to your students.
4. Consider the background knowledge students will need to comprehend the story, and think about how you will build or draw on this knowledge. Sometimes students need facts and sometimes they just need to be reminded of what they already know. Having students write about the topic before an instructional conversation is a good way of activating their background knowledge.
5. Think of a key word (such as *friendship*) or question that you can use to start the discussion. You might want to write the word or the question on the board or on a sheet of chart paper and then jot down the gist of students' responses. These responses can simply be listed or they can be organized into a web or map, as discussed in Chapter 5.
6. In your mind, imagine how the lesson will unfold. Think of the different directions the discussion might take as you move the group from one point to another and explore the theme. You might want to think of a personal experience to share to get the

discussion started. You will also want to think about how you will "chunk" the text, that is, divide it into sections for reading and discussion.

7. Last, decide on some activities for students to work on after the lesson. Consider what students can do to show what they have learned from the instructional conversation. For example, you may want to have students write about or draw the part of the story just discussed, or write a script and act out a scene from the story.

A special point should be made to engage students with special needs in instructional conversations even when they are in the first grade and kindergarten. At these grade levels students with special needs will generally be reading predictable texts such as *Brown Bear, Brown Bear* (Martin, 1967) or *Grandpa, Grandpa* (Cowley, 1990). Books of this sort do not have the substance needed to sustain an instructional conversation that develops students' reading comprehension ability. Instead, instructional conversations for younger students with special needs can be based on picture storybooks read aloud by the teacher. As mentioned in Chapter 2, picture storybooks present children with ideas and vocabulary more complex than those in the predictable texts they can read on their own. Books should be chosen that provide children with the opportunity to discuss the characters' dilemmas and to make connections between stories and their own lives. Authors whose picture storybooks meet these requirements include Tomie dePaola, Eloise Greenfield, Russell Hoban, Ezra Jack Keats, Leo Lionni, and Patricia McKissack.

Reciprocal Teaching

Teachers can improve students' ability to comprehend informational text by engaging them in reciprocal teaching (for a detailed discussion of informational text comprehension, refer to Chapter 4). Annemarie Palincsar (1984) developed reciprocal teaching to involve students with special needs actively in the construction of meaning from informational text. This approach targets four comprehension activities:

1. self-questioning (asking main idea rather than detail questions)
2. summarizing
3. predicting
4. evaluating (identifying and clarifying the meaning of difficult sections of the text)

The basic procedure can be adapted for use with small groups of children from kindergarten on up.

In reciprocal teaching the teacher engages the children in discussion by first modeling an activity. Then the children try to engage in the same activity, with the teacher guiding their performance by providing corrective feedback.

To introduce the procedure, begin with a group discussion of why people might sometimes have difficulty understanding reading material. Children are likely to come up with responses such as "hard words." Follow this introductory discussion with instruction in each of the four comprehension activities. For example, teach your students how to summarize by telling the main points and eliminating the details. Let your students know that these activities will help them focus their attention on the text and gain a better understanding of it. Finally, discuss the content areas, such as science and social studies, where these activities can be used, and how they can help with tasks such as writing reports.

In Palincsar's study, the students were introduced to reciprocal teaching in the following way. First, students were informed that each one in the group would have a turn to be the teacher during the reading lesson. Students were told that the one who took the role of teacher would be responsible for doing four things:

1. asking an important question of the group,
2. summarizing the text read up to that point,
3. predicting what the next part of the text might be about, and
4. sharing anything that seemed confusing or unclear.

The student in the role of teacher had to choose someone to answer the question and then say whether the answer was correct. The other students (the ones not teaching) had the job of commenting on the teacher's questions and ideas and adding to the discussion.

After working for several days on the information above, have the students begin to follow this procedure. First, give the students an expository passage of about 1,500 words. Shorter passages would, of course, be given to younger students. If you are working with kindergartners, first, or second graders, select passages to read aloud to them. If the passage is new to the children, have them make predictions based on the title. If they are already familiar with the passage, ask them to state the topic and the important points already learned.

Then have the children silently read a paragraph or two. If the children are just being introduced to the reciprocal teaching procedure, let them know that you will be acting as the teacher for this text segment. If the children are already familiar with the procedure, choose a child to be the teacher.

After the segment has been read silently, ask an important question about it or have the child teacher ask the questions. Then summarize and make a prediction or clarification, if appropriate. If a child is serving as the teacher, Palincsar recommends providing the following kinds of assistance:

Prompting, "What question do you think a teacher might ask?"; Instruction, "Remember a summary is a shortened version, it doesn't include a lot of detail"; Modifying the activity, "If you're having a hard time thinking of a question, why don't you summarize first?" and by soliciting the help of the students, "Who can help us out with this one?" (pp. 254–255)

Invite the other members of the group to offer comments or additional information. Provide praise and feedback to the child teacher, using comments such as the following:

"You did a good job with that question. I could tell exactly what information you wanted."

"That was a great prediction. Let's read on to see if it was accurate."

If the child teacher still needs help in some area, model that activity. For example, you might suggest another question that could have been asked, provide a summary, or point out a potentially confusing spot in the text.

Palincsar reports that it takes most teachers about a week to feel comfortable with these activities. She suggests that teachers practice with the materials they plan to use with the students. Teachers may wonder if their students will really be able to engage in reciprocal teaching. To ensure that the first few lessons will be successful, Palincsar recommends selecting well-structured expository passages, clearly written and with headings. Teachers should be prepared to do a lot of modeling and to call on more capable students to act as models for less capable members of the group.

To get an idea of the kind of progress students can make through participation in reciproal teaching, consider the following lesson excerpts (Palincsar, 1984, pp. 262–263). Here is a sample of the dialogue between the student and teacher on day 1:

S: What is found in the southeastern snakes, also the copperhead, rattlesnakes, vipers—they have . . . I'm not doing this right.

T: All right. Do you want to know about the pit vipers?

S: Yeah.

T: What would be a good question about the pit vipers that starts with the word "why"?

S: (No response.)

T: How about, "Why are the snakes called pit vipers?"

S: Why do they want to know that they called pit vipers?

T: Try again.

S: Why do they, . . . pit vipers in a pit?

T: How about, "Why do they call the snakes pit vipers?"

S: Why do they call the snakes pit vipers?

T: There you go. Good for you.

By day 7 the student was almost able to phrase questions based on the reading.

S: How does the pressure from below push the mass of hot rock against the opening? Is that it?

T: Not quite. Start your question with "What happens when?"

S: What happens when the pressure from below pushes the mass of hot rock against the opening?

T: Good for you. Good job.

By day 15 the student was successful in asking questions about important information in the text.

S: Why do scientists come to the South Pole to study?

T: Excellent question! That is what this paragraph is all about.

Notice how much help the student required in the beginning, and how he gradually became able to ask questions with less and less help from the teacher.

In short, teachers can use instructional conversations and reciprocal teaching to improve the reading comprehension of students with special needs. In using these approaches the teacher may need to modify interactions with students to be responsive to cultural and linguistic differences. Both approaches can be adapted for use with younger students, if texts are read aloud to students instead of having students read them on their own. As we will discuss in Key Concept 4, instruction of students with special needs should emphasize comprehension, and not just word identification, if students are to progress well as readers.

KEY CONCEPT 3   TEACHERS SHOULD USE INSTRUCTIONAL STRATEGIES THAT DEVELOP STUDENTS' ABILITY TO IDENTIFY WORDS WITH ACCURACY AND FLUENCY.

BUILDING WORD IDENTIFICATION ABILITY

Value of Writing

In Chapters 2, 3, and 4 we stressed the importance of conducting a writers' workshop where children can write about self-selected topics. In the writers' workshop, when children are drafting, they learn that the most important thing is to get their thoughts down on paper. So that children will not slow down and lose their train of thought, they are encouraged to use invented spelling. For example, a kindergarten child might write MI BR WZ SK for "My brother was sick." When the child has finished drafting her story, it will be edited in preparation for publication. During editing the teacher will help the child correct her spelling, and the child understands that conventional spelling will make it easier for readers to enjoy her book.

Daily opportunity to write and use invented spelling to explore the English spelling system gives young children an excellent start in learning about spelling-to-sound regularities, as mentioned in Chapter 2. Knowledge gained through invented spelling is reflected in children's ability to decode words (Clarke, 1988) and lays the foundation for them to become fluent readers.

Making Words

Some students with special needs may benefit from additional instruction in spelling, as a way to increase their knowledge of letter-sound relationships or phonics. Patricia Cunningham and James Cunningham (1992) developed an instructional strategy called Making Words, which helps children learn how letters go together to form words and to see patterns in the way words are spelled. Making Words capitalizes on the invented spelling children are already doing. The strategy has been tested with first and second graders and can also be used with older students.

In Making Words, each child is given a set of six, seven, or eight cards with the letters to be used for that day's words. One letter is writen on each card. In a 15-minute lesson, children progress from spelling words of two letters (*Ed*), to three letters (*red*), to four letters (*pies*), and so on. The final word spelled uses all the letters children have that day (*spider*).

The teacher begins by writing on the chalkboard the number of letters in the word to be spelled. The teacher pronounces the word and uses it in a sentence. The children use their letters to try to spell the word. The teacher then calls a child to come to the pocket chart and use the big letter cards there to spell the word. The pocket chart contains multiple pockets made of clear plastic strips so that the letters can be read through them. The child will almost always be able to spell the word correctly, but if not, the teacher provides assistance. The rest of the children compare their own spellings with that shown in the pocket chart, and they change their letters if necessary.

As the lesson nears a close, the teacher directs children's attention to the letter patterns with which they have been working. For example, the teacher might ask the children to identify a word that rhymes with *Ed* (red) or two words that rhyme with *side* (ride, pride).

She can point out that not only do these words rhyme but they have the same -*ide* spelling pattern. Details for planning and teaching Making Words lessons are shown in Figure 9.1.

Repeated Reading

Students with special needs may know quite a few skills and strategies but be slow to apply them when reading. Often, these students read haltingly, and it takes so much effort for them to decode the text that they lose track of its meaning. These students may benefit from an approach called repeated reading (Samuels, 1979), which is designed to improve reading fluency. Through repeated reading students experience ease in reading and improve their word-reading strategies. This approach can be used with students at all grade levels.

According to Jay Samuels, fluency has two components: speed and accuracy. He advises teachers to have students read with greater speed rather than with complete accuracy. This prevents students from being overly hesitant or fearful when reading. Each time students reread the text, they find it easier and easier to recognize the words. Because little attention is then required for word identification, more attention can be paid to comprehension.

Repeated reading may be used either with individual students, as Samuels suggests, or with a small group, as discussed by Carol Lauritzen (1982). Here we will describe how the approach can be used with a small group of students.

First, choose or help students select a text they will enjoy reading over and over again. For younger children, Lauritzen recommends selections with rhyme, rhythm, and a clear sequence of events, such as the familiar folktales *The Gingerbread Boy* or *The Three Little Pigs.* Older students might choose to read part of an exciting book or a magazine article. The text should be matched with the students' level of reading skill so they do not see it as overwhelmingly difficult. In the beginning, the passages selected for reading should be short, perhaps no more than 50 words.

Begin by reading the selection or passage aloud to the students. Have them follow along in their copies of the text. Then have them practice reading, first by echoing you and then by trying to read on their own. To make sure that students do not lose track of meaning, ask students questions about the text or have them retell what they have read.

You may wish to make a tape recording of the selection or passage. Then students can practice reading along with the tape until they feel they can read the passage on their own. Be sure students understand that they are trying to read the text quickly. Older students may wish to keep track of how quickly they are reading, perhaps timing themselves and making graphs of their times.

Planning Steps

1. Decide what the final word in the lesson will be. In choosing this word, consider its number of vowels, child interest, curriculum tie-ins you can make, and letter-sound patterns you can draw children's attention to through the word sorting at the end.
2. Make a list of shorter words that can be made from the letters of the final word.
3. From all the words you listed, pick 12–15 words that include: (a) words that you can sort for the pattern(s) you want to emphasize; (b) little words and big words so that the lesson is a multilevel lesson; (c) words that can be made with the same letters in different places (e.g., *barn, bran*) so children are reminded that when spelling words, the order of the letters is crucial; (d) a proper name or two to remind them where we use capital letters; and (e) words that most of the students have in their listening vocabularies.
4. Write all the words on index cards and order them from shortest to longest.
5. Once you have the two-letter, three-letter, etc., words together, order them further so that you can emphasize letter patterns and how changing the position of the letters or changing or adding just one letter results in a different word.
6. Store the cards in an envelope. Write on the envelope the words in order and the patterns you will sort for at the end.

Teaching Steps

1. Place the large letter cards in a pocket chart or along the chalk ledge.
2. Have designated children give one letter to each child. (Let the passer keep the reclosable bag containing that letter and have the same child collect that letter when the lesson is over.)
3. Hold up and name the letters on the large letter cards, and have the children hold up their matching small letter cards.
4. Write the numeral 2 (or 3, if there are no two-letter words in this lesson) on the board. Tell them to take two letters and make the first word. Use the word in a sentence after you say it.
5. Have a child who has the first word made correctly make the same word with the large letter cards. Encourage anyone who did not make the word correctly at first to fix the word when they see it made correctly.
6. Continue having them make words, erasing and changing the number on the board to indicate the number of letters needed. Use the words in simple sentences to make sure the children understand their meanings. Remember to cue them as to whether they are just changing one letter, changing letters around, or taking all their letters out to make a word from scratch. Cue them when the word you want them to make is a proper name, and send a child who has started that name with a capital letter to make the word with the big letters.
7. Before telling them the last word, ask "Has anyone figured out what word we can make with all our letters?" If so, congratulate them and have one of them make it with the big letters. If not, say something like, "I love it when I can stump you. Use all your letters and make _____."
8. Once all the words have been made, take the index cards on which you have written the words, and place them one at a time (in the same order children made them) along the chalk ledge or in the pocket chart. Have children say and spell the words with you as you do this. Use these words for sorting and pointing out patterns. Pick a word and point out a particular spelling pattern, and ask children to find the others with that same pattern. Line these words up so that the pattern is visible.
9. To get maximum transfer to reading and writing, have the children use the patterns they have sorted to spell a few new words that you say.

Note: Some teachers have chosen to do steps 1-7 on one day and steps 8 and 9 on the following day.

FIGURE 9.1
Planning and Teaching a "Making Words" Lesson
Source: Cunningham & Cunningham, 1992, p.108.

Students need an appreciative audience for their reading. After they have practiced reading, they can read to you, to other students, or to their parents. Using younger students as an audience may also be effective, as discussed in Key Concept 4.

Students with special needs may benefit from direct instruction in phonics and other word-reading strategies, as provided in activities such as Making Words, and they may also receive practice in applying skills and strategies in context through repeated reading. However, having students participate in wide independent reading will give them the best opportunity of all to become fluent readers. The reason is that, when students read independently, they must orchestrate or coordinate the use of all the word-reading skills and strategies in their repertoires. Voluntary reading (see Chapter 8) is not an extra or a luxury for students with special needs. Rather, it is at the very heart of a successful reading program for these students. Instruction in skills and strategies does the most good when students are motivated to apply what they have learned in reading on their own.

KEY CONCEPT 4

TEACHERS SHOULD ENGAGE IN A CONSISTENT EFFORT TO PROVIDE HIGH-QUALITY INSTRUCTION TO STUDENTS WITH SPECIAL NEEDS, CREATING SYSTEMS OF SOCIAL SUPPORT INVOLVING OTHER TEACHERS, CLASSMATES, AND FAMILY MEMBERS.

INSTRUCTIONAL PATTERNS THAT SUPPORT PROGRESS

In this key concept we first discuss the qualities of instruction that will prove beneficial to students with special needs, and then how the teacher can reinforce high-quality instruction by creating systems of social support for these students.

High-Quality Instruction

You may already have noticed that the approaches we have recommended for students with special needs are not different in quality from those we have recommended for students in general. For example, instructional conversations involve students in the kind of active engagement with text and meaning making that is beneficial to all students.

The idea that students with special needs require instruction that is similar in quality to that given to other students is highlighted in research conducted by Richard Allington (1983, 1991). As implied in the opening quotation of this chapter, Allington emphasizes that the reading difficulties experienced by many students with special needs is caused by the low quality of reading instruction they receive, rather than their inherent abilities. His research indicates five areas in which the instruction given to students with special needs (often referred to as "poor readers" or "low group" students) differs from that given to students who are perceived to be able readers (often referred to as "good readers" or "high group" students). These differences contribute to a widening of the gap.

1. *Allocation of instructional time.* Teachers seem to allocate about the same amount of time for teaching reading to good and poor readers. However, Allington argues that this treatment is in fact unequal, because poor readers need *more* instructional time to overcome their reading deficits.

2. *Engaged instructional time.* During reading lessons poor readers show more off-task behavior or less engagement with the reading task than good readers. According to Allington, the problem is *not* that poor readers are naturally inattentive or hyperactive but that the nature of their lessons allows them to be distracted by signals from many different sources. Poor readers are easily distracted because their lessons often center on oral reading rather than on text discussion.

3. *General instructional emphases.* While the lessons given to good readers tend to focus on meaningful discussions of text, those for poor readers are generally organized around letters and words and oral reading. Poor readers appear to receive more instruction on word identification and less on comprehension, and thus they seem to have less chance to gain an understanding of reading as the process of constructing meaning from text.

4. *Quality and mode of assigned reading.* In first-grade classes, Allington found that good readers did more reading every day than poor readers (about three times as many words). Furthermore, good readers do about 70 percent of their reading silently, while poor readers do most of their reading orally. This is a dangerous trend because, in general, the amount of time spent in silent reading seems to be positively related to reading achievement. Also, good readers tend to be questioned and evaluated on their understanding of the text, while poor readers are assessed on the word-for-word accuracy of their oral reading.

5. *Teacher interruption behavior.* Teachers tend to correct and interrupt poor readers much more frequently than good readers. These practices are damaging to poor readers, Allington suggests, because they prevent them from self-monitoring and self-correcting when reading. Both are important components of reading comprehension, but poor readers apparently have little opportunity to practice them.

Classroom teachers, Title 1 teachers, and other reading resource teachers can work together to avoid the pitfalls identified by

Allington. By following the recommendations below, they can provide students with special needs with the high-quality instruction required to spur their progress as readers.

1. Assess the teaching behaviors you use when giving lessons to students with special needs. Before changing anything, become aware of what you are already doing. Tape record a number of the lessons you give to your slowest learners, review the tapes, count such features as the number of interruptions, and identify behaviors to be changed. Try to make the needed changes and then tape record lessons again to make comparisons. Over time, see if you can detect any differences in the students' behavior. A good way to measure your success is by the number of students with special needs who are able to begin reading material typically used with students who are reading at grade level.

2. Give students with special needs a second daily reading lesson. Try to give students with special needs the extra instructional time they need to overcome their disadvantage. Remember, however, that these lessons must be of high quality. For example, the lessons might focus on instructional conversations or reciprocal teaching. Not just time, but what happens during reading lessons, is the critical factor.

3. Be sure students with special needs spend a substantial amount of time in silent reading. If you add a second reading lesson, Allington suggests that you allow only silent reading during this time. In any event, anticipate that the students will have difficulty with silent reading at first, since few of them will have had much previous experience with it. Be sure to set purposes for silent reading and remind the children to use strategies such as skipping over unknown words and then coming back to them later. Try not to offer too much help. In the beginning, break the story into relatively short segments for silent reading. Begin with texts the students should find quite easy.

4. Every day, give students the opportunity to read easy material for the purpose of increasing their reading fluency. Students with special needs often have developed the habit of labored, word-by-word reading. You want to give them the feeling, often experienced by able readers, of moving smoothly and effortlessly through the text. This is a matter both of selecting easier texts and of giving students with special needs the chance to develop reading habits more like those of able readers. To develop fluency, a suitable procedure is repeated reading, as described in Key Concept 3.

5. Teach students to monitor their own reading performance. Emphasize to students with special needs the importance of "making sense" when reading, and be sure to give them the chance to correct their interpretations of the text. Through tape recordings or other means, check to be certain that you are not encouraging them to become dependent on *your* monitoring. Do not jump in immediately and correct errors during discussion or oral reading, but give students the chance to correct themselves. For example, ask for an explanation of the answer or have the student reread. Set purposes for reading and have students check to see if their reading has met these purposes.

6. Have poor readers spend more time in independent reading, or in reading for information, and less time with worksheet and workbook assignments. The reading required by worksheet and workbook assignments is unlike the reading of text and tradebooks (Osborn, 1984). Valuable time is wasted if students—especially students with special needs—are doing these peripheral assignments rather than actually reading for meaning. Use easy texts for independent reading and hold students responsible for discussing their reading or for writing a brief response or report. If a teacher's aide is available, he or she can be asked to listen to students' retellings or summaries and to discuss their reading with them.

In short, the patterns of instruction described in these guidelines should be followed by all teachers and other adults who help students with special needs learn to read. These students require consistent, high-quality instruction to progress well in learning to read. In particular, teachers must be careful to provide students with ample instruction in reading comprehension and time for independent reading.

Social Support for Learning

Students with special needs will progress well as readers and writers if they are surrounded by systems of social support for their learning. Recall the point made in Chapter 1 that reading involves a dynamic interaction among the reader, the text, and the social context in which reading takes place. Certainly, as described earlier, a strong system of support for students' literacy learning needs to exist within the classroom, which is the main social context for students' reading in school. This system should include not only the teacher but other adults and students.

Reading Recovery, Title 1, and other resource teachers are certainly part of the system of support for students. We have already seen how Joan Lyons, Susan Meyers, and Jessie Michaels coordinated classroom instruction with that provided by the reading recovery and Title 1 teachers. Coordination was achieved through weekly meetings and through a shared philosophy of literacy instruction. These teachers were well aware of the importance of consistency in the instruction provided to students with special needs.

Other adults in the school may play an important role in the social system. For example, in some schools the principal comes into classes to read to students, the librarian helps students find just the right book, and there is a schoolwide time for sustained silent reading.

We have already mentioned many ways that students with special needs can be helped by their classmates. They can be seated next to classmates who are capable readers and writers, so they have someone to turn to when they have a question. Students may be involved in buddy reading, where they read literature and content-area selections with a partner who may be a better reader. They may engage in writing conferences with peers. Or students may be placed in small groups for literature discussions and projects.

The student helpers, who usually are already good readers and writers, do not have to be in a formal relationship to students with special needs, for example as peer tutors. However, the teacher should compliment the student helpers on their reading and writing accomplishments and suggest that they be willing to share what they know to help others.

Reading to Younger Students

Students with special needs often have numerous opportunities to receive help but few to give help. The chance to be the one doing the teaching can boost the self-esteem of these students as well as develop their reading and writing abilities. One way to give students with special needs the chance to be the teacher is to have them read to younger students. For example, sixth-grade students might read to first-grade students.

The teacher begins by finding the teacher of a class in the lower grades who would be interested in having older students visit to read aloud. The older student prepares for the lesson by selecting a book she thinks the younger child will enjoy. Then the older student engages in repeated reading of the book, until she can read it fluently and with expression. In preparation for the lesson, the older student also writes down two or three questions to ask the younger child. The teacher reminds the student that these questions should be on important points in the story.

In the first-grade classroom, the sixth grader meets with the younger child in a corner of the room. She first reads the story aloud and then asks the younger child the questions. Upon returning to her own classroom, she prepares a brief written report on her experiences, to be shared with her teacher as well as the first-grade teacher.

This is a good way of motivating repeated reading and the development of fluency, because the student can see the purpose for practicing—to read to the younger child. The student must comprehend the text in order to develop the questions to be asked. And in preparing the report, the student must use writing to reflect on her experiences.

Shirley Brice Heath and Leslie Mangiola (1991) describe a successful cross-age tutoring program in which low-achieving fifth-grade students learned to become teachers of first graders. The tutors received two weeks of instruction to prepare them to work with the younger students. They learned to model story reading with changes in intonation that would keep the listener interested. They learned to ask different types of questions, including those that would encourage the younger student to talk about personal experiences related to the story. Because the tutors had to account for what happened in the sessions, they developed the skills needed to take field notes, to analyze the videotapes of the session, and communicate with the first-grade teachers.

The tutors, who were all Mexican-American girls, gained in many ways from this experience. Although they began by speaking and reading only in Spanish, they gradually shifted to speaking and reading in English as well. Their teachers reported that they gained self-confidence, spoke up more in the classroom, and were more willing to act as leaders. By involving the first graders in reading and writing activities, they increased their own knowledge of literacy and language.

Support Systems Involving Family Members

Systems of support may also exist in the home and community. Students with special needs often have the support of family members, not only parents but grandparents, brothers, and sisters. Or students may participate in activities sponsored by an institution, such as a church or youth group, that provides them with tutoring or a place to go to do their homework. Other programs, such as story hours, may be offered by the community library.

Approaches for communicating with parents about their children's progress and for involving parents' in their children's literacy learning were discussed in Chapter 8. All of these approaches can also be successful with the parents of students with special needs.

Teachers must be sure not to underestimate parents' willingness and ability to help their children learn to read, particularly if parents speak a home language other than English. Goldenberg (1987), studying Spanish-speaking parents of first-grade children, found that the parents were highly concerned about their children's educational progress. For the most part, parents did not help their children with reading at home, because they did not know that their children needed this kind of help and no one from the school informed them otherwise. However, children whose parents took the initiative to help them made the strongest gains in achievement.

Goldenberg's work suggests that educators should reach out to the parents of students with special needs. Teachers often need to communicate to parents the critical role they can play in helping their children become proficient readers. In addition, teachers should acquaint parents with the value of new instructional approaches, such as the process approach to instruction and the use of invented spelling, which differ greatly from the approaches most parents experienced when they were in school.

If children bring books home from school, parents can be asked to read with children, to monitor children's reading, or to discuss the books with their children. Other children in the family, who may be more fluent in English than their parents, may be encouraged to help their younger siblings learn to read. Goldenberg points out that family members may assist students in other literacy activities as well, such as helping them write journal entries or teaching them to write the names of everyone in the family.

This discussion of the involvement of families in children's literacy learning seems a fitting note on which to end. In Chapter 1 we pointed out how literacy has its roots in family life. It makes sense to conclude that all students, especially those with special needs, will become better readers and writers if their literacy learning continues to be supported at home as well as at school.

SUMMARY

In this chapter we looked at ways that teachers can support the literacy learning of students with special needs, through both instruction and classroom organization. We began with examples taken from classrooms of the first, third, and fifth grade. Teachers in all three classrooms helped students with special needs become full-fledged members of the classroom community of readers and writers. They provided extra instruction but not in a way that set students permanently apart from others.

In the first key concept we considered ways that teachers could develop students' ownership of literacy, including promoting voluntary reading and inclusion in the classroom community. In the second key concept we introduced two approaches for improving the reading comprehension of students with special needs: instructional conversations and reciprocal teaching. Both approaches involve students in the kinds of active, complex thinking required to interpret stories and informational text. In the third key concept we described two approaches for improving students' word identification skills: Making Words, which helps children attend to spelling patterns, and repeated reading, which helps them to read more quickly and accurately.

Finally, in the fourth key concept we described typical patterns of instruction that have negative consequences for students with special needs and provided recommendations to counter these patterns.

We also suggested how teachers could boost students' learning to read by creating a system of social support, including other teachers, classmates, children in other classrooms, and members of students' families. Because reading is a social process, learning to read proceeds best in circumstances where teachers can organize a system of social support for students, drawing on resources in the home and community as well as the school.

◀ **ACTIVITIES**

Reflecting on Your Own Literacy

Think about your own strengths and weaknesses as a reader. What are you good at doing? What do you find difficult? What did your teachers do to help you to become a good reader?

Applying What You Have Learned to the Classroom

Arrange to observe a student who is having difficulty learning to read. What does the student know and understand about reading? With what aspects of reading does the student need help? What kind of reading and writing instruction is the student receiving? Does this instruction seem beneficial to the student? Why or why not?

BIBLIOGRAPHY

References

Allington, R. L. (1983). The reading instruction provided readers of differing abilities. *Elementary School Journal, 83*(5), 548–559.

Allington, R. L. (1991). Children who find learning to read difficult: School responses to diversity. In E.H. Hiebert (Ed.), *Literacy for a diverse society: Perspectives, practices, and policies.* New York: Teachers College Press, pp. 237–252.

Au, K. H. (1993). *Literacy instruction in multicultural settings.* Fort Worth, TX: Harcourt Brace Jovanovich College Publishers.

Cazden, C. B. (1988). *Classroom discourse: The language of teaching and learning.* Portsmouth, NH: Heinemann.

Clarke, L. (1988). Invented versus traditional spelling in first graders' writings: Effects on learning to spell and read. *Research in the Teaching of English, 22,* 281–309.

Clay, M. M. (1985). *The early detection of reading difficulties.* (3rd ed.). Auckland, New Zealand: Heinemann.

Cunningham, P. M., & Cunningham, J. W. (1992). Making words: Enhancing the invented spelling-decoding connection. *The Reading Teacher, 46*(2), 106–115.

Fielding, L., & Roller, C. (1992). Making difficult books accessible and easy books acceptable. *The Reading Teacher, 45*(9), 678–685.

Goldenberg, C. (1987). Low-income Hispanic parents' contributions to their first-grade children's word-recognition skills. *Anthropology & Education Quarterly, 18*(3), 149–179.

Goldenberg, C. (1993). Instructional conversations: Promoting comprehension through discussion. *The Reading Teacher, 46*(4), 316–326.

Harris, V. J. (Ed.) (1992). *Teaching multicultural literature in grades K-8.* Norwood, MA: Christopher-Gordon.

Heath, S. B., & Mangiola, L. (1991). *Children of promise: Literate activity in linguistically and culturally diverse classrooms.* Washington, DC: National Education Association, Center for the Study of Writing, and American Educational Research Association.

Herman, P. A. (1985). The effect of repeated readings on reading rate, speech pauses, and word recognition accuracy. *Reading Research Quarterly, 20*(6), 553–565.

Lauritzen, C. (1982). A modification of repeated readings for group instruction. *Reading Teacher, 36*(4), 456–458.

Mehan, H. (1979). *Learning lessons.* Cambridge, MA: Harvard University Press.

Moll, L. C., & Diaz, S. (1985). Ethnographic pedagogy: Promoting effective bilingual instruction. In E. Garcia & R. V. Padilla (Eds.), *Advances in bilingual education research.* Tucson: University of Arizona Press, pp. 127–149.

Osborn, J. (1984). The purposes, uses, and contents of workbooks and some guidelines for publishers. In R. C. Anderson, J. Osborn, & R. J. Tierney (Eds.), *Learning to read in American schools: Basal readers and content texts.* Hillsdale, NJ: Lawrence Erlbaum Associates.

Palincsar, A. S. (1984). The quest for meaning from expository text: A teacher-guided journey. In G. G. Duffy, L. R. Roehler, & J. M. Mason (Eds.), *Comprehension instruction: Perspectives and suggestions.* New York: Longman.

Philips, S. U. (1983). *The invisible culture: Communication in classroom and community on the Warm Springs Indian Reservation.* New York: Longman.

Pinnell, G. S., Fried, M. D., & Estice, R. M. (1990). Reading Recovery: Learning how to make a difference. *The Reading Teacher, 43*(4), 282–295.

Ridley, L. (1990). Whole language in the ESL classroom. In H. Mills & J. A. Clyde (Eds.), *Portraits of whole language classrooms: Learning for all ages.* Portsmouth, NH: Heinemann, pp. 213–228.

Robb, L. (1993). A cause for celebration: Reading and writing with at-risk students. *The New Advocate, 6*(1), 25–40.

Samuels, S. J. (1979). The method of repeated readings. *Reading Teacher, 32*, 403–408.

Shepard, L. A. (1991). Negative policies for dealing with diversity: When does assessment and diagnosis turn into sorting and segregating? In

E. H. Hiebert (Ed.), *Literacy for a diverse society: Perspectives, practices, and policies.* New York: Teachers College Press, pp. 279–298.

Tharp, R., & Gallimore, R. (1988). *Rousing minds to life: Teaching, learning and schooling in social context.* Cambridge, England: Cambridge University Press.

Tharp, R., & Gallimore, R. (1989). Rousing schools to life. *American Educator, 13*(2), 20–25.

Suggested Classroom Resources

Brenner, B. (1978). *Wagon wheels.* Illustrated by D. Bolognese. New York: Harper & Row.

Caines, J. (1988). *I need a lunchbox.* New York: Harper & Row.

Cowley, J. (1990). *Grandpa, Grandpa.* Bothell, WA: Wright Group.

Hargreaves, R. (1978). *The Mr. Men series.* London: Thurman.

Harvey, B. (1988). *Cassie's journey: Going west in the 1860s.* New York: Holiday House.

Martin, B. (1967). *Brown bear, brown bear, what do you see?* New York: Holt, Rinehart and Winston.

Ringgold, F. (1991). *Tar beach.* New York: Crown.

Waber, B. (1972). *Ira sleeps over.* Boston: Houghton Mifflin.

Young, E. (1989). *Lon Po Po: A Red-Riding Hood story from China.* New York: Philomel.

Further Readings

Delpit, L. D. (1991). A conversation with Lisa Delpit. *Language Arts, 68* (7), 541–547.

Hoyt, L. (1993). Many ways of knowing: Using drama, oral interactions, and the visual arts to enhance reading comprehension. *The Reading Teacher, 45* (8), 580–584.

Kameenui, E. J. (1993). Diverse learners and the tyranny of time: Don't fix blame; fix the leaky roof. *The Reading Teacher, 46* (5), 376–383.

Rigg, P., & Allen, V. G. (Eds.) (1989). *When they don't all speak English: Integrating the ESL student into the regular classroom.* Urbana, IL: National Council of Teachers of English.

Video Tapes

Johnson, K. (1991). Fostering a literate culture. In the six-part series *Teaching reading: Strategies from successful classrooms.* Urbana-Champaign: Center for the Study of Reading, University of Illinois.

ACKNOWLEDGMENTS

"Principles of Small-Group Instruction in Elementary Reading" by Institute of Research on Teaching. Reprinted by permission of Michigan State University.

American Educational Research Journal 14/1 "Frameworks for Comprehending Discourse" by Anderson, Reynolds, Schallert and Goetz. Copyright © 1994 by the American Educational Research Association. Reprinted by permission of the publisher.

"Teaching Students to Write Informational Reports" by Beach. Reprinted by permission of University of Chicago Press.

Excerpt from "Considerations of Some Problems of Comprehension" by Bransford and Johnson. Reprinted by permission of Academic Press.

Excerpt from "Voices of Readers: How We Come to Love Books" by Carlsen and Sherrill. Reprinted by permission of National Council of Teachers of English.

"The Best-laid Plans: Modern Conceptions of Violation and Education Research" by Corno. Reprinted by permission of Journal of Educational Research.

"Bequest of Wings: Three Readers and Special Books" by Cramer. Reprinted by National Council of Teachers of English.

Excerpt from "Reading the World and Reading the Word: An interview with Paolo Freire" by Freire. Reprinted by permission of National Council of Teachers of English.

"Arts As Epistemology: Enabling Children to Know What They Knew" by Gallas. Reprinted by permission of Harvard Education Review.

"Alternatives to Standardized Testing: An Interview with Howard Gardner" by Gardner. Reprinted by permission of Harvard Education Letter.

Excerpt from "One School's Adventure into Portfolio Assessment" by Lamme and Hysmith. Reprinted by permission of National Council of Teachers of English.

"What Is Authentic Assessment Portfolio?, the Newsletter of Arts" by Mitchell. Reprinted by permission of the publisher.

"The Quest for Meaning from Expository Text: A Teacher Guided Journey" by Palincsar, 1984. In Duffy, Roehler and Mason, Comprehension Instruction: Perspectives and Suggestions. Reprinted by permission of the author.

"A Framework for Authentic Literacy Assessment" by Paris and Calfee. Reprinted by permission of International Reading Association.

"Portraits of Whole Language Classrooms: Learning for All Ages" by Ridley. Reprinted by permission of Heineman Publishers and the author.

"What Facts Does This Poem Teach You?" by Rosenbaltt. Reprinted by permission of National Council of Teachers of English and the author.

"Concept of Definition: A Key to Improving Students' Vocabulary" by Schwartz and Raphael. Reprinted by permission of International Reading Association.

Excerpt from "The Child As Critic: Teaching Literature in Elementary and Middle School" by Sloan. Reprinted by permission of Teachers College Press.

Excerpt from "The Contexts of Reading" by Smith, Carey and Harste. Reprinted by permission of National Council of Teachers in English.

Excerpt from "A Portfolio Approach to Classroom Reading Assessment: The Why, Whats and Hows" by Valencia. Reprinted by permission of International Reading Association.

"Masking Words in a Big Book" by Holdaway. Reprinted by the author.

"Masking Words with an Overhead Transparency" by Holdaway. Reprinted by the author.

"The Gradual Release of Responsibility Model of Instruction" by Pearson & Gallagher. Reprinted by permission of Academic Press.

INDEX